THE]
in Sport

By
J. WENTWORTH DAY

With a Foreword by
' THE VISCOUNT CASTLEROSSE

CW01460237

OVER THE WALL

Miss J. Wykeham-Musgrave's Field Trial Champion Spaniel Poodle 'Crinkle'
retrieving a rabbit over a stone wall.

Photo Sport and General

Fr.

FOREWORD

So, MY DEAR JIMMY, you are writing about dogs, and I may tell you that a better subject does not exist. Dogs cannot contradict you, nor bring libel actions against you. Further, I can assure you that the greater nonsense you write about dogs the larger will be your sales among women.

At this moment, as you well know, I have a dog, Cinna by name. Those who read history will no doubt remember that that admirable gentleman had a head to conceive, a heart to resolve, and a hand to execute any mischief. So has Cinna to-day. I have just received a bill for a pair of curate's trousers.

The great necessity in dog-owners is patience. You, I know, are patient, for have I not watched you fish? It also requires patience to write about dogs, because dogs are frequently dull animals. Only occasional dogs are really clever. You remember, maybe, that dog of Dan Leahy's at Killarney, half Labrador, half heaven-knows-what. Well, whatever it is, herding sheep, tracking a deer, retrieving a snipe, or being petted, he always does the right thing.

Your dogs, I am sure, do the right thing, and you are doing the right thing in writing about them.

CASTLEROSSE

KARLSBAD

PREFACE

This is no book for the dog-breeder or the show-bench hot-gospeller. It is, I hope, a book for the ordinary man or woman who has had a lot of fun and friendship, a good deal of boyish enchantment, with dogs; who perhaps has discovered that the love of a dog is a balm for wounds.

I have known many dogs since my father's old retriever, Black Bess, loomed on my childish horizon as an all-wise Mother of Dogs. Black Bess, to five-year-old eyes, seemed to possess a wisdom and a divining sense denied to those grown-ups who ruled one's existence. There was a friendship between the dog and the child which somehow filled a gap that no human being could have stopped. That is no fantastic thought.

The dog has been the watchman of the house, shepherd of the sheep, warden of the oxen, nursemaid of the children, since the first skin-clad man slept shiveringly on the naked ground, fearful of the wolf in the night.

In those spheres the dog stands out as the servant of man.

But the dog in sport, from the dimmest days of Gaelic deer-hunts, from the magnificently pictorial boar-hunts of French chivalry, to the present day, when he shivers beside you in a duck-hole on a bitter winter tide-line—when he flusters the skulking pheasant from a brambly ditch bottom—when he hunts the hare or fox or ranges the windy miles of a Scotch moor—here the dog is not merely the servant, but the friend, the fellow-sportsman, the sharer in man's most primitive and masculine delights.

I have tried in these chapters to give pictures of days which I have known in the still unspoiled places of that older, lovelier England which lingers stubbornly where no factory smoke stains the upper air. There is, thank God, plenty of it still. And in those precious memories, a common heritage to most of us, the dog was our partner.

I have to thank that eminent present-day authority Mr Edward C. Ash, whose monumental *History of the Dog* and other works are present-day milestones in dog history, for having read and corrected the proofs and for many valuable suggestions. I thank also Mr Nigel Holder for his help with the chapters dealing with retrievers. My acknowledgments are due likewise to the honorary secretaries of the various breed societies for their kind assistance with the standards of points.

The Sport and General Photographic Agency gave invaluable co-operation in securing most of the photographs. That of the Egyptian Camel Corps was very kindly provided by His Excellency Ahmed Seddik Bey, Director-General of the Egyptian State Tourist Bureau, who is organizing sport for visiting sportsmen in Egypt.

J. WENTWORTH DAY

WICKEN, CAMBS

CONTENTS

CONTENTS

ILLUSTRATIONS

THE DOG IN SPORT

CHAPTER I

THE DAWN OF THE DOG

Egyptian and Norse, Remains—The Dog of 5000 B.C.—The
Wolf Type and the Desert Hound—The 'Dogs of War'—
When the Late Tsar's Bear Dogs killed a Child—The First
French Hunting Dogs—The Wolf Strain.

HAD WILLIAM OF NORMANDY not grounded the keels
of his war vessels on Pevensey beach and landed his
barons on English soil it is probable that there would
not be a foxhound in England to-day. The most
typically English of all sports—itself little more than
two hundred years old—might never have existed.
For we owe to France the direct roots of every form
of hound used for hunting in this country, whether
it is the Scotch or Irish deerhound, the foxhound, the
otter-hound, the harrier, the beagle, or the fleet
greyhound.

It is an odd fact that France and England alone
have kept the art of venery alive. Those two countries
are the Masters of Game so far as the pursuit of birds
and animals with hounds and dogs is concerned. In
the Norman era and in the Middle Ages the great
Teuton princes and barons preferred to shoot their
game, elk, bear, and fox, rather than hunt it. They
do so to-day.

It would be difficult to say which is the oldest breed
of dog. All the Arctic breeds are of remarkable
antiquity. We are told that the Norwegian elkhound
dates back in its present form to four or five thousand

years before Christ. It is only a short time since a number of Norwegian antiquarians, carrying out considerable excavations at Vistehollow, discovered, among a mass of skeletons of animals and men, those of four dogs. Two of these were pronounced by Professor Brinchmaun as being of undoubted elkhound type and at least four to five thousand years old.

Then we know that the ancient Greeks bred hounds for hunting. Their quarry was usually hare, and it is possible that the greyhound originated in Greece.

The Romans in the last decades of the Empire kept packs of hunting dogs in various parts of Gaul, and had their regular days for hunting parties.

Arrian describes a sort of rough-coated hound which he calls *segusii*. These were bred and kept by the Gauls. They were shaggy in appearance, deep-jowled, and with voices so sad that the Gauls said they were like beggars asking for charity. The Cretan hound was of much the same type and appearance. It is just possible that some of the French hounds of to-day are descended from those early *segusii*.

This study of the ancient roots of the breeds and races of dog is as fascinating as the study of the beginnings of the races of men. And it is as difficult. The dog was born in a mist of legend. He steps out of the dim panorama of the past, a shaggy, rough-coated attendant on man, in his large, mournful eyes that dumb adoration of his master which no other animal has ever exhibited or sought to emulate.

Through all history, through the agonies of

Europe's earliest birth pains, the dog moved obedient amid the changing scenes of wars and falling empires.

In the white snow-mists of the Arctic, where the ice-floes grind, the bull-seals bark, and the great snowy owls beat on noiseless wings, the dog stands in the centre of the picture as the Eskimo's friend, guardian, fellow-hunter, and beast of transport. Here is perhaps the most ancient of all dogs, the breed which so many authorities claim as being descended directly from a domesticated wolf. There is no proof of that. There are distinct wolf-like characteristics in all the species of the Eskimo breed, the Canadian husky, the Norwegian elkhound, and the Samoyede which is used between the Ob and the Yenesei for herding reindeer and for draught purposes. The chow is similar in type, with the difference that it is shorter in the muzzle, has a blue tongue, and is broader in the head.

The theory held for many years was that the domestic dog originated from a cross between the wolf and the jackal. That remarkably painstaking scientist Gerritt Miller pointed out that whereas the structure of the wolf's teeth coincided almost exactly with that of the domestic dog, the jackal's tooth structure is so different as to shake the theory.

The Eskimo group resemble the wolf in their pricked ears, size, build, shape of head, and the colour and texture of their coats. Like the wolf, they do not bark, but, unlike the wolf, they carry their bushy tails tightly curled over their backs.

But in all the conflicting theories, and there are

many, the mystery of the dog's origin remains un-
solved.

I have seen him sculptured on Egyptian tombs that
were built five thousand years before Christ. There
he is the companion of kings and Pharaohs, the fleet
gazelle-hound of the desert, ancestor of the graceful,
tassel-eared Saluki of to-day, of our own greyhounds
which you may see coursing their hares on the fens of
Hockwold and the Isle of Ely or chasing a stuffed
dummy at the White City.

Through the clash and carnage of Hannibal's wars;
amid the screams and bloodshed, the rape and burning
of Carthage, the sacked city of the sea, the dog stands
forth, grim and terrible, in fact and verity the ' dog of
war.' Those great dogs of war, heavy-jowled, prick-
eared, bull-like in structure, in size the height of a
calf, in strength able to throw a soldier to the ground
and tear out his throat, in courage brave enough to
spring full-throated at the trampling elephants which
led the invading ranks—these were hounds, bred out
of the old Molossian kind, whose like we shall never
see again.

If you were able to turn back nineteen hundred
years of history, to read the unwritten pages of
London's earliest birth, you would, I believe, find
such dogs of war set at the gate of the city, " that
city, small and white and clean," which sat upon its
seven hills and gazed out above the flooding, swirling
waters of the Thames, where the salmon splashed like
falling swords in the spring sunlight, and the great
sturgeon nosed their way upstream from the sea.

The armed hand of Rome set that capital city upon its seven little hills, even as their own imperial capital —born out of the wolf, mark you, and by that token a City of the Dog—stood proudly upon its own Seven Hills by the yellow Tiber.

London looked out upon the marshes of Bermondsey—Bermond's Ey, the Isle or Ey of Bermond the Saxon—it looked upon the wild forest land of Hampstead, the marshes of Hackney and Vauxhall, the heathy wastes of Charing Cross, and the forest glades of Kensington. The wild moorland surged like a tide against the wall of the city where stood Moorgate.

Those heaths, marshes, and wastes held always the threat of prowling bands, clad in shaggy skins, blue-painted in woad, their dark Celtic eyes burning with invincible hatred of the Latin, olive-skinned and tall, who had set his armed hosts on their land and in their village, who ruled with a sword. So the dogs were at the gate, watchdogs, quicker in sight and scent and hearing than any sentry of Gaul, any spearman from the Tuscan plains. They were quick and strong, fleet enough of foot to hunt a man through the twisting glades of bracken and forest trees, or over the quaking bogs where Pimlico now stands. They were strong enough to leap on him like a leopard, burying their fangs in his throat and bringing him crashing to the ground in a last snarling battle for life.

I suppose the last possible descendants of the original dogs of war were the great Medelans owned by the late Tsar of Russia, and kept by him at the

summer palace at Gatchina. These dogs were the size
of a calf, and quite capable of killing a man single-
handed. They were used for rousing bears out of the
thickets in summer and from their hibernating quarters in snow in winter. My friend Prince Nicolas
Galitzine, whose uncle, Prince Dimitri Galitzine, was
Chief Ranger of the royal forests and hunting-
grounds, tells an extraordinary story of the ferocity
of these hounds.

Prince Dimitri was standing in the courtyard of
the head gamekeeper's house at Gatchina one morning, talking to the keeper. Three or four Medelan
puppies, the size of Great Danes, were playing about
in the yard. The Prince wanted some papers brought
from the keeper's house. The keeper told his nine-
year-old son to cross the yard to the house and bring
them. The boy started to run on his errand.

Before the horrified Prince or the keeper could do
anything the puppies leaped on the running child and
mangled him to pieces in full view of his mother, who
was standing at her door. The wretched child was
torn practically limb from limb in less than sixty
seconds. I believe that the last of these dogs were
destroyed during the Revolution, and that there are
none now left in the world. The breed had been kept
alive by successive Tsars, but I can find no authentic
record of its original root and ancestry.

I will quote from a letter written on the 15th of
October, 1781, by Dr Pallas, the eminent scientist
and ornithologist. His remarks and those of Collinson, which I quote later, are worth studying in the

light of the theory that the original dog was a domesticated wolf. It is probable that Dr Pallas saw an ill-bred Samoyede, but there seems no reason to doubt that dogs will copulate with both wolves and foxes. Dr Pallas says:

"I have seen at Moscow about twenty spurious animals from dogs and black wolves; they are for the most part like wolves, except that some carry their tails higher, and have a kind of coarse barking. They multiply among themselves; and some of the whelps are greyish, rusty, or even of the whitish hue of the Arctic wolves; and one of these I saw, in shape, tail, and hair, and even in barking, so like a cur that, was it not for his head and ears, his ill-natured look, and fearfulness at the approach of man, I should hardly have believed that it was of the same breed."

Collinson says:

"It is certain that the Siberian dogs copulate with wolves and foxes. When confined they will not intermix; but at full liberty they willingly come together. With regard to the dog and wolf, I myself have seen them couple in England; but never met with any person who saw dogs and foxes intermingle. However, from a kind I saw produced from a bitch, which had lived at freedom in the woods, I have no doubt that she had been impregnated by a fox; and by the peasants this species is distinguished by the name of fox-dogs."

Daniel caps the lot by quoting Pliny, who, he says, observes that

"The Indians leave their bitches tied in the woods,

to be warded by the tiger; that the first and second litter of whelps were destroyed, as partaking too much of the fierceness of the sire; but that the third was kept, as superlatively excellent for their hunting."[1]

It is certain that the Alsatian, no matter what its show-bench defenders may say, is descended more nearly from either the wolf or the wolf strain than any other dog in Europe to-day. The characteristics of the two animals are almost exactly alike, with the differences that the Alsatian has a finer head, smaller teeth, and a more uniform coat. Its intelligence is undoubted, and probably far higher than that of the wolf in its wild state; but, much as I personally dislike the breed, we must admit that on any reasonable hypothesis we have here the undoubted progenitor of most of the breeds of dog which we know and use to-day.

The Egyptian and Chaldean tombs and carvings show two types of dog, one a distinct greyhound and the other a much shorter-legged, long-bodied animal, rather resembling a Scotch terrier. It was probably used in actual fact as a terrier for bolting small animals from the rocks. The very word ' terrier,' derived from the old French *terriere*, means an animal which goes to ground.

These monuments are the first pictorial record of the dog in history, but we know from the researches of Professor Sedgwick, Canon Greenwell, the late

---

[1] The meaning of this sentence is obscure, but I imagine that " the third " refers to a third cross with a dog from the original tiger-dog cross —that is, if the whole story is to be taken at all seriously, which I doubt.— J. W. D.

AN IBEX TREED BY A TERRIER IN THE RED SEA HILLS
IN EGYPT

A remarkable photograph taken in the country which can claim to be a "cradle
of the dog" by Mr Theodore Karam, of Alexandria and reproduced by courtesy
of Mr Alec Ralli of Alexandria.

THE SALUKI

(1) The Egyptian Camel Corps on patrol in the Sinai Desert; a Saluki following the camels.

By permission of His Excellency Ahmed Seddik Bey, Director-General of the Egyptian State Tourist Bureau

(2) Miss S. Kerrison's 'Giafar,' 'Ali Baba,' and 'Razali' arriving in the van at the Saluki Coursing Club's meeting at Sarsden Pillars, Chipping Norton.

Photo Sport and General

Professor McKenny Hughes, whom I knew well, and other archæologists that the peoples of the Stone, Bronze, and Iron Ages possessed a domestic dog. Their bones have been found in the remains of lake dwellings, middens, cave dwellings, and burial-places. What sort of animal it was we do not accurately know, but it is presumed that it was a herd dog or watchdog, of about the same size and shape as the Alsatian.

What has always puzzled me is that I have never been able to find any record that the Danes, Jutes, or Norwegians ever introduced a dog into this country in the course of their numerous forays and settlements. It is only since the War that those canine Vikings the Norwegian elkhound and the Dutch barge-dog, or *Keeshond*, have crossed the North Sea, in the track of the forbears of their own masters who sailed those old seaways a thousand years ago, their beaked galleys dripping in the swell and follow of the waves, their long-banked oars threshing, their raven-blazoned sails bellying, with the stuffed bird of Odin at the prow and masthead, the scent of war going before them on the wind.

Both Roman and Danish civilizations swept over our land, leaving great legacies. The Romans gave us roads, laws, and a code of justice. The Danes bequeathed us our sea-sense. Their fighting stock hardened our national character and physique. Their forthrightness offset and overmastered the cunning and deception of the native Celt. They brought a breed into the nation which has helped perhaps more than any other to make this Empire.

The Roman brought the pheasant. The Dane brought the sailor and the fisherman. Both brought the sword and the fighting spirit wherewith to use it. But neither brought the dog, who, as Aristotle said, is "man's greatest triumph of conquest."

That was left to the French. The grim, steel-clad barons of Normandy; the dashing Gascon knights; the squires from Poitou and Touraine; the gentlemen-adventurers from the lands of La Vendée—all that precious, fighting, filibustering crew brought with them their hounds of the chase, the love of hunting, the artist's knowledge of the finer points of venery— the foundation of the Englishman's greatest sport of the day, the root and branch of that love of the dog in sport which came to its most ironical climax when Wellington hunted both Frenchmen and foxes with a splendid impartiality in the Peninsular War.

CHAPTER II

THE SALUKI, THE HOUND OF THE DESERT

Hunting Gazelle in the Libyan Desert—A Long Chase in the
Wadi Natrun—The Oldest Hound in the World—A Heritage
of Sporting History.

WE BUMPED OVER THE SANDS in a desert car,
which merely means an ordinary car fitted with low-
pressure balloon tyres. The Shell rest-house, midway
on the Cairo–Alexandria desert road and eighty miles
at least from either city, lay behind us. Ahead was the
uneven ocean of the Libyan Desert, its endless horizon
broken by scarps and ridges of sand. The sand beneath
our wheels was rippled by the desert wind—long,
flowing ripples, like petrified waves on a vast pond.

Here and there small tufts of juicy vegetation three
or four inches in length sprouted miraculously. Once
that lovely bird a cream-coloured courser whipped up
at our feet and fled on graceful wings, banking suddenly against the apple-green of the early morning
sky. For this was very early in the morning indeed.
Moreover, it was illegal. We were poachers. And had
my friend Major Bather, of the Camel Corps, who
patrols the Western Desert, seen us he would very
properly have run us in and roped us up for the
malefactors that we were.

But there were three thousand miles of unbroken
desert in front of us, three hundred miles behind us,
broken only by the slim green valley of the Nile. To

25

the north the sands ran on for a hundred miles to the lonely, houseless shores of the Mediterranean. To the south they stretched unguessed, unmeasured leagues into the heart of all Africa.

The sun came up. It broke along the rim of the desert in flat, burning streaks of vivid crimson, flame-yellow, dark blue, shading upward into a lucent green. It was sheer, extravagant loveliness. The wind still blew sharp and cold, cold with the last chill of the desert night. Ahead the first rays of the sun showed in a flash of silver on the long, winding chain of those salt lakes of the Wadi Natrun which lie like a broken sword across fifty kilometres of treeless desert.

There is no equal to those lakes in all Egypt. At the lower end they are so salt that if a man wades in them he comes out with his feet and legs pickled. But the top three, the two lakes of Gaar and the farthermost Beda, are barely brackish. Dense reed-beds, vast forests of bulrushes, surround them. Their waters are black with duck, their solitudes thunderous with the sudden roar of wings. They are a desert reincarnation of the fens of Caroline England. On one's first sight of this incredible wildfowl paradise set in the encompassing desert the mind flies back through alleyways of history to a fanciful recapturing of the bird glory of the meres of Whittlesea, Soham, Streatham, Ugg, and the other besieging waters of the Isle of Ely as William the Conqueror found it when Hereward defied him.

Hundreds of acres of rough, broken, tussocky moorland fringe the lakes and lie between them.

Dense thickets of giant reeds, bulrushes, and low bushes hide herds of half-wild, ferocious-looking water buffaloes and hybrid, indeterminate cattle. A few palms break the flat waste, but there is no house, no tent, and no man.

Half a mile above the water-line of the top lake of Beda lies a miserable hamlet set in the bitter desert. There is one wooden hut with a crude, cranky watch-tower, two Arab shacks built of reeds, sugar-canes, bits of board—shelters that no English farmer would use for anything except his pigs. In them live a head *ghaffir* and his family. The *ghaffir* is the gamekeeper, the desert watcher, the man whose job it is to keep poachers at bay.

He came out, wild, unkempt, his dirty *galabia* blowing in the dawn wind, a double-barrelled hammer 12-bore slung over his shoulder on a strap.

Seeing us, knowing us, he touched his forehead in a sweeping salute, waved us on. We bumped on, down a desert slope, down towards the lake where the duck were moving back and forth in long, wavering lines like thunder-clouds.

The car swung left-handed, squelched on to the first boggy ground, trundled forward, slipping and sliding, through splashes of water, across a neck of land between two lakes. Snipe sprang screaming before our wheels. Spur-winged plover, whistling shrilly, swept back and forth. A herd of Egyptian geese, croaking like bullfrogs, passed high overhead. Teal jumped from every splash. Shoveller grunted as they swept by on creaking wings.

"What a morning for a gun!" said Dick, beside me. But we had no gun, no weapon more double-barrelled or dangerous than a pair of field-glasses. For a moment we stopped the car and scanned the lakes. Duck of every sort and description rode their barely rippled waters in squadrons and flotillas. There were mallard and widgeon—how that shrill whistle took my mind back to beloved dawns on the Essex Blackwater! There were pintail by the hundred, graceful as ballet dancers, their heads proudly erect, their tails cocked in the path of the rising sun. There were teal in urgent, whistling bunches. Shovellers swarmed. Once six great white birds—I swear they were storks—passed high, very high against the sun, so faint and far and white that they looked like blown ghosts in the dawn sky.

White cattle egrets, those ubiquitous birds of all Egypt, barely moved out of our way. And the dunlin were in thousands. They swarmed like mice along the shores. They fed within six feet of the car. Even the redshank in this desert paradise had forgotten his native shyness, forsworn almost his irritating whistle of alarm.

But we were after bigger, swifter, and rarer game. The car jerked forward, its wheels spinning in the boggy ground, gathered way, and bumped across a wide strip of swampy moorland to the white blown sand of the desert edge.

There we turned left, the car wheels sending up a fine spindrift of sand that stung the under-side of the mudguards like frozen rain. Mile after mile we drove in the lightening dawn, the lakes on our left, the desert yawning empty on our right.

Ahead loomed a clump of palm-trees. Beneath them figures stirred—horses and men. A camel stood solitary, humped and sneering. We drew up under the trees. There were four Arabs in long white, flowing *galabias*, four Arab horses, all of them stallions. One was a magnificent white, a very prince of the desert. There was a dapple-grey, two lightish chestnuts. And held on leashes were four Salukis, gazelle-hounds of the desert, the oldest sporting dog in the world.

I told you we were poachers. We were out to hunt the gazelle on Arab horses with Arab hounds, as Arabs have hunted them since Christ walked in Galilee. But to-day you must not hunt or kill the gazelle. The Egyptian Government has said so. That is the law. And, being the law, it is in Arab eyes made to be broken. And surely this was too good and great a chance to be missed, too gallant and rare an adventure.

I am no great shakes as a horseman. In fact, an occasional electric day's hunting, a high point of adventure, had so far been my equine portion. So I was a little frightened of the look of these Arab stallions, their distended nostrils, their arched necks, their tails carried high and proudly like banners, their eyes wide and brilliant. Here were no mounts for beginners. These were horses for real men! What would happen if one was run away with by one of them in the desert, the desert where no English

29

beginner had the right to set his ignoble foot? Paralysing thought! It was easy enough to be lost in those long valleys of sand with neither compass, star, nor fixed landmark to guide one. I had a sudden sick feeling.

But no one else felt sick. There were long, chattering discussions in liquid Arabic, wavings of hands, shruggings of shoulders. Plans were being made.

An Arab turned to me, bowed with a calm dignity which squashed my fears like a rotten apple, and handed me to, of all horses, the white stallion.

I put my foot in the stirrup, swung myself into the saddle, quaking. Then I stopped. He who quakes to begin with quakes longest. It was an effort of will, but it worked. I settled myself. Thank heaven there were English reins, an English bridle, and, miracle of all, an English saddle. Memories of other Arab saddles, of rotten reins, of patched head-stalls and contraptions made to hold a lion, but so botched that they would not control a mouse, had prepared me for the worst.

We moved off, walking our horses up a long, shallow *wadi*, their feet kicking the sands with cat-like steps. Two Arabs on foot kept pace with us, leading the hounds on leashes. For a mile we walked, not a word being said. Then the sheik motioned us to a standstill with a wave of his hand, walked his horse gently up the side of the valley, and stood below the crest of the rise looking intently before him. Without turning his head he waved one of the footmen to approach him. The man stole up, his pair of hounds sliding obediently at his heels. They looked the picture of grace and beauty, their long, silky, sandy-coloured coats blending almost imperceptibly with the sand.

For a few moments the two men, the sheik on his dapple-grey and the footman at his stirrup, stood motionless, conferring in whispers. Their robes stirred in the wind. The dapple-grey's tail swished idly sideways; the hounds stood, their heads raised, their tasselled ears cocked, the light of interest in every fibre of their graceful bodies.

Then the footman was off, slinking away to the right, sliding across the sands, almost imperceptibly. He vanished behind a shoulder of desert outcrop. For ten minutes, a quarter of an hour, twenty minutes, the sheik sat motionless on his horse. My white stallion had cocked his ears forward and raised his head, was smelling the wind. He knew the game.

Abruptly the sheik turned his head, sudden excitement on his face, beckoned us forward, and with a plunge was over the rise, galloping madly. My stallion sprang forward. There was no question of trot or canter. It was a full gallop. The sheik was a hundred yards in front, his robes billowing. Ahead of him, flying across the desert, was the sudden spectacle of a full-grown gazelle buck, travelling like the wind, the two Salukis hard on his heels. I sat down to ride. It was an armchair ride. No English hunter, no park hack, was ever so comfortable as the Arab horse on his native desert.

I believed now the words of Shafi, my *shikari*, who

had said the night before, comforting me, "Sheik's horse all good. That horse ride like silk." He rode indeed like silk.

The wind whipped my face. Sharp and cool it came from Libya, from far Cyrenaica, from Tripoli beyond, from all the hills and deserts that lay between my horse's wide nostrils and the far Atlantic beaches. This was riding. An English gallop, even a hunting run, seemed a patchwork affair, a back-garden compromise.

On and on, the sharp, soft beat of hoofs thudding on the desert, the lithe, tireless energy beneath one, the smooth flowing action—here was a gallop to dream of.

Gazelle and hounds disappeared over a rise. We came to the top to see beneath us a sudden yawning slope, cut sheer away, dropping at an angle of thirty degrees. I thought suddenly, fantastically, of those pictures one sees of Italian cavalrymen sliding, stiff-backed, on their horses down cliff-faces steep as house-sides. We did it. The stallion took charge—more or less. And at the bottom the gazelle jinked suddenly to one side, gliding like a shadow up a narrow *wadi* that doubled back almost on our track. The hounds overshot him, wheeled, pulling up suddenly in a flying storm of sand, and came racing back on his tracks. But they had lost a good fifty yards. One knew that *they* knew that they had made fools of themselves. The beat of hoofs echoed back from the *wadi* walls like muted drum-beats.

The gazelle was now a hundred yards ahead, going

like the wind. Arabs tell you that they travel at from
forty-five to fifty-two miles an hour. I can believe
every mile of it. And those who have timed them
from motor-cars confirm it.

Suddenly there came a wild whoop ahead. Down
the *wadi*-side came tearing the two hounds we had
left behind, their Arab footman standing on the rise
against the skyline, his *galabia* blown out like a
banner.

The buck jinked again. He jinked twice. But it
was near the end. The two fresh hounds, turning like
taxis, almost in their own length, doubled and gained
on him. Again he jinked, and the leading hound took
him in the shoulder like a torpedo, bowled him over
like a shot rabbit. Horsemen and hounds arrived in a
clutter. The sheik was off his mount in a flash,
whipped out a thin knife, plunged it into the buck's
throat. That was my first gazelle hunt with the
hunting dogs of the desert.

The Saluki is probably the oldest sporting dog in
the world. It has been preserved since the earliest
Pharaonic times by the Bedouin of the desert. To
them the Saluki is the nobleman among dogs, so noble
that he is never referred to as a dog, but as a hound.
His pedigree is transmitted from generation to generation by word of mouth. No mongrel-breeding is ever
allowed. The Sahara Desert tribes call the Saluki
Barake, or " Specially Blessed." Nowhere in North
Africa or Arabia is the Saluki ever sold between tribes
or members of tribes. He is always given as a present

of honour either to an eminent guest or to a favoured friend. In the Libyan Desert the tribesmen speak of this graceful hound as *el Hor*, " the Noble One," and they say of him as they say of their horses, " Are not these the herited of our fathers, and shall not we to our sons bequeath them ? "

This pride of ancestry applies to horses, hounds, and themselves. But the ordinary herd dogs or sheep-dogs are beneath contempt, just as the mule, the donkey, and the camel are beasts of burden, on an infinitely lower plane than the Arab horse. Usually the puppies are brought up by the women of the tribe. They alone among dogs are allowed in the sheik's tent. When the tribe moves the Salukis travel in state on the backs of camels, so that their feet shall not be blistered by the hot sand.

They are usually entered to desert rats and jerboas when they are about six months old. After that comes desert hare, and finally the supreme trial—the hunting of the gazelle. Gazelle have been timed, as I said, at forty-five to fifty-two miles an hour, but it is estimated that the Saluki does not exceed forty miles an hour. The method of hunting, therefore, is that the gazelle chosen is separated from the herd, and then coursed down until it is tired out. It is often hunted in a circle and killed near the spot where it was first started, much after the fashion of coursing a hare at home. If by the end of two years a hound does not shape well it is considered to be useless and is got rid of.

I cannot discover the origin of the name. Some historians consider that it is derived from that long-

vanished city in Southern Arabia, Saluk, noted in its
time for the making of armour and the breeding of
swift hounds. Seleucia, which the Turks call Seleikeh,
is a runner-up for favour, as is the town of Saleuzia,
not far from Antioch. We shall never know the truth.

But it is interesting to find, as I did on a visit to
Upper Egypt in 1936, a wall-painting in the tomb
of Rekh-Ma-Ra at Western Thebes dating from
1400 B.C. in which three Salukis, respectively golden,
cream, and white, are led in the train of the conqueror
among the spoils of war.

Apart from the fact that on a long trek the Bedouin
carry their Salukis, particularly the puppies, on camel-
back, they are unsparing of them when it comes to
real hunting. Not only four-footed game but winged
game are caught by the really well-trained Saluki. He
will stalk a desert partridge or even a bustard, startle
it into sudden flight, and, quite surprisingly, often
catch it in the air, leaping from the ground at full
gallop to a height of several feet. I have not the
slightest doubt that they could be taught to catch
English partridges in the same way. Watch a Saluki
when he sees a covey get up at his feet. The old urge
to pursue them is still latent in even the most South
Kensington of the breed. But I have no doubt that
the desiccated dowagers into whose hands have fallen
the one or two drawing-room specimens which I occasionally encounter mournfully in London would regard
such a manifestation of masculine doghood as a gross
and unjustifiable negation of the principles of the
League of Nations, the R.S.P.C.A., and the other

tea-drinking bulwarks of our slightly shaken civilization.

I wonder that no one has employed Salukis for falconry in this country. Falconry from the earliest days has demanded the use of a hound, a hound long of vision and fleet of feet. He must mark the falcon as he towers, watch him as he stoops like a thunderbolt to the quarry, see him bind to it and bring it to the ground in a flurry of stricken feathers. Then falconer on horse and hound on foot are off like arrows, both having marked the spot where the hawk and his quarry have fallen. If the cover is thick it is the Saluki's task to find it.

The Arabs employ them constantly in this manner. Sometimes when they are hawking gazelle in the desert the Saluki must not only mark the gazelle, but get there before his master and hold it.

The earliest references which I have been able to find for Salukis date from the pre-dynastic period, long before the Pharaohs, roughly 5000–6000 B.C. The carved ivory head of a Saluki exists in this period. Then they are shown on a tablet of the Pharaoh Antef about 2500 B.C.

Better examples can be seen at the tomb of Kenhetep at Beni Hasan. He was the Governor of the Western Desert. A good many mummified bodies of Salukis have been found from time to time in the Tombs of the Kings, near Luxor; and the " Stables of Antar," in the Assiut district, where I was in 1936, also provided one.

The Greeks knew them, and there is every reason

to believe that they were known in the times of the
Old Testament. You will remember that the Book of
Proverbs speaks of a hound which is one of the four
things " comely in going."

Albuquerque, the navigator and adventurer, writing
in 1506, said, speaking of his raids at Ormuz, on the
Persian Gulf: " There are many who hunt with
falcons and take by their aid creatures smaller than the
gazelle, training swift hounds to assist the falcon in
catching the prey."

It would be wearisome to go in detail into the many
Arab sayings and proverbs connected with this unspoiled and probably earliest breed of hound. But that
it was early known in Europe, being probably introduced by the Crusaders, is shown by that magnificent
picture in the Dresden Art Gallery in which Duke
Henry the Pious is shown with a Saluki. The Duke
wears the pilgrim's collar, evidently to prove that he
had been to the Holy Land.

The connexion of the Saluki with the Arab horses
which are the root of our present-day bloodstock is
shown in many paintings, notably Watton's painting
of the Byerly Turk in the possession of the Dunn-
Gardner family, and in the same artist's painting of
the " Bloody-shouldered Arabian " in the Duke of
Portland's collection. The first picture was painted in
1703 and the second in 1704. Lord Derby has another
Watton of an unknown Arab horse with a Saluki
prominent in the foreground.

I believe that the originals of the most recent im-
portation of the Saluki breed into England were a pair

given to the Hon. Florence Amherst in 1897. Colonel
Jennings Bramley got them from the Sheik of the
Tahgwi Bedouin, in the Saliha Desert, in Egypt. This
pair were the beginnings of Miss Amherst's famous
kennels to-day.

Miss Lucy Bethel soon after imported some from
Syria, and also from the Western Desert of Egypt.

Indeed, we owe it to Miss Amherst and to Brigadier
Lance and his wife that the breed has grown to its
present importance in this country, just as we owe to
Baroness Wentworth and her father, the late Wilfred
Scawen Blunt, the establishment in England of what
is now by far the finest stud of Arab horses in the
whole world.

One of the most lovable characteristics of the
Saluki is its homing instinct. Its admirers say that if
you buy one you must impress upon it that it has come
to a new home, that it is expected to live there. Otherwise it may return to its former owner, no matter how
far away. A great many stories, some of them quite
fantastic, are told of the manner in which Salukis
have returned, either miles across the desert or
through intricate city streets to the houses of their
previous owners.

It is an ideal dog for the man or woman who lives
for a horse. The Saluki can keep up at a full gallop,
seldom tires, and thoroughly enjoys it.

For those who are actively interested in the breed
there exists a Saluki or gazelle-hound club of which
the Hon. Florence Amherst is president and Mrs
Lance is honorary secretary. The breed is, of course,

recognized by the Kennel Club, and is shown annually at all the leading dog-shows.

For the benefit of those who may think of taking up this graceful, dignified, and intelligent breed, I commend the following standard of points drawn up by the club:

Head. Long and narrow, skull moderately wide between ears, not domed, stop not pronounced, the whole showing great quality. Nose black or liver.

Ears. Long, and covered with long, silky hair hanging close to the skull, and mobile.

Eyes. Dark to hazel and bright, large and oval, but not prominent.

Teeth. Strong and level.

Neck. Long, supple, and well muscled.

Chest. Deep and moderately narrow.

Forequarters. Shoulders sloping and set well back, well muscled without being coarse.

Forelegs. Straight and long from the elbow to the knee.

Hindquarters. Strong, hip-bones set wide apart, and stifle moderately bent, hocks low to the ground, showing galloping and jumping power.

Loin and Back. Back fairly broad, muscles slightly arched over the loin.

Feet. Of moderate length, toes long and well arched, not splayed out, but at the same time not cat-footed, the whole being strong and supple and well feathered between the toes.

Tail. Long, set on low, and carried naturally in a curve, well feathered on the under-side with long, silky hair, not bushy.

Coat. Smooth and of a soft, silky texture, slight feather on the legs, feather at the back of the thighs, and

sometimes with slight woolly feather on thigh and
shoulders.

Colours. White, cream, fawn, golden, red, grizzle and tan,
tricolour (white, black, and tan), and black and tan.

General Appearance. The whole appearance of this breed
should give an impression of grace and symmetry,
and of great speed and endurance coupled with
strength and activity to enable it to kill gazelle or
other quarry over deep sand or rocky mountain. The
expression should be dignified and gentle, with deep,
faithful, far-seeing eyes. Dogs should average in
height from 23 to 28 inches, and the bitches may be
considerably smaller, this being very typical of the
breed.

In the smooth variety the points should be the same
with the exception of the coat, which has no feathering.

If only for the sake of comparison it is interesting
to read how the Arabs judge Salukis.

The first thing the Arab always looks at is the
chest: this must be deep and strong.

Head. There should be two fingers' width across the top
of the head between the ears. There should be plenty
of loose skin in the cheek. Ears should be long and
finely feathered.

Forelegs. Elbows should be difficult to press together.
Wrists should be small, and paws point forward at a
small angle.

Loins should be very narrow. There should be a width of
three or four fingers between the two hip-bones on
the top of the back; a deep hollow between these
bones is thought very good.

Back Legs. Hock must be very pronounced, and the
lower the better.

Rear Paws. There should be a pronounced flatness here, showing easy, quick turning at speed.

Tail. Feathering must be fine and regular. The tail when pulled down between the legs and round up the back should reach to the point between the hip-bones.

General. The main slope of the body should be from tail to shoulder, giving an impression of speed, the hindquarters being higher than the shoulders. An arched back with spine showing is considered a sign of speed.

CHAPTER III

ON FOXHOUNDS, HARRIERS, AND BEAGLES

The Origin of the Foxhound—His Norman Blood—The Talbot
Hound and Bloodhound—The Staghound Cross—The Old
Southern Hound—The West Country Harrier—The Kerry
Beagle—The Fastest Hounds in the World.

I SAID IN THE FIRST CHAPTER that we owe the
modern foxhound to a French stock introduced into
this country. I do not propose to go into the various
French breeds. Like French women, they are varied,
enchanting, and occasionally a nuisance. It would
take too long, and Sir John Buchanan-Jardine has
already done it better than anyone else in his excellent
and invaluable book *Hounds of the World*. But to
take a brief survey of the subject—very brief, for foxhounds, harriers, and beagles alone deserve a book to
themselves—we must cast our minds back to the
Norman Conquest. The Normans brought to this
country a big, upstanding hunting dog known as a
Talbot hound, forerunner of those Talbot hounds
which were used in medieval England as guards for
the pack-trains of merchandise which crossed and recrossed England. Hence the common occurrence of
the Talbot as a public-house sign.

The straight descendant of the Talbot to-day is the
bloodhound, who has preserved many of the characteristics of the earliest hunting hound, including the
" sad and wild " appearance, deep jowl, and voices

42

"like beggars asking for charity" which Arrian described.

Shakespeare refers to them as "crook-kneed and dewlapped like Thessalian bulls." He certainly knew something about it, the old poacher, for Sir Thomas Lucy's keepers caught him deer-stealing in Charlecote Park. And the Talbot hound was the dog used by the deer-stealer.

From these Talbots developed what was known as the Northern hound, a fairly fast animal, bred in Yorkshire, Northumberland, and Cumberland in Queen Elizabeth's reign. Gervase Markham, writing about 1600, and comparing them with the Southern hound, says of them:

"The light, or Northern, hound has a head more slender, with a longer nose; ears and flews more shallow, broad back, belly gaunt, joints long, tail small, and his general form more slender and greyhound-like: but the virtues of these Yorkshire hounds I can praise no further than for scent and swiftness, for with respect to mouth they have only a little shrill sweetness, but no depth of tone or solemn music."

Away over in the west, in Lancashire, Cheshire, among the deep valleys of Shropshire, and on the savage moorlands of Staffordshire, they had a somewhat slower and bigger hound. In the Midlands, from Worcestershire down to Berkshire, the hounds were of middle size and quite fast, admirably suited to the flat, galloping pastureland and open down country.

All these various local breeds differed considerably in the quality of their coat, their bone, shape, and even stamina. It was reckoned that the Northern hound had the greatest staying power of all.

But the French hound across the Channel was still considered to be vastly superior. That was why Henry IV of France sent James I of England a pack of his staghounds, of the best blood in France. There is no doubt that these contributed markedly to the improvement of the British types.

So there you have both staghound and bloodhound blood contributing to the modern foxhound. Several authorities, notably Johnson, who wrote his *Hunting Directory* in 1850, and Youatt, author of *The Dog*, published in 1845, make no bones about their conviction that a greyhound or lurcher cross was introduced also. Horlock, better known as " Scrutator," author of *The Science of Foxhunting*, allowed that this cross was possible. He said:

" The greyhound shape is there, and, moreover, the greyhound tongue and the greyhound ear, but this cross must have been of ancient date, since for more than one hundred years pedigrees of foxhounds . . . have been scrupulously and carefully registered."

This was written in 1867.

In the same book he lays down the thesis that the wolfhounds used in England in the reign of Edward I were also a cross between the deerhound and the bloodhound, and as such are merged in the foxhound to-day. Indeed, he quotes having seen in the North Warwickshire Kennels a few years previously a cross between a foxhound and a bloodhound, " upon which Peter Collison, the huntsman with the Cheshire, pinned his faith as the most efficient hounds in the pack, quite equal in speed and swiftness to any other, and showing better nose than the majority."

Then he quotes a hound from the Badminton Kennels, sent to him by Will Long, which he named Marmion. This, he says, showed a definite deerhound cross in both colour and the shape and structure of the head, neck, and chest.

Now, "Scrutator" was a Master of Hounds, a breeder, and a highly knowledgeable man. We may take his views with the utmost seriousness.

The result of these crosses, these dim stages of evolution down the centuries, is a hound to-day which can do its fourteen or fifteen miles from the kennels to the meet, hunt all day on heavy plough, through dense woodland, gallop over grass, swim brooks and rivers, tire out a couple of horses, and, having sent the fox-hunters home weary, will then return to its kennels full of spit and fire and ready to repeat the dose two or three days later.

The foxhound deserves a monument. He gives more sport to more people than any other hound in the country. He is the means of distributing between ten and twelve million pounds a year in British money which, but for hunting, would probably be spent in Switzerland or the South of France. He is a grand 'mixer,' for every man, rich and poor, hunting or non-hunting, is stirred by the sight and music of a pack of hounds. I have seen porters at a London railway station, men who had probably never seen a fox in their lives, unloading a draft of hounds from a van with the enthusiasm of schoolboys. They showed far more real interest in them than they would have done in any other animal.

To-day you will find English hounds hunting the fox or the nearest approach to it all over the world, in practically every European country, the United States, Australia, Canada, India, China, New Zealand, and even Palestine.

Yet as a type the modern foxhound is only about a couple of centuries old. It has been gradually fined down, knitted into one or two distinct types from the many local types which were once indigenous to different parts of England.

Even to-day the Welsh hound, the Belvoir, the Milton, and probably some of the Scottish packs all show marked individual characteristics.

That, after all, is not surprising. A hundred years ago or less, when transport was long and difficult, when railways were practically non-existent, when the sending of hounds to a distance was a trouble and a vast expense, there was no great reason to breed with blood from a distance provided your local hounds stood up to their local conditions.

Hugo Meynell, Master of the Quorn, which he took over in 1752, was the father of the modern foxhound. The time, trouble, research, and scientific judgment which he gave to the study of hound-breeding place him for all time at the top of the tree as the man who helped first to make the English foxhound.

But even before his day breeding had been taken sufficiently seriously for several packs to keep their records clearly. The Brocklesby lists begin in 1746, while at Badminton the then Duke of Beaufort began his hound lists as far back as 1728. Lord Lonsdale claims that the present Cottesmore hounds derive from a pack kept by Viscount Lowther at Lowther Castle, in Westmorland, in or about 1695. He has a picture of that year which shows the pack as it was just prior to being sent off to Northamptonshire. The present-day Cottesmore hound lists do not, however, begin before 1732, and the Milton come later—in 1765.

If we want a picture of the difference between various well-known packs in about 1830 we have only to turn to "Scrutator's" recollections, published in 1861, in which he says:

"Some thirty years ago, when making a tour of inspection to some of the first kennels of the country, I was much struck with the difference in the appearance of the Belvoir and Cottesmore Packs. The Duke of Rutland's hounds, then under the management of Goosey, were, respecting framework, as nearly perfection as possible, looking as neat and bright in their coats as a new pin, averaging in height about 23 inches.

"A very striking contrast was presented in the late Lord Lonsdale's pack, which was of a totally different character, particularly perceptible in the doghounds. Some of these stood 26 inches in height, with rather wide, long heads, and a good share of neckcloth; they were also put loosely together, although possessing straight legs and good feet, with plenty of bone and muscle.

47

" The characters of these two packs were also very different in the field. The Duke's were quick, active, and mettlesome—forcing the fight and running into their fox in the open. The movements and tactics of the Cottesmore just the reverse—hunting the fox being their forte, and this they certainly accomplished to perfection. Their style of going was like that of a large thoroughbred horse, striding over the ground at a long, lurching pace; but their noses were always in the right place, and they could get forward with a bad scent, hold to the line, and wind up their fox at last with untiring pertinacity.

" But the pack which approached nearest to my own ideas of what foxhounds ought to be was that of the Earl Fitzwilliam, their standard ranging between 24 and 25 inches, with immense power and muscle."

So much for a brief survey of the foxhound. I do not propose to enter into the up-to-date standards of points or any dissertation on breeding. Those are matters best left to experts, and I am not one. Enough has been written on hound-breeding to fill a library, let alone a volume of this nature, which pretends to treat generally of ' dogs ' rather than of ' hounds.'

But since we cannot very well omit the part played by the foxhound in the sporting life of England I have outlined the history of development in this brief and general manner. I am, I hope, no fool to rush in where the wise man fears to tread.

The Welsh hound deserves more attention than he gets; for, if we are to believe the earliest authorities, here we have a hound which, according to some, is

THE ENGLISH SCENE

The Heythrop Hounds moving up from the lake in the park at a meet at Blenheim Palace, Oxfordshire.

Photo Sport and General

(1) THE BRAES OF DERWENT DOG HOUND 'COMRADE'
First-prize winner and Champion Dog Hound of the Peterborough Hound
Show, 1937.

(2) CHAMPION 'DAUNTLESS OF REYNALTON'
Mrs N. Elms' beagle, winner of 100 prizes and 20 championships.

Photos Sport and General

descended, just possibly, from those original hounds of Gaul which Arrian mentioned as being rough in coat, with sad voices. The Welsh hound is probably, or so his admirers believe, the oldest type of hunting hound in England, descended from the original Celtic rough-haired hound.

Sir John Buchanan-Jardine, who is an acknowledged authority on these matters, believes they may probably have a touch of Breton blood in them. He points out also that the hounds which originated from Margam Abbey, in South Wales, where they were kept by the monks, came probably from a monastery of St Hubert in the Ardennes. If so these hounds have a double claim on history, for not only are they the old stock of Gaul, but they derive also from the monastery of the patron saint of hunting.

The Reverend Jack Russell, that grand old sportsman of the eighteen-hundreds who, like my friend Sir Jocelyn Lucas, at one time lived on £80 a year and hunted hounds on it—though Lucas found it infinitely more difficult than Russell can ever have done—had a hand in the breeding of the Welsh hound as we know him to-day. For they are said to have a touch of staghound. And this apparently came from three staghound bitches which Parson Jack sent to " Smash " Lewis in 1825. Here is the story, as Mr E. W. L. Davis tells it in his memoir of Jack Russell:

" In 1825, to Russell's great regret, the old-fashioned staghounds, a grand pack, that stood nearly 27 inches high and for more than a century had been bred for the sport, were sold at Tattersall's and for ever lost to the country. 'They went to Germany,' writes Russell, 'but I kept three bitches for twelve months, hoping some one would begin again; then, having only £80 a year to live upon, I gave them to 'Smash' Lewis for a Welsh friend of his—a Mr John Dillwyn Llewellyn, of Penllergare, near Swansea; and thirty years after I picked out their descendants in his kennel.'"

There are here and there to-day in Wales occasional big, upstanding, rough hounds, which merely shows the touch of the staghound, and I dare say that my friend Captain J. D. D. Evans, late Master of the Brecon, would be able to put any interested person on the track of them. What Captain Evans does not know about the Welsh hound is not worth writing about. But what is worth hearing are his views on those who suggest that a dash of, say, Brocklesby or Badminton blood might improve the Welsh strain!

What was known as the Jelly hound descended from the original Margam pack. They were mostly black-and-tans, with a heavy, bloodhoundy look about them, not much above 21 inches in height, somewhat finer in the throat than the average Welsh hound, and possessing the most wonderful musical voices. It was said that when they were in full cry in a wild valley in the hills the mountains reverberated their music as though it were the tones of a cathedral organ.

It is a grand picture—the wild valley, the bracken slopes turning to rusty brown, rowan-trees flaming red, splashing the hills with magnificent colour, somewhere ahead a big mountainy fox sneaking up through the rocks, and behind him a black-and-tan pack dappling the moorland, their grand music chiming in a thousand echoes. No wonder the old Welsh squires were proud of their stock; no wonder they claim, with all the magnificent ideology of the Celt, such misty roots of antiquity for these hounds.

That old Jelly strain runs through most of the Welsh packs to-day. The original pack was broken up somewhere about the middle of last century—regrettable, but perhaps all to the good, for it meant that the music of those precious voices, instead of being confined to one pack alone, is now distributed throughout the Principality.

Most of the Welsh hounds are a bit lighter in bone than the English, and smaller in size. As to colour, they run from white, lemon-pie, black and tan, rusty red, black, white and tan, to a blue mottle. In fact, you can have them almost any colour.

Their drawback, if it is a drawback, is that they are extremely individual, apt to hunt on their own, lacking in the spirit of concerted discipline. They have excellent noses and a free, fine action, but more than one authority swears that they are not up to the English hounds in stamina. I remember once asking Captain Evans if this was true. The smoking-room of the Fly Fishers' Club in Piccadilly nearly caught fire in consequence.

Up in the Lake District, where they are just as individual, just as stiff-neckedly local as any Welshman, they have the fell-hound. Mr Richard Clapham, of Troutbeck, Windermere, is the man to tell you all about them. The fell-hound is probably more like Peter Beckford's original foxhound than anything else we have to-day. He hunts the fox up the sides of screes of sliding shingle and perilous slates, where only a man with the agility of a wasp and the persistence of a flea can hope to follow. They are a lightish hound, of first-class quality, usually standing about 23 inches, short-coupled to a degree, and full of muscle but not of bone.

I have never tried fell hunting, but it is an experience that no one with a real interest in the essentials of foxhunting should miss. The Blencathra, Melbreak, and Ullswater are specialists in this type of hound.

The harrier is the hare-hound. As such he may spring from any one of three different strains. It may be the old Southern hound, or 'fleet' harrier, which is really at least a quarter foxhound, or the West Country harrier, descendant of the old staghound. On the other hand, he may be a beagle, thick-quartered, neither so high nor so sharp as the harrier, but none the less pertinacious, capable of hunting a twisty line, and, mercifully, so low that foot people can keep up with him.

I like these distinctions of the various hounds used for hunting the hare. Nowadays, when we worship 'efficiency' and 'progress'—two slapdash catch-phrases for standardization and the lack of careful thought and individuality—it is refreshing to find that the science of hound-breeding, like a few other sciences almost forgotten in the present day, tends to perpetuate the old doctrine that if a man wishes to succeed he must work hard by thought, by care, by attention to detail, by a proper recognition of the values of the past and with a long-sighted, constructive eye for the future.

I rather agree with Somervile, who, as you will remember, wrote in *The Chase*:

> A different hound, for every different chase,
> Selected with judgment; nor the timorous hare
> O'ermatched destroy, but leave that vile offence
> To the mean, murd'rous, coursing crew, intent
> On blood and spoil. Oh, blast their hopes, just Heaven!

To start with the old Southern hound. Sir John Buchanan-Jardine, who two or three years after the War tried to breed a pack which would perpetuate this type, went on the theory that the Southern hound was derived from the Gascon hound, and that it came to this country during the three centuries when England possessed the Duchy of Gascony—that is, between 1150 and 1450. He considers therefore that the Southern hound is a younger breed than those which spring from the old Norman hound or Talbot.

He bought two or three couples from the old Hailsham Harriers, which were a blue-mottled type, and a few more old English harriers from other packs. Then he got some Gascon hounds from France. The result was that when the three lots were put together no one could tell the difference between any of them. He had, by the way, a bitch from the Holcombe Harriers, who hunt a wild country in Lancashire, claim two hundred years of history, and are probably the most representative pack of what remains of the old Southern hound to-day.

This Southern hound has notable stamina and pertinacity on a line. They can hunt a cold line long after beagles have given it up, but they have the odd peculiarity of hunting individually rather than collectively, going entirely by nose—so much so that they never miss a yard—and sometimes running one behind the other in Indian file, each chiming with a magnificently mellow deep note. They give, however, a great deal of trouble in breeding, suffer from rickets, and have a lot of trouble with their feet when young. It seems unlikely, therefore, that we shall find anyone else as public-spirited as Sir John who will endeavour to revive this now almost forgotten breed.

However, it is worth quoting two writers of the last century whose remarks on the breed are now historic. *The Sportsman's Cabinet* published in 1803 said of the Southern hound:

"This hound, formerly so very highly estimated, is readily distinguished by his superior size, great strength, and majestic solemnity of appearance; in the body he is long, in the carcass round, chest deep, ears long and sweeping, with a tone in the cry peculiarly deep, mellow, and attracting. From the particular formation of the olfactory organs, or from the extra secretion of glandular moisture, which always adheres to the nose and lips, or from some other latent cause, it is endued with the most exquisite sense of smelling, and often distinguishes the scent an hour after the lighter beagles have given it up: their slowness affords them opportunity to receive the assistance and instructions of the huntsman in a much greater degree than those of a fleeter description; but, as they are so well enabled to hunt a cold scent, they are too apt to make it so, by their tardiness in action and too minute exactness.

"These hounds were once universally known, and equally common in every part of the kingdom, and the breed were then cultivated much larger than those now to be found in the low and marshy parts of the country, where they are still in use for the purposes of the chase; although it has been said, 'that the breed, which has been gradually declining, and its size studiously diminished by a mixture of other kinds, in order to increase its speed, is now almost extinct.'

"The assertion of this author, however, savours much more of speculative conjecture than of experimental practice; for the present writer hunted the winter of 1775, in the neighbourhood of Manchester, with each of the two packs supported by subscription in that town: one of which was denominated the Southern hounds (uniform of the subscribers blue, with white cuffs and capes), the other called the beagles (the uniform scarlet, with silver buttons and green velvet capes).

"The Southern (or old English) hound is, most undoubtedly, the original real-bred harrier of this country, and most particularly in those swampy parts where the chase is wished to be protracted without prolonging the distance.

"The reverend editor of *Rural Sports* corroborates the above remark of the Southern hounds being adapted to the low, marshy, and moory countries by

55

saying he once saw at Mr Wild's, in Lancashire, a numerous pack of hounds kept to hunt hare, the least of which stood *twenty-two inches*, and the huntsman went with *a pole on foot*; and true this is, for in some of the peat-moors and coal-pits in the environs of Manchester, and its surrounding neighbourhood, no horseman whatever, however well mounted, would be able to go with the hounds."

Then comes Blaine, who in his *Rural Sports* said:

" The old Southern hound . . . was formerly strong and large, with a monstrous head, overhanging chaps, full in the throat and dewlapped. This dog is now rarely met with; but a somewhat lengthened type is occasionally seen, and they still preserve the general character. In colour the Southern hound is mottled, pied, or liver-coloured, and sometimes nearly black, but in such cases the tintings are elegantly relieved with tan markings. . . . Until within thirty or forty years the heavy, deep-flewed Southern hound was to be met with in several inclosed and very deep-earthed counties.

" As irrigation drained the lands, and cultivation improved the soil, and enabled the sportsman to follow the chase on horseback, a lighter breed was employed. But even within a very few years the Weald of Sussex has hunted by these slow hounds, whose bass music raised the echo around and made the welkin ring. The want of speed in this dog is admirably compensated for by his unerring nose and his determined perseverance, which thus makes the trial between the pursuers and the pursued on an equality, and also enables the followers to become witnesses of every stratagem of the hare and every hit of the dogs. The general *rush* to the head, which would delight the modern hare-hunter, would have outdistanced the olden one, even had he been mounted on the stately palfrey or the domestic pad.

"The old Sussex blue-mottled harriers, which formed perhaps the first step in the fining of the original stock, are now nearly extinct, and only to be met with in the Weald of that county, some heavy parts of Kent, and a few other vicinities."

Just as one West Country parson, the Reverend Jack Russell, was responsible for a breed of terriers, so another Devon divine, the Reverend John Froude, Vicar of Knowstone, in North Devon, was responsible for what is known to-day as the West Country harrier. These had a good deal of staghound blood in them, as was conclusively shown one day in 1825 when his pack, hunting a hind for four hours, killed her near Tiverton. Every hound was up, and the run was done with one slight check only.

Jack Russell, writing of Parson Froude's hounds, says:

"His hounds were something out of the common; bred from the old staghound—light in their colour and sharp as needles, plenty of tongue, but would drive like furies. I have never seen a better nor more killing pack in all my long life. He could not bear to see a hound put his nose on the ground and 'twiddle his tail.' 'Hang the brute!' he would say to the owner

57

of the hound, ' and get those that can wind their game when they are thrown off.' "

Parson Froude's hounds were dapple-grey, stood about 21 inches, and are represented to-day, so far as type is concerned, in such packs as the Sparkford Vale, the Taunton Vale, the Axe Vale, the Cotley, the Dart Vale, the Modbury, the Quarme—who have one or two lemon-and-white pies—and the Haldon, who probably have the longest history of all. They have a mellow, beautiful cry.

Beagles probably give more fun to budding fox-hunters than any other hound in the world. They are a charming little breed of foxhounds in miniature, purely English in origin, and known as far back as the reign of Henry VII. So far as I can find out no country but this has ever produced anything approaching the beagle type. Johnson, the author of *The Sportsman's Cyclopedia*, published in 1830, says:

" A beagle is the smallest of the hound tribe, and principally, if not altogether, used in the pursuit of the hare. All those who have written on the subject of beagles have never been sufficiently definite in their mode of expression as to give a clear idea of the animal to those who were not previously acquainted with it: for the word ' beagle,' although it designates the smallest kind of hound, also signifies one of such a peculiar formation as to be obvious at first view. Thus, the animal under consideration is remarkable for an elongated form and short legs; and it presents to the eye altogether the appearance of a dwarfhound.

" Although the Talbot, or old English bloodhound,

may be very justly considered as the original stock, whence have sprung all the various ramifications which we see at the present day, yet the peculiar cross which produced the beagle is now unknown. They were originally employed for the purpose of coursing: they would trail a hare to her form, or, by opening, give notice that one was at no great distance. . . . Those who are desirous of procuring these interesting little hounds may suit their own taste as to size, strength, etc., as they are to be met with in great variety in almost all parts of the kingdom.

"The large, bony beagle mentioned above is well calculated to endure fatigue, and to show good sport, while the smaller kinds will not answer so well; and as to the very smallest, distinguished by the name of the lap-dog beagle, though they are very pretty in appearance, and may occasionally kill a hare, yet ultimate satisfaction cannot be expected from their exertions. Finally, if an opinion is to be formed from the appearance of the animal of the cross whence sprung the dog under consideration, it might seem that the deep-mouthed hound, and something of the turnspit breed, had been the original progenitors."

The Sportsman's Cabinet of 1884 tells an amusing story of a Colonel Hardy who had a pack of beagles so small that the whole ten or twelve couple used to be "carried to and from the field of glory in a large pair of panniers slung across a horse." Apparently these diminutive beagles could kill almost any hare they found, or, as the author says, "tease her to death."

However, one night the barn in which they were kennelled was broken into, the entire pack was stolen and taken away in their own panniers, and in spite of the most careful search they were never recovered.

The present-day beagle stands about 14½ inches. If he is any taller it is almost impossible to keep up with him on foot. Most of the present-day packs are composed of splendid little hounds, quite first-class. I can imagine nothing more delightful to a man of moderate means with a little time to call his own than the ownership of a pack of these grand little hounds. They cost very little to maintain, and one can very often hunt rough country, particularly marshes, with them, where it would be suicide to ride a horse.

The Kerry beagle, which stands about 22 to 23 inches high, descends from various packs kept by the Butlers at Waterville in the sixties—still carried on under the name of the Waterville—and by the O'Connells at Lake View, that lovely mansion on the shores of Killarney, and the Chutes of Chute Hall, Kerry. The Scarteen, who hunt in Limerick, claim a history going back to 1735. They are owned by Mr John Ryan, whose family founded the pack, and later bought up most of the best blood in the Chute and O'Connell packs.

Colouring in the Kerry beagle generally runs to black and tan, sometimes black and white, with an occasional blue mottle.

The heads are a little bloodhoundy, their voices remarkable for both depth of tone and mellowness, and they have terrific drive. In fact, the Master of the

Scarteen, Mr Price, claims that his hounds are the fastest in the world, and that no fox could stand up to them for more than twenty-five minutes!

It is always said that the founder of the pack, Mr John Ryan, bought some Gascon hounds from France in 1735, and that this is where the marvellous music of to-day comes from. Sir John Buchanan-Jardine believes that at some time or another there was a cross of Talbot blood. He points out that the Talbot hound was quite extensively used in the South-west of Ireland right through the eighteenth century, and that a probable cross with the descendants of the French hounds accounts for the bloodhound look about some of them. The Talbot was, of course, the forerunner of the bloodhound. From which you will see that the Kerry beagle has a lot to commend him and a most interesting background behind him.

CHAPTER IV

THE FIRST GENTLEMAN IN AMERICA

The Chesapeake Bay Dog—An Individual and an Aristocrat—
The Romance of his Beginnings—Points to look for.

I FIRST MET HIM KNEE-DEEP in water on my own fen in the wilds of Cambridgeshire. He gave me a most independent stare without the courtesy of a nod, and went on with his shooting. I was hurt but interested. He was obviously a foreigner, but I guessed from that gruff air of independence that there was a touch of British blood somewhere. So I asked his companion, one of my partners in the shoot, where the old boy came from and who he was.

"Good Lord, he's not old—he's a youngster! He's an American, the only pure-bred one in the whole country. In fact, he claims the longest and most authentic pedigree in the whole of the United States. What's more, he is the first one of his family ever to come to England."

"I could have sworn there was English blood in him somewhere," I answered. "What is he, then— Red Indian?"

"No, just pure-bred American, real native stock evolved and bred on the spot. Here, Bruce!" He whistled up the pure-bred American.

That was my first introduction to the Chesapeake Bay dog, the dog which Americans claim to be the finest water dog in the world, just naturally bred by Providence to make wildfowlers happy. But when they claim that he is pure-bred American I have my biological doubts. Listen to Mr Anthony A. Bliss, president of the American Chesapeake Club. This is what Mr Bliss says:

" The Chesapeake Bay retriever is a pure American dog. Only the Boston bull-terrier can claim with the Chesapeake the United States as its origin, and no other sporting dog has ever been developed in this country. Beyond this I do not believe that the Chesapeake has ever been imported into another country, and I am almost sure that none has ever been taken to England." Since Mr Bliss said that several Chesapeakes have come to England. They have even poked their noses into Cruft's Show. And they have made a few friends and a great many admirers.

The Chesapeake is not the sort of dog to make friends easily. He is an exclusive, almost an esoteric, person. Like all people of discrimination, he makes few friends and has lots of acquaintances. But, again being a person of discrimination, he sets a wide gulf between friends and acquaintances. I am sure he gets more fun out of life that way.

He is one of the most individual dogs I have ever known. Each dog, indeed, is an individual, and responds to particular and individual treatment. He decides in his own mind who is his master, and that is the only man he will work for. The mere fact that you own a Chesapeake does not by any means imply that you are the Chesapeake's master or that he will work for you. He is the person who decides that, and his decision depends on you—but you don't *make* the decision. Like all people of real character, there is nothing either showy or stylish about him, but he is faithful to a degree, highly sensible, a magnificent guardian, a companion without equal, and the greatest man that ever walked into a child's nursery. Any child that is at all a likeable child, fit to make friends with dogs, will at once agree with you on that point.

The odd thing about the Chesapeake is that you always think of him, quite instinctively, as "a grand old dog." That is precisely what I felt about my friend Mr Nigel Holder's seven-months-old Chesapeake, when I found him plugging through the water on his own on my fen in Cambridgeshire. He struck me as being slightly rude in his stand-offish way, but obviously a person to know, to admire, and, later on, to like. That applies to all Chesapeakes.

Their impression of power is remarkable. They give one the feeling of immense reserves of energy, of great reservoirs of knowledge, of tolerance of disposition, obstinacy of purpose, and tenacity of principle. They are responsive, and they have a lot of quiet good sense. It will take many generations of stupid women in Bayswater and *suède*-footed young men in Kensington to ruin the character of this eminently sensible working dog. He has all the dignity, the native aristocracy, the quiet good sense, and the instinctive judgment of human nature of the British working man. Foreigners can never understand that it is because of those qualities that revolutions happen in this country with, to them, such distressing infrequency.

THE 'JELLY DOGS'

The opening meet of the Guildford and Shere beagles, who hunt a large country in Surrey, and are one of the most popular packs with London followers.

Photo Sport and General

64

DR HELEN INGLEBY'S CHESAPEAKE BAY RETRIEVER

A grand upstanding example of a breed which is rapidly gaining in popularity.

Photo Sport and General

It is just the same with the Chesapeake. If you have two or three Chesapeakes in the kennel there will never be any disturbances in your shooting routine—none of that hoity-toity flightiness of the Gordon setter, the kiss-me-quick slobberings of the spaniel or the mental whimperings of the golden retriever. Do not imagine for a moment that I dislike any of these three excellent breeds of sporting dogs. But I mourn for individuals among them. The show-bench and the drawing-room have made fools of them, undermined their character, ruined their stamina, set their nerves on edge, reduced them from working dogs to park paddlers, tea-table sycophants, and drawing-room druggets. I doubt if you could ever do that with the Chesapeake. He will probably bite some one finally, just as a protest, and then walk out of the house, a dog in search of a man for a master.

They say that there are none of them which are highly strung—that is, none that have been brought up from a healthy puppyhood. I should like to believe that. I have met a few, and so far every one has borne out every claim made for it by its proud possessor.

How did this paragon evolve? What were its original parents, and of what crosses is it compounded in order to justify the claim that it is a native American dog?

The Chesapeake, like Venus Anadyomene, was born of the sea. It was in 1807 that an English brig went to pieces on the rocks off the coast of Maryland. The American ship *Canton* stood inshore as near as she dared, lowered her boats, and rescued the crew and the cargo, including a pair of Newfoundland puppies. The bitch was named after the rescuing ship, while the dog was appropriately christened " Sailor." When the crew were landed a number of settlers owning houses and plantations on the coast gave them hospitality and shelter. In return the crew presented them with the Newfoundland puppies. These were very soon found by the local sportsmen to be wonderful retrievers. We are told that the dog was a dingy red and that the bitch was black, both being of a much shorter-leg type than the present-day Newfoundland. A lot of nondescript dogs in the neighbourhood were bred to the pair, but there is no record of whether Sailor and Canton were ever actually mated. Queer out-crosses were produced, and the present upholders of the Chesapeake claim that the breed derives from one of these out-crosses, in which flat-coated dogs played a governing part. More detailed information on these obscure beginnings of a pedigree are being sought most carefully at the present time by the American Chesapeake Club.

By 1885 the present type had largely evolved, the main differences being that the breed then possessed one colour only, a dark brown shading into a reddish sedge. The dead-grass colour was quite unknown. The heads were more wedge-shaped, and the coats were even thicker and longer than you find in the best specimens to-day. The dog was particularly noted as being the favourite animal in use among the wild-fowlers of Chesapeake Bay, and its hardihood and strength in the rough, cold waters of that bitter coast became famous.

Just before the War shooting men in the Western states took a great fancy to the Chesapeake. Hence the dead-grass colour which was evolved to suit the Mid-Western stubble fields. The dog became smaller, its colour lighter, and, many maintain, its stamina less. The East did not tamper with colour, but they did increase the size of their dog. For a time it seemed as though there would be a wide and unbridged gulf between the two varieties, but, fortunately, since the War the breeders of the East and West have very sensibly resolved to reduce their two extremes to something more nearly appropriate to a uniform type.

The result is that the Chesapeake to-day is settling down gradually but surely into a very fine, reliable, likeable type of gun dog, full of intelligence, absolutely trustworthy, and something of which the United States has every reason to be proud. Lest I should be thought harsh in my previous remarks on the disposition of the show-bench to ruin almost any dog, let me quote the American Chesapeake Club on their ambitions for the future: " Our primary purpose is to promote field trials to such an extent as for ever to prevent bench shows from fashioning and spoiling the Chesapeake Bay retriever."

Here are the standard points of the breed as adopted by the American Chesapeake Club on the 1st of July, 1933, and approved by the American Kennel Club on the 12th of September of the same year. They are worth giving, since I hope that this excellent breed will become popular in this country—popular, that is, among real sportsmen who require real dogs, and not among show-bench exhibitors who require a tailor's dummy among dogs. First of all for the general disqualifications. They are:

1. Black or liver-coloured.
2. White on any part of body, except breast, belly, or spots on feet.
3. Feathering on tail or legs over 1¾ inches long.
4. Dew-claws, under-shot, over-shot, or any deformity.
5. Coat curly or tendency to curl all over body.
6. Specimens unworthy or lacking in breed characteristics.

Here is the general description and standard of points officially approved and drawn up, which should be noted in conjunction with the disqualifications:

Head. Skull broad and round with medium stop, nose medium, short muzzle pointed but not sharp. Lips thin, not pendulous. Ears small, set well up on head, hanging loosely, and of medium leather. Eyes medium large, very clear, of yellowish colour, and wide apart.

Neck. Of medium length, with a strong, muscular appearance, tapering to shoulders.

Shoulders, Chest, and Body. Shoulders sloping, and should have full liberty of action with plenty of power without any restrictions of movement. Chest strong, deep, and wide. Barrel round and deep. Body of medium length, neither dobby nor roached, but rather approaching hollowness, flanks well tucked up.

Back Quarters and Stifles. Back quarters should be as

high as, or a trifle higher than, the shoulders. They should show fully as much power as the forequarters. There should be no tendency to weakness in either forequarters or hindquarters. Hindquarters should be especially powerful to supply the driving power for swimming. Back should be short, well coupled, and powerful. Good hindquarters are essential.

Legs, Elbows, Hocks, and Feet. Legs should be medium length and straight, showing good bone muscle, with well-webbed hare feet of good size; the toes well rounded and close pasterns slightly bent, and both pasterns and hocks medium length. The straighter the legs the better.

Stern. Tail should be medium length—varying from : males, 12 inches to 15 inches; females, 11 inches to 14 inches; medium heavy at base, moderate feathering on stern and tail permissible.

Coat and Texture. Coat should be thick and short, nowhere over 1½ inches long, with a dense, fine, woolly under-coat. Hair on face and legs should be very short and straight, with tendency to curl not permissible.

Colour. Any colour varying from a dark brown to a faded tan or dead-grass. Dead-grass takes in any shade of dead-grass, varying from a tan to a dull straw colour. White spot on breast and toes permissible, but the smaller the spot the better, solid colour being preferred.

Weight. Males, 65 to 75 lb.; females, 55 to 65 lb.

Height. Males, 23 inches to 26 inches; females, 21 inches to 24 inches.

Symmetry and Quality. The Chesapeake dog should show a bright and happy disposition and an intelligent expression, with general outlines impressive and denoting a good worker. The dog should be well proportioned, a dog with a good coat and well balanced in other points being preferable to the dog excelling in some but weak in others.

69

The texture of the dog's coat is very important, as the dog is used for hunting in all sorts of adverse weather conditions, often working in ice and snow. The oil in the harsh outer coat and woolly under-coat is of extreme value in preventing the cold water from reaching the dog's skin, and aids in quick drying. A Chesapeake's coat should resist the water in the same way that a duck's feathers do. When he leaves the water and shakes himself his coat should not hold the water at all, being merely moist.

Colour and coat are extremely important, as the dog is used for duck-hunting. The colour must be as nearly that of his surroundings as possible, and with the fact that dogs are exposed to all kinds of weather, often working in ice and snow, the colour and texture must be given every consideration when judging.

Courage, willingness to work, alertness, nose, intelligence, love of water, general quality, and, most of all, disposition should be given first consideration in the selection and breeding of the Chesapeake Bay dog.

POSITIVE SCALE OF POINTS

	Points
Head, including lips, ears, and eyes	16
Neck	4
Shoulders and body	12
Back quarters and stifles	12
Elbows, legs, and feet	12
Colour	4
Stern and tail	10
Coat and texture	18
General conformation	12
Total	100

Note. The question of coat and general type of balance takes precedence over any scoring table which could be drawn up.

APPROXIMATE MEASUREMENTS

	Inches
Length, head, nose to occiput	$9\frac{1}{2}$ to 10
Girth at ears	20 ,, 21
Muzzle below eyes	10 ,, $10\frac{1}{2}$
Length of ears	$4\frac{1}{2}$,, 5
Width between eyes	$2\frac{1}{2}$,, $2\frac{3}{4}$
Girth, neck, close to shoulder	20 ,, 22
Girth of chest to elbows	35 ,, 36
Girth at flank	24 ,, 25
Length from occiput to tail base	34 ,, 35
Girth forearms at shoulders	10 ,, $10\frac{1}{2}$
Girth upper thigh	19 ,, 20
From root to root of ear, over skull	5 ,, 6
Occiput to top shoulder-blades	9 ,, $9\frac{1}{2}$
From elbow to elbow over shoulders	25 ,, 26

Explanatory Notes (Not Official). Hocks should be well let down, with a moderate bend to stifle. Straight or cow-hocked hind-legs are a fault. Dark brown or dead-grass colours are equally preferable. A sound mover is essential.

CHAPTER V

A LAMENT FOR THE DACHSHUND

The Drawer of Badgers—The Sussex Squire and his Bell-mouthed Beagles—A Real 'Rabbity Day'—And a New Use for the Dachshund.

THERE IS A LAMENT for the dachshund. His lovers complain that he is a miserable drawing-room pet. This is true. I have never seen a dachshund bite a rabbit. But he was bred and brought up to bite badgers. Hence his name. *Dachs* is German for 'badger,' and *Hund* is, naturally, the basis of our English word 'hound.'

The dachshund was bred with short legs, a long body, incisor teeth, and trap-like, pointed jaws in order that he might follow the badger into the farthest, darkest subterranean caverns of his 'sett,' and thence drive him forth into the broad daylight and the iron tongs of the badger-digger—a job which is performed in England by miserable but lion-hearted terriers.

Thus we witness the declining glory of the sleek 'sausage dog.' Born a fighter, bred a warrior, nurtured on Nordic aims of war, he has become a mere paddler about carpets, a licker-up of chocolates, a sycophant at women's knees. So the days of dogs decline. The fighter has fallen. The drawer of badgers has become a lowly squire of dames.

But I am perhaps a little hard on the dachshund. For all his drawing-room popularity he is a gallant little dog, happy in a sunny ditch-bottom on a mild autumn afternoon when the ferrets are working, the rats bolting. Run the fat off him, and he will twist and snap, turn and chase, almost with the best of the terriers. Put him, singly or by the half-dozen, into a square of gorse on a slope of downland that falls verdant into the sparkling Sussex sea, stand at one corner, gun-barrels balanced lightly, ready for the instant shot, and hear the badger-dog drawing through the gorse, weaving in and out like a serpent, sudden terror to the rabbits which dwell therein. They soon bolt, and you will get those grand, flat-out shots when Brer Rabbit, hit clean in the head, does a double somersault down the slope, to finish up twitching, white belly uppermost.

Years ago there was a Sussex squire who regularly used a pack of the old slow-footed, bell-mouthed Sussex beagles for such rabbit days. He put bells on their collars. The bracken on his downland slopes was rided into broad squares.

The old squire would collect his friends, his ruddy-faced neighbours in beaver hats and buskins, his tenant farmers in brass-buttoned, green cutaways and kersey-mere breeches. They turned up from miles, in dog-carts and gigs, tooling along the white, dusty Sussex lanes, their long-barrelled guns between their knees, for the great rabbit day of the year.

For twenty-four hours beforehand the head keeper, his men and boys, had stunk out every rabbit-hole within a square mile. The party gathered at the chalky gateway which opened between grass-grown, bracken-covered banks on to the down that fell in

73

verdant folds to the cliff's edge, where sparkled the sea to the rim of the sky. There was a great sorting out of cartridges, flasks, even shot-belts, for one or two still used the long-barrelled muzzle-loader; a flying back and forth of greetings between neighbours, chucklings over past days, rumbling jokes at easy shots missed last twelvemonth but still remembered.

Then the beagles turned up, a motley, parti-coloured, magpie-looking lot, undulating down the narrow lane, their little bells tinkling. Somehow they provoked a sudden, fantastic image of undersized sheep.

Rabbits lay out on the turf by the hundred, some crouching, some sitting bolt upright, ears cocked, eyes alert for the commotion at the gateway, the march of men and dogs that presaged war.

Then the party moved off. The rabbits scuttled to cover. Guns drew lots, took up their positions. The beagles were put in. The chime of little bells broke musically on the sunny morning. Then the first rabbits were afoot. The bell-mouthed chorus crashed out.

Presently they began to bolt. Shot after shot rang out. The heavy bang of black powder echoed across the empty downs. A blue haze of pre-smokeless powder hung thinly on the air, stung the nostrils sharply. Soon it was a crackling, irregular volley. The turf was alive with racing rabbits, fireworky with rabbits which turned sudden somersaults, catapulted themselves a foot into the air in the death-spring. It was dotted with rabbits that lay dead.

So the morning went on. It was the day of the

sheep-farmer's revenge, the ultimate answer to acres of green turf nibbled down to the chalk. And at midday they gathered in a sunny quarry, their backs to sun-warmed chalk, sand-martens dodging in and out of their holes, a kestrel swinging high in the blue. Cold rabbit and bacon pie, great wicker-covered jars of home brew, home-made cake, Ribston pippins that crackled sweetly on the teeth, cheese whose memory lingers like a dream, pats of yellow butter, and great flat, crusty loaves, still smelling of the wood ashes. That was the high point of the day, crowned if you wished with a glass or two of the squire's ' put-wine.'

Nobody shoots rabbits on sunny Sussex downlands with such packs of slow and musical beagles in these hurried days. We hurry so much we miss the half of life, the charm of the quiet things, the simplicity of the easily attainable.

Perhaps one could not even find the like of such slow-footed, bell-mouthed beagles, with their heavy ears, their loving, sleepy eyes, to-day. I dare say they have been show-benched into a Never-Never Land, a land peopled by the misty dreams of old-fashioned sportsmen who have no use and less wonderment for dog-show poodledom.

But it was a pleasant way of shooting rabbits. It combined a smack of hunting with the quickness and zest of real snap-shooting. So if we cannot find the beagles, why not turn the dachshund to this very simple form of sport? I will bet a last year's hat that he would like it. It would revive in his lowly breast the dormant Teutonic ardour of the chase. Who knows but that the grey shape of the crouching rabbit might not wake some atavistic dream of far-off generations of German brocks! Surely it is fair to the dachshund to give him this humble chance of recovering his lost manhood.

I have a suspicion, more than a suspicion, that the dachshund derives from the French basset hound. Of course, there are dachs fans who will tell you that if you gaze into the tombs of two-thousand-year-old Egyptian ladies you will see sculptured the profiles of the faithful dachshund. But I have gazed into these tombs, and I cannot believe that the prick-eared, coffin-headed, jackal-like little beasts there delineated have anything to do with the dachshund we love to-day.

I prefer to stick to the basset-hound theory. That dead-and-gone writer " Wildfowler," who discoursed so learnedly on duck-shooting and dogs, delivered in the first edition of *British Dogs* the following opinion:

" . . . A black-and-tan or red basset *à jambes torses* cannot, by any possible use of one's eyes, be distinguished from a dachshund of the same colour, although some German writers assert that the breeds are quite distinct. To the naked eye there is no difference; but in the matter of names (wherein German scientists particularly shine), then, indeed, confusion gets worse confounded. They have, say, a dozen black-and-tan bassets *à jambes torses* before them. .Well, if one of them is a thoroughly good-looking hound they call him *Dachs Bracken*; if he is short-eared and with a pointed muzzle they cap him with the appellation of *Dachshund*. Between you and me, kind reader, it is a distinction without a difference, and there is no doubt they both belong to the same breed. I will, at a fortnight's notice, place a basset *à jambes torses*, small size, side by side with the best dachshund hound to be found, and if any difference in legs, anatomy, and general appearance of the two can be detected I shall be very greatly surprised."

But then, in a later chapter on the dachshund, he produces the following bombshell:

" The head, when of proper [dachshund] type, greatly resembles that of a bloodhound. The ears are also long and pendulous; . . . the muzzle should finish square, and the flews should be fairly developed. . . . We have a brood bitch from one of the best kennels in Germany in which the dewlap is very strongly pronounced. . . . The forelegs are one of the great peculiarities of the breed: these are very large in bone for the size of the dog, and very crooked, being turned out at the elbows and in at the knees. . . . The feet should be very large, and should be well splayed outwards."

I wonder where one would find a bloodhound-headed dachshund to-day!

The breed is probably about two hundred years old, and in England it dates from about 1850. Somewhere in the sixties it poked its long nose into the boudoirs of Queen Victoria and the Princess of Wales, later Queen Alexandra. Its popularity was immediate, and from Royal circles the snaky ' sausage dog ' permeated downward through the aristocracy to the ranks of the common or show-bench exhibitors. I believe the first event which actually gave separate classes for the breed was the show at the Crystal Palace in 1873. From that day to the present the dachshund has grown steadily in popularity. The first champion that I can discover was Mrs Merrick Hoare's Dessauer, bred by Count Picked, a black-and-tan dog which she imported into this country in 1874. Then there was Mr Arkwright's famous old Champion Xaverl, who came to England in 1876, direct from the Royal kennels at Stuttgart. These two, with Champion Jackdaw, a descendant of Xaverl, are really the cornerstones of the breed in England to-day.

The wretched dachshund suffered severely during the War. It is odd, after a lapse of years, to reflect that because of his Germanic ancestry the harmless, friendly dachs was subjected to an actual and literal hymn of hate between the years 1914 and 1919. One well-known judge of the breed was furiously attacked by a gang of toughs in a Scottish town in 1915, because he had walked down the street leading a dachshund bitch. The dog was only saved from lynching by the arrival of the police.

I am far from being a wholehearted believer in show-bench or field-trial standards of points as the ultimate criterion of the working qualities of any dog. Too much has been made of the importance of these machine-made standards within the last twenty or thirty years. In some cases rigid adherence to show-bench rules and points may even lead to a definite deterioration in a breed. But every sensible person recognizes that a standard of points is necessary, if only as a definite framework on which the future development of the breed must be founded.

So here is the modern standard of points, adopted by the English Dachshund Club, after the old standard had been cancelled in 1907. This new standard follows the basis laid down by the Teckel Klub of Germany in 1891, and applies to smooth-haired dachshunds only. The wire-haired, long-haired, and miniature dachshunds are sufficiently rare for me to deny them space which they might legitimately claim in a more specialized work. Here is the up-to-date standard of points for the smooth dachshund:

General Appearance. Long and low, but with compact and well-muscled body, neither crippled, cloddy, nor clumsy, with bold, defiant carriage of head and intelligent expression.   10 *points*

Head and Skull. Long and appearing conical when seen from above and from a side view, tapering to the point of the muzzle. Stop not pronounced, and skull slightly arched in profile and appearing neither too broad nor too narrow.   9 *points*

Eyes. Medium in size, oval, and set obliquely. Dark in colour, except in the case of chocolates, in which they may be lighter, and in dapples, in which one or both wall eyes are permissible.   3 *points*

Ears. Broad, of moderate length, and well rounded (not narrow, pointed, or folded), relatively well back, high, and well set on, lying close to the cheek, very mobile; when at attention the back of the ear directed forward and outward.   5 *points*

Jaw. Neither too square nor snipy, but strong; lips lightly stretched and fairly covering lower jaw. 5 *points*

79

Neck. Sufficiently long, muscular, clean, showing no dewlap, slightly arched in the nape, running in graceful lines into the shoulder, carried well up and forward.   *3 points*

Forequarters. Shoulder-blades long, broad, and set on sloping, lying firmly on fully developed ribs or thorax, muscles hard and plastic. Chest very oval, with ample room for heart and lungs, deep, and with the ribs well sprung out towards the loin, breast-bone prominent.   *10 points*

Legs and Feet. Forelegs very short and, in proportion to size, strong in bone. Upper arm of equal length with, and at right angles to, the shoulder-blade; elbows lying close to the ribs, but moving freely up to shoulder-blades. Lower arm short as compared with other animals, slightly inclined inwards (crook), seen in profile moderately straight, not bending forward nor knuckling over; feet large, round, and strong, with thick pads; toes compact and with distinct arch in each toe; nails strong. The dog must stand true—*i.e.*, equally on all parts of the foot.   *25 points*

Body or Trunk. Long and muscular, the line of the back slightly depressed at shoulders and slightly arched over loin, which should be short and strong; outline of belly moderately tucked up.   *9 points*

Hindquarters. Rump round, full, broad; muscles hard and plastic; hip-bone, or pelvis, not too short, broad, and strongly developed, set moderately sloping; thigh bones strong, of good length, and joined to the pelvis at right angles. Lower thighs short in comparison with other animals; hocks well developed and, seen from behind the legs, should be straight (not cow-hocked). Hind-feet smaller in bone and narrower than forefeet. The dog should not appear higher at the quarters than at the shoulders.   *10 points*

(1) THE DACHSHUND IS STILL IN ROYAL FAVOUR

Here is the King's Warrener ferreting in Windsor Park with one in attendance.

(2) A GOOD SPECIMEN OF THE ATTRACTIVE LONG-HAIRED
DACHSHUND

Mr R. E. Chamberlain's 'Nathaniel of Stutton.'

Photos Sport and General

"SLIPPED!"

Mrs Oliver Lucas's 'Blondie Locks' and Lieut.-Colonel Heseltine's 'Joe's Hunger' being slipped in the Sussex Oaks at the South of England Coursing Club's meeting at Woodhorne Farm, Bognor Regis, in 1937.

Photo Sport and General

Stern. Set on fairly high, strong and tapering, but not too long and not too much curved or carried too high. *5 points*

Coat and Skin. Short, dense, and smooth, but strong. The hair on the under-side of the tail coarse in texture. Skin loose and supple. *3 points*

Colour. Any colour. No white except spot on breast. Nose and sinal should be black. In red dogs a red nose is permissible, but not desirable. In chocolates and dapples the nose may be brown or flesh-coloured. In dapples large spots of colour are undesirable; the dog should be evenly dappled all over. *3 points*

Weight. Heavy-weights: up to 25 lb. for dogs, and up to 23 lb. for bitches. Light-weights: up to 21 lb. for dogs, and up to 19 lb. for bitches.

There, then, are the points which should give any ordinary supporter of the breed as much common-sense guidance as he desires so far as the smooth-haired type is concerned.

One final word of advice is worth remembering: that is, that if you want a dachshund to be of any use as a sporting dog it is no good having one with a mincing, dancing gait. This may look all very well in the house, but it is not the slightest use in the field. A dachshund which is to be a sporting dog must have a free, easy, swinging gait, throw its legs forward with a smooth, flowing motion, plenty of room between the hocks, nothing wobbly or unsteady. So if you are going to buy a dachshund for fun as well as decoration, have him trotted out and walked round just as you would with a horse. It is worth the extra five minutes of observation.

CHAPTER VI

THE GREYHOUND: I

Man-hod I am; therefore I me delyght
To hunt and hawke, to nourishe up and fede
The greyhounde to the course, the hawke to th' flight,
And to bestryde a good and lusty stede.

VISCOUNT WENTWORTH wrote an urgent letter to
the Earl of Carlisle on the 30th of November, 1632,
saying that he had been asked by his cousin Wandes-
ford to "furnish your Worship with some couples of
fleet hounds; it is grown a very rare commodity in
these parts, all men, as they tell me, having given
over breeding that kinde of cattle."

I wonder what Lord Wentworth would have to
say to-day were he to return to this twentieth-century
England and witness the "kinde of cattle" which we
are breeding in every back street and alley, every publican's paddock and bookmaker's backyard, in order
to race them at some one or other of the little coursing
meetings which dot the country?

I think the noble viscount would have no very good
word to say of some of the "fleet hounds" which
we see walked up and down suburban side-roads by
dirty-necked fellows in cloth caps and chokers.

The greyhound is a noble beast of the chase, with
an ancestry as long as time. He deserves more than
a full chapter in the history of English sport. He is,

indeed, the only hound which hunts to-day the last beast but one in England that deserves the noble name of a Beast of Forest or Venery; for the fox is still nothing but vermin—a fact which some of the camera-catching young women in Leicestershire might well remember when next they smirk from the pages of the shilling weeklies.

There were five animals which were properly Beasts of Forest or Venery—namely, the hart, hind, hare, boar, and wolf. Let me quote old W. B. Daniel on the matter. His ticklish English of 1801 is so neatly definitive as to be worth a resurrection:

" The hart is so named when in his sixth year; being called in the first year *hind-calf*, or *calf* ; in the second a *knobler*; in the third a *brocket*, or *spayard*; in the fourth a *staggart*; in the fifth a *stag*; in the sixth a *hart*; after being chased by the king or queen, if he escapes, he is a *hart-royal*.

" The hind in the first year is called *calf* ; in the second a *hearse*, or *brocket's sister*; in the third an *hind*.

" The hare is a *leveret* in the first year, a *hare* in the second, and a *great hare* in the third.

" The boar in the first year is a *pig of the sounder*; in the second an *hog*; in the third an *hog steer*; in the fourth a *boar*; at which age, if not before, he leaves the *sounder*."

Turbervile states, at the end of his volume, that he could find nothing in the foreign works that he had translated relative to coursing with greyhounds, but that in England they set great store by the pastime of coursing with greyhounds "at deare, hare, foxe, or such like, even of themselves, when there are neyther hounds hunting, nor other means to help them."

He sets forth that in coursing deer (especially red deer) the greyhounds were divided into three leashes, "teasers, sidelaies, and backsets," which were set at the deer in turn. In the coursing of hares a quaint method of procedure is laid down in detail. Thus:

"Let him which found the hare go towards and say, 'Up, pusse! Up!' until she ryse out of her forme. . . . When you go to course eyther hare or deare or to hunt any chace, it is a forfayture (amongst us here in England) to name eyther beare, ape, monkie, or hedgehogge; and he which nameth any of those should be payd with a slippe upon the buttockes in the field before he go any furder."

I would give a five-pound note to see Miss Fawcett or Mr Baxter or Mr Rank advancing upon a hare in its form at Altcar, crying, "Up, pusse! Up!" And how many fivers would it not be worth to see one or two of our more pompous pillars of the coursing world "payd with a slippe upon the buttockes in the field"! They had a nice sense of values in those days.

Turbervile's last words in his treatise of 250 pages on hunting are warmly in favour of coursing with greyhounds, "which is doubtlesse a noble pastime, and as mete for nobility and gentlemen as any of the other kinds of venerie before declared: especially the course at the hare, which is a sport continually in sight, and made without any great travaile: so that recreation is therein to be found without immeasurable toyle."

84

The 1481 *Boke of St Albans* gives this enchanting list: "Thyse be the names of hounds. Fyrste there is a grehound; a bastard; a mengrell; a mastif; a lemor; a spanyel; raches; kenettys; teroures; butchers' houndes; dunghyll dogges; tryndeltaylles; and pryck-eryd currys; and smalle ladye's popees that bere awaye the flees and dyvers small sawtes."

General Critchley may take it kindly that the "grehound" heads the list. The terrier is thinly hidden beneath the mantle of "teroure," while the "dunghyll dogges" and the "tryndeltaylles"—any sort of down-at-tail cur—is a fine, free way of brushing away all further attempts at classification. But one may be permitted the sly question whether the "smalle ladye's popees that bere awaye the flees" were the Pomeranians, Pekinese, and lap-spaniels of the day.

The historian goes on to give the methods of what he describes as "Royal hunting," and, as the greyhound enters largely into the picture, the description is worth quoting. But I wonder what the busybody humanitarian societies of to-day would have to say to the parks and chases "where the game was usually enclosed with a . . . fence-work of netting."

"*Royal Hunting.* Several methods of hunting were practised by the sportsmen of this kingdom, as well on horseback as on foot. Sometimes this exercise took place in the open country; sometimes in woods and thickets; and sometimes in parks, chases, and forests, where the game was usually enclosed with a haye or fence-work of netting, supported by posts driven into the ground for that purpose. The manner of hunting

85

at large needs no description; but, as the method of killing game within the enclosures is now totally laid aside, it may not be amiss to give the reader some idea how it was performed, and particularly when the king with the nobility were present at the sport. All the preparations and ceremonies necessary upon the occasion are set down at large in the manuscript made for the use of Prince Henry, mentioned before; the substance of which is as follows.

" When the king should think proper to hunt the hart in the parks or forests, either with bows or greyhounds, the master of the game, and the park-keeper, or the forester, being made acquainted with his pleasure, was to see that everything be provided necessary for the purpose. It was the duty of the sheriff of the county, wherein the hunting was to be performed, to furnish fit stabling for the king's horses, and carts to take away the dead game. The hunters and officers under the forester, with their assistants, were commanded to erect a sufficient number of temporary buildings for the reception of the royal family and their train; and, if I understand my author clearly, these buildings were directed to be covered with green boughs, to answer the double purpose of shading the company and the hounds from the heat of the sun, and to protect them from any inconveniency in case of foul weather.

" Early in the morning, upon the day appointed for the sport, the master of the game, with the officers deputed by him, was to see that the greyhounds were properly placed, and the person nominated to blow the horn, whose office was to watch what kind of game was turned out, and, by the manner of winding his horn, signify the same to the company, that they might be prepared for its reception upon its quitting the cover.

" Proper persons were then to be appointed, at different parts of the enclosure, to keep the populace at due distance. The yeomen of the king's bow, and the grooms of his turored greyhounds, had in charge to secure the king's standing, and prevent any noise being made to disturb the game before the arrival of his Majesty. When the royal family and the nobility were conducted to the places appointed for their reception, the master of the game, or his lieutenant, sounded three long mootes, or blasts with the horn, for the uncoupling of the hart hounds.

" The game was then driven from the cover, and turned by the huntsmen and the hounds so as to pass by the stands belonging to the king and queen, and such of the nobility as were permitted to have a share in the pastime; who might either shoot at them with their bows, or pursue them with the greyhounds at their pleasure.

" We are then informed that the game which the king, the queen, or the prince or princesses slew with their own bows, or particularly commanded to be let run, was not liable to any claim by the huntsmen or their attendants; but of all the rest that was killed they had certain parts assigned to them by the master of the game, according to the ancient custom.

" This arrangement was for a royal hunting, but

similar preparations were made upon like occasions for the sport of the great barons and dignified clergy. Their tenants sometimes held lands of them by the service of finding men to enclose the grounds, and drive the deer to the stands whenever it pleased their lords to hunt them."

CHAPTER VII

THE GREYHOUND: II

How his Name Began—The Duke of Norfolk's Rules—The
Swaffham Coursing Society—Lord Orford's Dramatic Death—
A Winter's Tale on Newmarket Heath.

I WAS PERHAPS A LITTLE LONG-WINDED historically
in the previous chapter. But then the greyhound has
a long-winded history. He is almost the oldest hunting
dog in the world—probably quite the oldest if you
regard him in his different forms.

As for the etymology of the name, there are all sorts
of views. Whitaker derives it from the ancient British
word *greg* or *grech*, which means a dog. But various
Scottish writers, including Sir David Lindsay, suggest
that the word *gre* means a dog of degree or rank. One
or two of the more classically minded historians of the
breed have suggested that the word comes from *Graius*
(Grecian), because greyhounds, or a whippet form of
them, were popular with the Greeks. Then there is a
Dutch name *Gruss-hund*, which derives from the word
grypun, meaning 'to grip.'

Canute passed a law which laid it down that nobody
below the rank of a gentleman could keep a greyhound. So that might suggest that it was a 'great'
hound—or the hound of the great.

In any case it seems quite definite and unmistakable
that the breed in this country came from Egypt, the
Levant countries, and Western Asia generally, having
as their common root a dog approximating to the

89

Saluki of to-day. There seem to have been three types to start with: the first an East Russian and Tartary type, which was rough-coated; the second a smoother, more silky-haired dog which came from Egypt, Persia, and Natolia; and the third the two rough-haired and smooth-haired dogs which we know to-day as the Scotch or Irish deerhound and the ordinary greyhound.

Egyptologists who have given a little time to dogs when they could spare their thoughts from mummies have suggested that the oldest type of all was yellow in colour, to match the sand, wire-haired, with short prick ears. This is the type of animal which I have seen on Egyptian temple walls, and no doubt it was a desert hunting dog of a very common type, widely distributed.

At any rate, the greyhound has one unchallengeable boast to his credit—he can claim to be among the oldest of all dogs, the dog most seen in the company of kings, the dog most frequently chosen by artists, and the dog whom men have chosen again and again to be sculptured on their monuments and mural memorials—the dog who, above all others, was rated as the fittest companion for the voyage to the other world.

You will find the greyhound on old Greek cameos, on the Greek terra-cotta vases in the British Museum, in Dürer's picture of St Hubert, in Pisano's *Vision of St Eustace*, painted before 1438. Vulcan forged the first greyhound in brass, named it Lailaps, and then, because he liked the look of it, gave it life.

You will know, if I remember my mythology rightly, that this was the dog that Vulcan gave to Jupiter, from whom it passed to Europa, to Minos, to Procris, and then to Cephalus. It "had a nature so irresistible that he overtook all that he hunted, like the Teumesian fox, and Jupiter, to avoid confusion, then turned both these incomprehensible beasts into stone."

The great Molossian dogs, which I mentioned in the first chapter of this book, are supposed to be descended from that original bronze hound of Jupiter.

Coursing in England to-day derives in the first place from the original rules laid down by a Duke of Norfolk, which led to the foundation of the immortal Swaffham Coursing Society in 1776. There were twenty-five members; the Earl of Orford was the founder, and, merely to show that modern young women who think that female 'independence' is something like a fireman's brass badge, to be flaunted, it is worth noting that the Lady Patroness was the Marchioness of Townsend, the Vice-Patroness was the Countess of Cholmondeley, and Mrs Cooke was the assistant Vice-Patroness.

The so-called Duke of Norfolk's rules of coursing given by Taplin are worth quoting as a picture of coursing practice in his (Taplin's) time:

" 1. No hare to be coursed with more than a brace of greyhounds.

" 2. The hare-finder to give the hare three *so-hos* before he put her from her form, that the dogs might have notice to attend to her being started.

" 3. The hare to have law of twelve score yards

before the greyhounds were loosed, unless the small distance between the hare and the covert would not admit it without danger of immediately losing her.

"4. The dog that gave the first turn and during the course, if there was neither cote, slip, nor wrench, won.

"5. A cote is when a greyhound goes endways by his fellow, and gives the hare a turn.

"6. A cote served for two turns, and two trippings or jerkins for a cote; if the hare did not turn quite about she only wrenched, and two wrenches stand for a turn.

"7. If there were no cotes given between a brace of greyhounds, but that one of them served the other at turning, then he that gave the brace most turns won; and if one gave as many turns as the other, then he that bore the hare won.

"8. If one dog gave the first turn, and the other lose the hare, he that bore the hare won.

"9. A go-by, or hearing the hare, was equivalent to two turns.

"10. If neither dog turned the hare, he that led last to the covert won.

"11. If one dog turned the hare, served himself, and turned her again, it was as much as a cote—for a cote was esteemed two turns.

"12. If all the course was equal the dog that bore the hare won; if the hare was not borne the course was adjudged dead—that is, undecided.

"13. If a dog fell in a course, and yet performed his part, he might challenge the advantage a turn more than he gave.

" 14. If a dog turned the hare, served himself, and gave divers cotes, and yet in the end stood still in the field, the other dog, if he ran home to the covert, although he gave no turn, was adjudged the winner.

" 15. If, by accident, a dog was run over in his course, the course was void, and he that did the mischief was to make reparation for the damage.

" 16. If a dog gave the first and last turn, and there was no other advantage between them, he that gave the odd turn won.

" 17. He that came in first at the death, took up the hare, saved her from being torn, cherished the dogs, and cleansed their mouths from the fleck was allowed to retain the hare for his trouble.

" 18. And those who were appointed judges of the course were to give their decision before they departed from the field."

This Lord Orford who founded the Swaffham Club was a curious fellow. A man of undoubted ability, great mental quickness, and terrific enthusiasm, he is very well summed up in Taplin's words:

" Nothing in art or science, nothing in mental or even in manual labour, was ever achieved of superior excellence, without that ardent zeal, that impetuous sense of eager avidity which to the cold, inanimate, and unimpassioned bears the appearance and sometimes the unqualified accusation of insanity."

One of Lord Orford's engaging habits was to drive a phaeton round about Newmarket with four red stags harnessed to it. This was a very pleasant, spectacular method of progress. But he was caught rather badly on it one day a mile or two outside Newmarket, when a pack of hounds, crossing the road behind him, got the wind of the deer and hunted them into Newmarket at top speed. The old record says that the deer, scared out of their wits by the hounds, dashed off with the " celerity of a whirlwind," dragging the phaeton behind them bumping and bouncing over the road until it was nearly shaken to pieces.

Luckily for Orford, the deer were accustomed to be stabled at the Ram Inn, at Newmarket. And they swept into the stable-yard full tilt, nearly wrecking the phaeton on the gate-posts as they dashed in. The ostlers just managed to slam the door on the hounds' noses in time.

Lord Orford took a lot of trouble over the breeding of his greyhounds. He tried every sort of cross, including Italian greyhounds and English lurchers—the latter of the same type as you still find in use as ' warren dogs ' on the big heaths round about Thetford. He even tried a bulldog cross. Finally, after seven generations of breeding, he got what were acknowledged to be the best greyhounds of the time. They had " small ears, rat tails, and skins almost without hair, together with that innate courage . . . rather to die than relinquish the chase."

He used to turn up at the meetings on Newmarket Heath in the most bitter weather, riding a cobby, broad-backed piebald pony, a cocked hat stuck belligerently on his head, no coat or gloves on, blue and red with cold. He was a great figure, and the crowd loved him.

In the end he went off his head. His relatives shut him up. Newmarket Heath and its coursing meetings saw him no more.

The end was sad but rather fine. He had a bitch named Czarina running in trials of more than ordinary importance. You must imagine the crowd collected on a winter's day, somewhere between the town and the Devil's Ditch, a sky of bleak and bitter blue, the wind cutting keenly off the Fens. All Swaffham Prior, Burwell, Swaffham Bulbeck, Reach, and the farther watery wastes of Wicken lay glistening in the sun, their meres and fen pools shining in the distance like beaten silver.

The eighteenth-century crowd, in their rough, fustian country clothes, their heavy highlows, coarse, gay-coloured scarves, and flat-brimmed hats, with their long coats down to their heels, stood stamping and shivering on the heath. A few of the gentry, the local lords and squires, were cantering up and down on their blood hacks. A coach or two was drawn up as a grandstand.

You can see the coachman, red-faced, red-nosed, with his flat beaver hat, his many-caped greatcoat, blowing down his nose, wheezing out the odds, rumbling out the praise of his fancy.

Rough "Fen tigers" out of the Fens, in round moleskin caps and moleskin waistcoats, their long leather fowling boots drawn up to their thighs, watched impassively, murderous-looking lurchers and ginger-coloured ' 'coy dogs' at their heels. It was just such a rough and tough sporting day as that splendid bit of English country has produced for centuries past. Every man among them had a sneaking thought, a passing regret, for the fine old Norfolk earl who had been the heart and soul of the meetings for so long and now was 'shut away.'

Suddenly, across the heath from Newmarket, thundered a fat galloping pony, a broad, dominating figure in the saddle, a cocked hat stuck grimly on his head. It was Lord Orford. He had escaped from his family prison, evaded his guardian, jumped on his old favourite piebald pony—and here they were together—master and mount, waiting to see Czarina run.

A ragged cheer went up. The old boy sat bolt erect on his horse, his face as crimson as of old in the biting Fen wind, no greatcoat on his back, no gloves on his hands. He watched Czarina run her trial. Czarina won. And Lord Orford raised his cocked hat to her, swayed in his saddle, toppled on his back—and died.

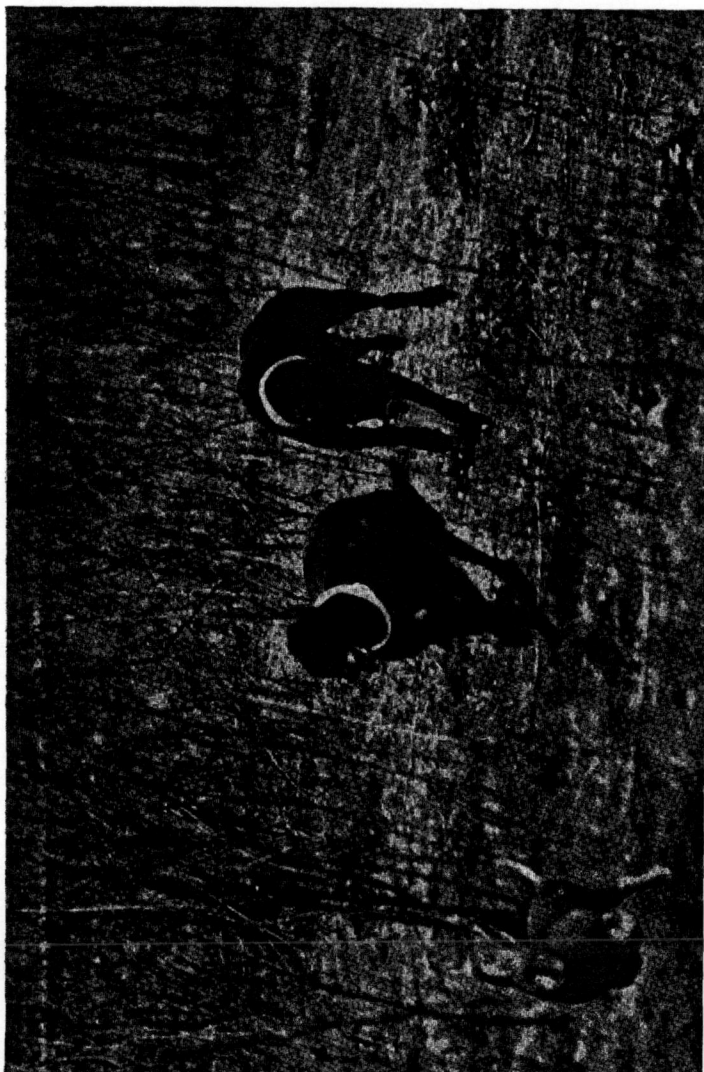

A REAL HARE THIS TIME!

The track greyhounds 'Just Hypnotic' and 'Waxen' in a course for the London Cup at Hockwold, in West Norfolk, in January 1938.

Photo Sport and General

(1) MRS PERCY ADAMS'S 'BELLA DONNA'

A notable specimen of the best type of whippet of to-day.

(2) GREYHOUND RACING AT STAMFORD BRIDGE

The start of the Smuggler Stakes, won by 'Genial Rajah.'

Photos Sport and General

CHAPTER VIII

THE GREYHOUND: III

Some Great Greyhounds, their Feats and Owners—The Great Snowball Family—Freak Bets and Challenges—Dame Juliana Berners' Points of the Perfect Hound—The Amazing Miss Richards and her Love Affairs—Lobengula's Italian Greyhound.

THAT EXTRAORDINARY MAN COLONEL THORNTON, one of the most eccentric sportsmen of all time, bought the best of Lord Orford's kennels after his death, taking most of them up to Thornville Royal, his place in Yorkshire. This made more than a mark on coursing history in the North, and greatly improved the local strains in Yorkshire. The Colonel paid from thirty to forty guineas apiece. His purchases included Jupiter and the immortal Czarina. She had then won forty-seven matches, and, so far as I can trace, had never had a defeat. But although the Colonel was most anxious to breed from her, she produced nothing until she was thirteen years of age, when she suddenly made up her mind to give Yorkshire a little bit of Norfolk quality. The result was eight puppies by Jupiter.

Two of these made coursing history, for Claret and Young Czarina beat every greyhound in Yorkshire. Claret sired Snowball and Major, both of whom made historic names. Snowball was reckoned to be the perfect type of greyhound. During his lifetime he beat a Scotch greyhound which was the champion of Scotland. In Yorkshire he was regarded as unbeatable by any dog except his full brother, Major.

G   97

Most coursing men know the famous story of " Snowball and the Hare." It is one of the landmarks in sporting history, and even stirred Sir Walter Scott to write a poem eulogizing " Fleet Snowball," which I do not propose to quote.

The actual course lasted about four miles, included forty or fifty turns of the hare, and it took Snowball and the hare twice up and down a hill a mile high.

It took place at the village of Flexton Brow, which stands on the hilltop. The course started with Snowball, a young dog twelve months old, and a sister of Snowball, all coursing the same hare. The other two dropped out about two-thirds of the way through, and Snowball was left to finish the course on his own, which he did, killing the hare in fine style in the village.

This achievement, coupled with the general fame of the family, resulted in one of the biggest farces in sporting history. A Mr Durand, who lived near Epsom, sent a challenge to Colonel Thornton for a thousand guineas, to match his greyhound Bellissima against any of the Snowballs, " play or pay."

On the appointed day about five hundred people on horseback and as many again in carriages, whiskies, tax-carts, buggies, and other strange vehicles gathered on Sutton Heights to witness this momentous match.

The Colonel, as usual, did things in terrific style. He was a great believer in pomp and majesty, and considered no one more majestic than himself. Everything that could be done to impress was done on every possible occasion. So it was on this day.

98

First of all two of his retainers led out of the van
two brace of the Colonel's greyhounds, sheeted in blue
and buff. These were merely canine heralds for the
dog Major, who then appeared in rich buff. On his
right side was emblazoned the arms and crest of
Colonel Thornton. On his left, in bold gold lettering,
blazed the challenge, " Major Aut Ne Plus Ultra,"
which, being modestly interpreted, means, " There is
nothing better than Major."

Mr Durand was overwhelmed. His heart, confidence, and his thousand guineas failed him on the spot.
He announced that he was quite satisfied that no dog
of his could possibly beat the magnificent Major.
The match was off. The disappointment of the onlookers was " prodigious." The Colonel scarcely concealed his disgust.

But Mr Durand merely begged blandly that a box-
hare should be liberated in order that the onlookers
might see something of Major's powers. So the
wretched box-hare was let loose. Major "made a
spring of many yards" and killed it. Whether this
means that he took a standing leap immediately the
hare dashed out of the box can best be left to the
imagination.

Those were the days of odd challenges and odd bets.
The next freak meeting took place at Doncaster in
December 1800, when a pair of racehorses were
matched against a greyhound for a hundred guineas,
over a distance of four miles. The contest must have
been more than interesting to watch, although of no
great practical value. What happened was that a mare

and the greyhound bitch raced over the distance, practically neck and neck the whole way, giving, so the record says, " an excellent treat to the field by the energetic exertions of both." The betting at the distance post was 5 to 4 on the greyhound, but it evened as they were passing the grandstand. The mare won by about a head.

No intelligent person, however, would take this race seriously, for it is almost certain that the greyhound would merely endeavour to keep level with the mare for the fun of the thing, but would almost certainly not attempt to race it. Anyone who has seen greyhounds following a hack or a hunter at exercise would realize this. But it does suggest that the greyhound might have been able to beat the racehorse had there been some inducement to make her do so.

Of the many remarkable courses on record I always like that quoted by Taplin of a brace of greyhounds which were being walked out by a man in the year 1792. On the way a hare got up. The greyhounds plunged after it, and were away at top speed with the leash still holding them. In spite of this handicap they actually coursed the hare over four miles and killed her.

I cannot find out the record length of a course in actual distance—if, indeed, there is any such record. Old sporting history, magazines, books, and records are so full of such fantastic claims and boasts that the truth is almost impossible to discover.

But there is a record which I think we may take as authentic, of a brace of greyhounds which in February

1798 coursed a hare from a field on the banks of the river Swift near Carlisle to Clemmell, a full seven miles in a straight line. They killed her in good style, having covered the distance in "remarkably short time," though how short the time was we are not told.

Then there is the tale of a Mr Moore, living at Windsor, who bought a greyhound from a man in Yorkshire. The greyhound was sent by coach from Yorkshire, consigned to the " Bell-Savage, an inn upon Ludgate Hill." There it was handed over to the guard of the Windsor Coach, who duly delivered it to Mr Moore.

A few days later it disappeared. Mr Moore had taken every possible care of it, and had become rather fond of it. He searched high and low. Finally he wrote to the seller in Yorkshire to tell him that the greyhound had disappeared mysteriously. Back came an answer to say that it had just turned up at its old home, rather footsore but in good fettle. I wish I knew the exact location of the seller in Yorkshire, so that one might work out the actual mileage covered by the dog, but neither the location of its old home nor the actual time which it took to cover the distance is given. None the less it is a remarkable instance of homing instinct.

Yorkshire has always kept up its reputation of pro-ducing something remarkable in sport, sportsmen, and the instruments of sport. It was a Mr Hodgson, of Stamford Bridge, in the East Riding, who produced probably the most remarkable strain of greyhounds seen in this country. He had three bitches, known as "the Dents," of quite remarkable appearance. They had short curled tails, small ears, and completely smooth skins, and are said to have resembled "a very light, smart rabbit dog." Their principal quality in actual performance was that they turned with the hare. As they were fast into the bargain, with lots of stamina, they naturally went for high prices. Mr Richard Darley, of Aldby Park, added to the family fame engendered by the Darley Arabian by buying one of them, Sir Francis Boynton, Bart., of Burton Agnes, had another, and a Major Topham got the third.

The main point about these three bitches was that they are said to have shown in every detail, except for tails, the famous set of points laid down by Dame Juliana Berners in *The Boke of St Alban's*—to wit, "the *head* of a snake, the *neck* of a drake, the *foot* of a cat, the *tail* of a rat, the *side* of a bream, and the *back* like a beam."

You can compare that neat summary with the points laid down by Edward, Duke of York, in *The Master of Game*. He says that the ideal greyhound should have "shuldres as a roe buck; the for legges streght and grete ynow, and nought to hind legges; the feet streight and round as a catte, and great cleas; the boones and the joyntes of the cheyne grete and hard as the cheyne of an hert; the thighs great and squarred as an hare; the houghs streight, and not crompying as an oxe."

Master McGrath will probably go down in history as the best greyhound ever bred, although many authorities do not consider him such a perfect model of points as Bed of Stone (Portland-Imperatrice), the dark fawn bitch who won the Waterloo Cup in 1872 for Mr J. Briggs, of Altcar. Bed of Stone weighed then 47 lb., Master McGrath round about 52 lb., and the immortal Fullerton about 62 lb. (I say 'about' owing to varying weights at different times.)

There is an engraving somewhere by James Armstrong of Bed of Stone. Anyone who can pick it up will have the perfect picture of points.

I do not propose to go into lengthy details of Waterloo Cup history in this work. It would be merely a record of statistical details which can be found elsewhere in works on the subject.

There is an excellent book called *Fifty-six Waterloo Cups*, by "Vindex," the pen-name of Mr James Lowie, of *The Sporting Chronicle*. In it he gives every conceivable detail of the various meetings which have been held since the first one in 1826. The year before that there had been a sort of village meeting on Lord Sefton's estate at Altcar, and as the Waterloo Hotel was the headquarters of the patrons, the meeting took its name from that. In the early days the prize was a silver collar and a stake, but in 1903 a cup valued at £100 was put up. Nowadays the winner of the Waterloo Cup gets £500 prize money in addition to the cup, while the runner-up receives £200, and the owners of the third and fourth dogs, £50 each; numbers five, six, seven, and eight receive £30 each; the next eight get £20, and after that £160 is shared between the owners of the next sixteen dogs—so there are pickings for all, or most of them.

The famous Master McGrath appeared to fame in 1868, when he beat Lobelia, that remarkable bitch who had the signal honour of having the church bells of Christ Church rung for her when she won the Cup in 1867. The parson discovered half-way through the ringing what the noise was all about, and indignantly ordered the bell-ringers out of the church.

Master McGrath was not greatly fancied in 1868, while Lobelia was a hot favourite, but he beat her. Altogether this remarkable dog won three Waterloo Cups, the last in 1871, after he had been used for stud purposes.

Then there was Coomassie, a famous little bitch who only weighed 42 lb., probably the smallest greyhound ever to win the Cup, which she did twice. "Vindex" says of her, "It is no exaggeration to say that a Waterloo Cup was never more brilliantly won." Cerito won the Cup three times, but Fullerton eclipsed this record by carrying it off four times, four years running, his last victory being in 1892.

Probably the most remarkable character in the whole history of coursing is that extraordinary woman Miss Ann Richards, of Comptom Beauchamp, an estate near Ashdown Park, high up on the Berkshire Downs. She was the complete sporting squiress. Her estate both of land and money was large. She was a first-class horsewoman, devoted to dogs, an ardent coursing enthusiast, and not a bad-looker into the bargain.

The local lords and squires besieged her like a swarm of flies. But Miss Ann Richards was having none of them.

The method of courting in those days was amusing. The suitor arrived on horseback accompanied by a servant carrying a large bandbox containing his ceremonial wig—what you may describe as his wig for calling purposes. So at Comptom Beauchamp they had what was known as the Wig Avenue. When you went to call on the lady you pulled up your horse at the end of the avenue, took off your riding wig, and put on the long, elaborately dressed curls of ceremony—hence the phrase 'setting his wig at her.'

But no amount of wigs, lords, squires, or gentlemen could win Ann from her dogs. Every morning she was driven in her coach up to the high downs, where she coursed hares, walking anything from fifteen to twenty-five miles a day. She kept up fine, old-fashioned customs of giving free beer and refreshments to any callers at the house, and all sick visitors who wanted a little blood-letting were attended to by William Carter, her old coachman. William was a rough-and-ready hand with a lancet and cup, but in spite of his hedgerow surgery the number of sick men in the near-by villages who required blood-letting—and beer—was phenomenal.

It was always said of Ann that when she engaged a servant she asked, " Young man, or young woman, do you love dogs?"

" Yes, please, your ladyship, in their proper place," was the answer.

" Very well," Miss Richards replied. " Remember that their proper place in my home is anywhere they think fit to go."

Her whole house was crawling with dogs, upstairs and down. Each room contained a settee for the especial use of any dog which took a fancy to it.

This remarkable woman had an adopted daughter, Miss Watts, to whom she left all her spaniels, setting dogs, pointers, and greyhounds, with the order that they should be looked after as though they were her children. Miss Watts honoured this instruction so faithfully that some of the dogs lived until they were twenty.

Among other things Ann left was her own epitaph, which I think is worth quoting:

> Reader, if ever sport to thee was dear,
> Drop on Ann Richards' tomb a tear,
> Who when alive with piercing eye
> Did many a timid hare descry;
> Well skill'd and practis'd in the art,
> Sometimes to find and sometimes start,
> All arts and sciences beside,
> This hare-brained heroine did deride:
> An utter foe to wedlock's noose,
> When poaching men had stopt the meuse.
> Tattle and tea! she was above it,
> And but for her form appeared to love it.
> All books she laughed at, Pope and Clarke,
> And all her joy was Ashdown Park,
> But Ann at length was spy'd by death,
> Who cours'd and ran her out of breath;
> No shifting, winding turn could save
> Her active life from gaping grave;
> As greyhound with superior force
> Seizes poor puss and stops her course,
> So stopp'd the fates our heroine's view,
> And had her take a long adieu
> Of shrill so-ho! and loud halloo.

I can find no record that Miss Richards was ever sufficiently feminine to succumb to the charms of that delightful little dog the Italian greyhound, useless from the sporting point of view, but most attractive as a decorative pet. Some were minute. Indeed, a Mr Knowland, of Bachelors' Walk, Dublin, owned one which was only 9 inches high. It was properly described as " a vast soul in a little carcass."

Taplin, commenting on these little dogs, says that they were so delicate that if you held one up by its legs against a strong light you could see most of its internal organs. The average weight was between 6 and 8 lb.

I have, I think, seen one or two genuine specimens in the last ten years, but not many . As far back as 1867 " Stonehenge " described it as " the rarest dog of the day."

In Staffordshire, where bull-terriers govern the canine horizon, this greyhound was occasionally mated with a small bull-terrier, producing a blue-tan puppy, which was rather like the blue terrier once popular in London, and known as a " blue Peter."

The Italian greyhound figures as a decorative element in a great many portraits by Kneller, Van Dyck, Watteau, Lely, and the rest of the fashionable portrait-painters of the seventeenth and eighteenth centuries. Every one knows the picture of Queen Anne at Hampton Court which shows her about to mount her horse, attended by a negro servant and Italian greyhounds.

The most charming story I know of them is that of Lobengula, King of the Matabele, and a mighty man in the long line of African fighting potentates. When Mr Murcombe Searelle, the traveller, visited this forbidding monarch he presented him, as a flight of fancy, with an Italian greyhound. The King was so delighted that he retaliated with a herd of 200 cattle!

The whippet, a larger version, so to speak, of the Italian greyhound, was really responsible for the beginning of greyhound-racing in Great Britain. The breeding of the original whippet was a cross between an Italian greyhound and a greyhound, or sometimes a terrier. The result to-day is a very sporting, attractive little animal, graceful in the extreme, weighing from 8 to 28 lb. and about 18½ inches high.

They were bred originally for rabbit-coursing, and it is generally reckoned that the bitches are faster than the dogs. To-day no miner in the North of England considers himself properly equipped if he is not the owner or part-owner of a whippet. Apart from rabbit-coursing in the open, a great deal of whippet-racing goes on in industrial and mining districts, and in a good many country villages all over England. Racing is generally known as 'straight running.' The dogs race down a series of lanes or tracks divided from one another by string. The 'lure' is a handkerchief or coloured rag which the owner waves frantically at the end of the track.

I must say that, provided they are well handicapped, a good whippet race is well worth watching, and I have seen some amazing bursts of speed put up by these little dogs. The standard distance is 200 yards, and a tip-top dog will do it in 12 seconds. They race with a curiously springy, elastic action, taking tremendous jumps, sometimes as much as fifteen feet in length.

On the whole, whippet-racing is well conducted and honestly run. There seems to be very little dirty business about it.

Whippets are not expensive to buy, charming little pets about the house, and delightful to look at.

Some of the stake money is quite big, £100 handicaps not being uncommon at Newcastle and other North Country towns.

The points of the whippet as laid down by the Whippet Club are:

Head long and lean, rather wide between the eyes and flat at the top; the *muzzle* finely chiselled, rather long and free from bluntness; the *jaws* powerful yet clearly cut, neither over-shot nor under-shot; *teeth* level and white. *Eyes* bright, quick, and denoting animation. *Ears* small, fine in texture, and rose-shaped. The natural ear carriage should be in a semi-erect position, and not bolt upright.

Neck long, straight, narrow, and rather lean, fairly muscular, and must be well let into the shoulders. *Shoulders* oblique and rather muscular but not overloaded with muscle or fat. The tops of the shoulder-blades should be fairly close together.

Chest deep and hatchet-shaped, showing plenty of heart room. *Brisket* very deep, and should reach almost down to the elbow joint. *Ribs* well sprung, but not barrel-shaped. They should not be visible, but just nicely covered. The *thigh bones* should also be well hidden, but not loaded with flesh.

Forelegs rather long, perfectly straight, firm, and upright; must be well set under dog, and should possess plenty of bone. *Elbows* should be firm and rigid, neither turning inward nor outward. *Pasterns* must be very firm and absolutely upright. *Feet* round, neither turned inward nor outward; *toe joints* well arched, but must be close together and not sprawly; *toenails* must be kept short, and the soles should be round and firm. *Back* broad and rather long (to allow for covering plenty of ground, and to be free from short-coupling). The *loin* should be slightly arched, very firm, and nicely moulded. *Hindquarters* strong and broad across, possessing plenty of driving power; *stifles* well bent and gracefully curved, *thighs* broad and muscular, *hocks* well let down. *Tail* long, tapering, and slightly curved, carried not higher than the level of the back while in motion. *Coat* short, fine, close, and glossy.

The ideal *height* (at shoulder) for dogs is $18\frac{1}{2}$ inches, and that for bitches $17\frac{1}{2}$ inches. The ideal *weight* for dogs is 21 lb., and for bitches 20 lb.

Colours black, red, white, brindle, fawn, blue, and the various mixtures of each.

CHAPTER IX

COURSING DAYS ON FEN AND
SEA-MARSH

High Fen and the Gypsies—Farmer-sportsmen of the Right
Sort—Old Essex Days—Memories of Potton Island—The Devil
in Blue Fire.

Up at six, a breakfast of great, thick gammon rashers, hot, strong tea, home-made bread and butter, and then, still tingling from the effects of an ice-cold sluice in a tin bath, we are bowling along the highroad, through fields of dun-brown stubbles, a nip of frost making one draw the horse rug closer round the ankles.

In the stern-sheets a brace of the real Fen longtails curl up in the straw, their snaky heads and wet black noses nuzzling confidentially at one's calves. They may be 'look-dogs,' but I will lay half a sovereign that they can smell the three great mutton sandwiches stuffed hastily in the right-hand pocket of the old shooting jacket. There is more than mere dog-devotion in the persistence of those exploratory nuzzlings.

By eight o'clock we are on a wide and windy upland, the November stubbles glittering with melted drops of hoar-frost under the sharp blue of a winter sky. Miles of cattle pastures, seamed with dykes, dotted with bullocks, clamorous with gulls and pewits, stretch away to the winding snake of the Cam, a blue thread coiled through the green.

Smoke from a gypsy's hedge-fire curls up in a straight, thin column from the shallow ditch which

111

bounds the long, green Roman road that runs from Upware to this Fen farm of High Fen, our meeting-place. There have been gypsies camping in that lane, Lees and others, for the last two centuries. It is their immemorial squatting-place. Winter after winter they are there. Neither snow nor Fen gales, neither blizzard of rain nor driving storm of sleet, daunts them.

There was one winter when my great-uncle sent men through waist-deep snowdrifts to dig them out, for my grandmother, a woman of tender heart, was convinced that they must all be frozen dead. But when the men got there—and it took them nearly half a day to do so—they found the gypsies' wigwam-like tent buried deeply in the snow, the drifts banked up steeply around it, the smoke of their camp-fire redolent of roast pork. From somewhere they had purloined a sucking-pig. The little family, father, mother, and three strapping children, were as fit as fleas, over-whelmed with joy at the Christmas pudding, the joint of beef, and the bottle of rum which had been sent to them through the snow.

That was over forty years ago. But the memory of that one womanly act of kindness and Christian charity was preserved in the gypsy family. They knew that "the Guv'nor" lived for his harriers and grey-hounds. So the unwritten gypsy law went out that no hare should be touched on his lands. Rabbits they took, and were blessed for it. Dead chickens they filched gratefully from farmyard dunghills. Hedge-hogs they baked in clay. I ate one with them once—as good as chicken. Dead sheep they accepted as an act

(1) WAITING TO BE SLIPPED

Mr G. E. F. Tenison's 'Tricky,' Mr F. C. Minoprio's 'McSirtan,' and
Mr G. E. F. Tenison's 'Tussaur' at Altcar in 1938.

Photo Sport and General

(2) OVER THE JUMP

A remarkable—and probably unique—photograph of a racing greyhound in
action at the White City, the Mecca of the sport to-day.

By permission of the Greyhound Racing Association, Ltd.

(1) MR H. S. LLOYD'S 'EXQUISITE MODEL OF WARE'
A black-and-white cocker which won seventeen championships in 1937.

(2) THE LATE KING GEORGE'S 'SANDRINGHAM SPARKLE'
Considered to be one of the best specimens of the Clumber spaniel breed.

Photos Sport and General

of God. They once even excavated a litter of still-born piglets from the muck-heap where they had been born. And, of course, mangolds, turnips, potatoes, field-beans, and the hedgerow fringes of the orchard paid their proper tolls to these children of the earth. But the hares were safe.

That is why, on this pre-War morning which I ask you to imagine, we are met, at the old red-brick bridge over the lazy dyke which unites High Fen Pits with the Cam, by a long, swarthy, hawk-eyed fellow in a red choker, who informs us that a hare lies under yonder hedge, that another has her seat on Fodder Fen, and that a third has been using the same form in the field behind the draining mill for the last three weeks. It is the custom of that gypsy family, born of that dead-and-gone grandmother's act of grace long before the War.

Presently other people join us. One or two farmers in brown buskins on stout cobs, schoolboys in jerseys and chilly shorts, the vet. on his own lanky legs, a parson from over the river on a raking white horse that must be nineteen if it is a day, young Wilfred, the miller, with a face like a rising sun and two fists like hams, a couple of undergraduates from Trinity—none of your *suède*-footed, whey-faced, sniffling little intellectuals who nowadays clutter the pavements of the university, but a couple of the right sort of young Englishmen who in a few years' time will be worth something tangible to their country and their families.

There is not much formality about this village meeting of ours, no cups to be won, no prize money. There

H 113

are a few bets: "Half a quid on young Joe's dog," and "I'll lay ye three to one in half-crowns on my bitch"—and that is about all. Sport with these Fen farmers needs neither cash prizes, cups, nor bets to give it its proper edge.

We are out to match each other's dogs, to give our lungs a good blowing, kill a few hares for the pot, and to wind up the day with an appetite that will make a side of beef look silly and a quart of beer look small.

The first hare is soon roused. Young Wilfred's long-tails are slipped at her, and then it is gallop and jump, puff and blow, over the stubbles, through a straggly thorn hedge where the redwings and fieldfares start up in chacking clouds, across a cattle marsh where the bullocks career wildly in front of us, tails up, snorting and bellowing.

Then there is a dyke, broad and glittering, edged by rusty fringes of dead rushes, brown in the sun. We speared eels there in the summer, took moorhens' eggs from squashy nests, netted bream, fat and floundering.

But now it is cold and clear. No tench move goldenly through subaqueous forests of green weed. No water-lilies lift their maiden faces to the song of larks.

But the parson goes at it on his old grey Rosinante as though he were Dick Christian himself taking the Whissendine. He clears it beautifully, puss and the longtails streaming away in front of him. One of the farmers' cobs jibs violently on the bank. Pot-hat, red face, green shooting coat, cord breeches, brown bus-kins, and thumping great boots fly through the air like

a projectile from a Norman arbalest. He hits the
water like a sack of wheat, goes right under in a
mighty surge, scrambles out on the other bank,
squelching cascades from every limb. That has made
the day. There is a gust of laughter which quickens
even the flying hare to greater speed.

But, like another and more immortal ducking, " the
pace is too good to stop and inquire." The rest of us
are over or through somehow. As for the schoolboys,
there is not a dry one among them.

Two quick turns on the big bullock fen beyond and
the leading greyhound runs into puss, kills her neatly.

We are near enough, by the grace of fortune and the
hare's direction, to that other hare which Jack the
gypsy told us had her seat by the poplars on Fodder
Fen.

So after a few minutes of chat and laughter, a
strong pull at the rum-flask for the farmer who took
the dyke—for he caught his cob and came up with us
riding like a windmill—we are off again. There is
another course down there on the Fen by the river.
But she beats us this time by jumping boldly into the
Cam and swimming it from bank to bank. Good luck
to her!

But there was the sight of a hen-harrier beating the
windy levels, an echo of Elizabethan England in the
vision of six great grey herons blown windily across
the sky, like gaunt rags.

Four wild swans came high overhead, the chanting
wave-beats of their wings making a windy threnody
in the great silence of the Fen sky.

There are always these compelling sights and consoling visions in any day of sport on the Fen, no matter how otherwise fruitless it may be.

We have half a dozen hares by the end of the day as the sun drops down in a red bale fire through the ragged willows which stand Valkyrian against the western sky.

There is a gleam of firelight through the red curtains of the sanded bar-parlour of the " Five Miles From Anywhere—No Hurry," that Elysian pub of my boyhood which stands brooding, whitewashed and red-roofed, by the ferry at Upware, where the waters of Wicken, Burwell, and Reach gurgle through their lock-gates into the parent stream of Cam.

It was the obvious place to make for at the end of such a day. What stories of dog and gun, of fish and fowl, of punt-gunning and plover-netting, of eel-spearing and pike-fishing, of battles with bargees and forays after geese and duck, that old place could tell!

It was there, in the sixties, that the famous " Upware Republic " flourished. That fantastic club of sporting undergraduates made it their headquarters for shooting and fishing, for drinking and fighting, for crazy water frolics, for the compilation of a set of records which are crisp fun to read even to this day. And what is more, in spite of their drinking and fighting, the " Republic " turned out men who in later life occupied some of the highest positions in the State and the professions. Sir John Eldon Gorst was one who comes to my mind.

But here we are. Some one has kicked the door

open. There is a clatter of heavy boots in the boarded passageway, a snaky twisting of greyhounds through one's legs, eager for a smell of the fire; the sudden, thick, warm smell of niggerhead tobacco, wood-smoke, wet corduroys, clay pipes, and mulled beer. They are all in there, jammed as tight as fleas.

Here are the sons of Fenland, the men who live by plough and boat, by eel-spear and turf becket, by sedge-cutting and dyke-dydling.

Here is Charlie Crisp, rosy and rotund in his corner, his long water-boots stuck out straight in front of him, his clay pipe redder almost than his nose, his old brown-and-white spaniel—the best snipe dog in the Fen—curled at his feet. Charlie could beat any man for miles at skating. Put him on his long Fen-runners, and he whirled across the ice like a squat and jolly windmill. Alas, he is dead!

Charlie was a character, of that strongly individual type which the villages of last century produced. They could neither read nor write, but they were bigger, better, more workmanlike and more lovable men in many ways than half the board-school products of to-day who clutter the cinemas and Soccer football fields, aping the film gangster in their dress—a dreary period in Evolution.

"Come in, marster! Set ye down, all the hull bloody lot on ye. I'll warrant yew made them there owd Aunt Sallies blow their bellers suffin hot tu-day! Yew kin walk a pint down now, I'll lay ye!"

Then there is a great chat back and forth on the day's sport. There is the bargee from Lynn who tells

117

us with the slyest of digs that his old long gun that very morning "puncturated" an 11-lb. Fen hare on the river-wall. "An' the b——'s a'hanging up in my cabin aboard now, if so be as any o' yew gennlemen ood loike tu see as how an owd Sally can be ketched without them there long dorgs a-tomhossin' about all over the place." That brings down the house.

It is the proper wind-up to a good day. And when the wagonette comes, and we clatter off in the November darkness, full of hot rum and happiness, you would not, I warrant, change it for all the Altcar days that ever were.

There were those other rough days on almost similar country at Potton Island, on the Essex coast. But it was wilder, colder, with the smell of the sea and salt mud-flats strong on the air. Potton is a thousand and twenty-five acres of rough marsh pasture, of salting and fleet, pear-shaped, girdled by a great sea-wall. It lies between the estuaries of the Crouch and the Blackwater, one of that lonely archipelago, whose other islands bear the musical, lovely names of Foulness and Havengore, New England, Wallasea, and Rushley. It is a place of vast, windy silences, of crawling creeks where the tide flows in like silk. There are great herds of curlew that go shrieking up the tideways like blown clouds of lost spirits. There are redshank who flirt with the wind, and in springtime chime their million bells in the sweet silence of salty evenings. There are long teams of duck that in winter come dropping in over the sea-wall to light with a scuttering splash on the snaky fleets. There are geese which clang in the frosty moonlight and shelduck whose ghostly cackle sounds in the fog on the tideline like the laughter of drowned sailors.

There are only two houses on the island, no roads, no drinking water, two plum-trees, a baaing multitude of sheep, moving in woolly waves, and nothing else. But the big old farmhouse was built in Charles II's day, when Nicholas van Cropenbrough and his Dutch drainers reclaimed all these flat levels from the groaning sea.

I had that island for five years, a place of everlasting joy—and everlasting hares. There never were such hares. They said locally that if you stopped to look at one he would sit up and box you as bold as brass. They were "as big as small donkeys," as strong as steam-engines. They could fly dykes like Grand National winners. And if any old buck had his eye on a doe on the mainland he thought nothing of jumping into the salt creek with a four-knot tide flowing and swimming it. "Armour-plated they is, and paddle-wheeled like a Margit steamer," as one old fisherman put it to me.

Once upon a time the Rochford Coursing Club—in its day one of the grandest sporting bodies in all England—held its meetings there. That was when the club was composed mostly of sporting farmers and yeomen, of local people, of the doctor, the parson, the lawyer, the squire, and the cattle-dealer—all men who could ride and run. But then the Southend publican and Cockney butchers, the paunchy people, came along. Potton was too rough and tough a place for them. The dykes were too wide, and there were too many bellows to mend.

So when I had Potton I had it all to myself with only the sheep and the gulls and poor old Fred Keeble, the fisherman of Paglesham, to keep me company. Poor old Fred. He once saw the devil, covered in blue fire, swim the creek on a summer night and run up the mud " all glowering."

We were in my boat drifting down the tide under the moon, listening to the sibilant sounds of the birds in the night when he told me about it.

" And believe me, master," he said, " I was that scairt that I whopped on me knees on the bottom boards of me boat and prayed to the good Lord to deliver me. Then the davvle topped the wall, and I seed what he wur—a bloody great hare! So I ups wi' me gun an' shot the b——! "

CHAPTER X

THE WILD IRISHMAN

The Red Setter—His Ways, Charm, and Drawbacks—Some Records and Roots of the Breed—The Loftus Diary and other Notes of Early Types.

The ' Irishman ' is a handsome devil and perhaps the " least taste in de wurruld " of Hibernian recklessness in his affectionate nature. He ranks next to the typical Gordon in size, " an' he is a darling. God bless 'im." Keen-nosed, lean, sinewy, ragged-hipped, he can show them all how to cover the country, his methods are full of vim and dash, he has any amount of pluck, he is excitable, but he can stay to the end and can fight " wid the best of them." *In fine*, he's IRISH.—EDWARD W. SANDYS.

AND THAT QUOTATION, of course, means also that he can be unreliable as well as attractive, deceitful as well as gallant, ungovernable as well as full of dash— in fact, a person not to be relied upon for the sober, hard-fact demands of the one-dog shooting man. As the lyrical Mr Sandys exclaims, " he's Irish."

None the less, I have a likeable memory of the wild Irishman. I would not have one in my kennel other than for decoration and charm. But if I wanted to scatter my birds, disturb my ground, play merry hell, I would certainly buy the first Irishman I saw. He might turn up trumps as a good gun dog and torpedo my sardonic pessimism. And he might not.

In any case the women would admire him. The woman is yet to be found, at any rate an attractive woman, who does not fall for the dashing, unreliable, admiration-stealing, sympathy-demanding qualities of the Irishman.

He is not a person of long pedigree. No one can say with certainty when the Irish setter began, but it was somewhere about the beginning of the eighteenth century. He derives from the spaniel. The Irishman of the eighteen-hundreds called him *modder rhu* (the 'red dog'). But they were not all red. There were then, and still are, two sorts of Irish setter, the all-red and the red-and-white. A hundred years ago they were pretty evenly balanced in popularity and numbers. To-day the red-and-white has very largely gone out of fashion. The red dog is sweeping the board. And if you look at the pictures of the Welsh red-and-white spaniels of about 1820 you will see a quite notable resemblance to the red-and-white Irish setter of to-day. They were known as 'red spaniels' within living memory.

All setters spring from the spaniel stock, and the Irishman holds it to his credit that he is the least like them in appearance. Perhaps the scanty diet and the scarcity of grouse on Irish hills tended early on to produce that " lean, sinewy, ragged-hipped " type which Mr Sandys regards as the epitome of the Irishman.

No one, in any case, can say when the spaniel changed into the setter. It was probably about the time of Charles I, when hawking more or less went out of fashion among the nobility. Then, about 1700, the flint-lock gun came into fashion. Soon after country gentlemen went out to shoot partridges flying

—a very dashing proceeding. The man who could hit them on the wing was more than a chap, so the setter, with a docked tail and a very spaniel look about him, swam into the picture, particularly into those of George Morland.

Here, or hereabouts, was the time when the long-legged spaniel changed into the "setting dogg." It was about the time when the wolf died out, the capercailzie became extinct, the great white stork ceased to nest widely, and plans were on foot to drain the Fens. They will tell you in Ireland that at about this time the Carlow foxhounds were hunting the wolf. That by the way.

The earliest record that I can find of a setter is from some manuscripts in the Dublin Public Record Office which Miss A. Lloyd unearthed some years ago. The records are dated more than two hundred years back, and constitute the first direct reference I have been able to find of actual dog-training.

Here are the notes:

"A setting 'dogg' belonging to the seventeenth century has strayed into the Public Record Office at Four Courts under covering of a permit to one Michael Flynn to keep and teach the said setting dog. The document runs as follows: 'It being represented unto us that one Michael Flynn, of New Road, Ormond Gate, Dublin, has a white dogg with black about the head, a large white spot on the near side, and a small black spot on the same for the use of his Grace the Duke of Ormond, we therefore direct and require the chief ranger or master of the game, the under-keeper, and all officers and other persons whom it may concern to permit the said Michael Flynn to keep, carry, and teach the dogg above mentioned as he shall have occasion and thinks fit without any hindrance, disturbance, or molestation whatsoever. Given May 24, 1698.' "

That grand old Essex sportsman the Reverend W. B. Daniel gives a much more complete contract for training a " spanill bitch . . . to sitt." It is dated from Ribbesford, whose whereabouts is a mystery to me, under the 7th of October, 1685, and you will find it in his *Rural Sports*, published in 1807, the three volumes of which, bearing the book-plate of my dear old friend and boyhood hero the late Dr W. H. Salter, that king of dog-breeders, of Tolleshunt D'Arcy, Essex, take the high place on my bookshelves. Here is the contract, which may or may not be genuine:

I, John Harris, of Willdon, in the parish of Hastlebury, in the County of Worcester, Yeoman, for and in consideration of ten shillings of lawful English money, this day received of Henry Herbert, of Ribbesford, in the said County, Esq., and of thirty shillings more of like money by him promised to be hereafter pay'd me, doe hereby covenant and promise to and with the said Henry Herbert, his exors and admors, that I will from the day of the date hereof, until the first day of March next, will and sufficiently mayntayne and keepe a Spanill Bitch named Quad this day delivered into my Custody by the said Henry Herbert, and I will, before the said first day of March, fully and effectually train up and teach the said Bitch to sitt Partridges, Pheasants, and other game, as well and exactly as the best sitting dogges usually sett the

124

same. And the said Bitch, so trayned and taught, shall and will deliver to the said Henry Herbert, or whome he shall appoint to receive her, att his house in Ribbesford aforesaid, on the first day of March next. And if at any time after the said Bitch shall, for want of use or practice, or orwise, forgett to sett Game as aforesaid, I will at my costes and charges mayntayne her for a month, or longer, as often as need shall require, to trayne up and teach her to sett Game as aforesaid, and shall and will fully and effectually teach her to sett Game as well and exactly as is above mentyon'd.

Witnesse my hand and seale the day and year
first above written
JOHN HARRIS
his × *mark*
Sealed and delivered in presence of
H. PAYNE
his × *mark*

Daniel adds a note at the foot of this contract to the effect that a setting dog was broken to the net in 1555. John Dudley, Duke of Northumberland, was the first man who ever broke a setting dog to the net, and that was about 1555.

It is amusing to find that Daniel states quite solemnly that before 1747 all forms of shooting game were regarded as poaching. The original idea of the setter was that he should find the bird so that the gunner might take a pot-shot at it on the ground. But when it became the fashion to shoot birds flying the setting spaniel was a bit too slow. He could not always follow running birds. Nor could he round up coveys at a distance and hold them—nor follow the winged bird which might drop, a strong runner, at, say, fifty yards' distance. So the setter was gradually born.

The Irish seldom keep pedigrees of dogs, although they boast a good deal about their own usually rather misty claims to antiquity. It is not surprising, therefore, that if you start hunting out the early records of the Irish setter among the uneducated Irish you will usually find that they date things by such events as the Great Wind of 1839—not, as you might suppose, a patriotic ebullition of political oratory, but merely another and simpler Act of God. Or there is the Famine Year of 1849 and, earliest, the Year of the Rebellion, 1798. How often the Year of the Rebellion has been repeated as a national landmark is beyond my computation as a student of history, and probably governable only by the recurrent ebullitions of Irish self-consciousness.

But it is possible, nevertheless, to trace some of the main strains through the kennels of the old Irish families, the few which Ireland has allowed still to exist. Mr Arthur French, father of the first Lord de Freyne, had a brace of which he was very proud in 1793. This started the French Park strain. The second Lord, the Reverend John French, who flourished in the early eighteen-hundreds, was a great red-setter man. He kept them going well up to the day of his death. But by 1879 the breed had practically died out, and the few that were left were so inbred that they were destroyed. Thus, through sheer inattention to breeding principles, a really beautiful strain died. One thing we do know about them, and that is that they were all red, or practically so.

Colonel J. K. Millner, who has written the best book extant on the Irish setter, says that the late Mr A. F. Nuttall told him that he bred from one of these setters, and that it had " a shower of hail through its coat "—a most attractive-sounding dog.

Then there was a local strain of red setters in the King's County. Mr Maurice Nugent O'Connor, of Gort-na-mona, bred them up to a peak of perfection round about 1779. I can find little about these O'Connor setters beyond the fact that Maurice died in 1818, and the kennel apparently went to the La Touches, of Harristown, in County Kildare, and by them was sold to Sir A. Chichester, one of the Devonshire line of baronets who claim that they descend from the days of King Harold—which must have put even the Irish chieftains of that day in their place.

These setters were apparently a dark, rich red colour, rather light in bone. Chichester bought one dog named York for what was then the terrific price of seventy guineas.

The O'Connor-La Touche strain is, I fancy, well represented to-day. I cannot help quoting a tribute to the breed contained in Colonel Millner's book. It is in the form of a letter written to him by a Colonel Gresson, and as he refers to the breed maintained by my mother's family, the Stapleses, Baronets, of Lissan, County Tyrone, I feel a twinge of family pride—although I hasten to add that the Staples family were English settlers!

"Newberry
 "Harriston
  "Co. Kildare

" My father often told me of the La Touche setters, red spaniels, as he always called them; the late Mr Tom Hendrick, of Kerdiffstown, the owner of Squib, etc., and Mrs Falconer (Miss Warburton), the owner of Venus and Lily: Venus an ancestor of your Frisco. They also often spoke of the La Touche setters. As far as I have been able to find out, these setters were red, but, like the setters of old, were given to throw pups with white on face, neck, and hind-feet.

" My grandfather bred red-and-white setters nearly a hundred years ago, and I remember some of this breed at home when I was a very small boy, but my father gave up the red-and-whites when he got a brace of reds from my mother's uncles, Robert and Edward Evans, of Gortmerron, two brothers who were breeding red setters as far back as between 1812 and 1820. Robert died in 1868, and Edward blew off the fingers of his right hand loading an old muzzle-loader, whence the breed passed into the hands of the late Cecil Moore and others."

Robert Evans crossed his breed with that of the late Sir Thomas Staples, of Tyrone, a relative of my mother; the Staples strain, I believe, went back farther than the Evans strain, probably well into the seventeen-hundreds.

" Jimmy Wright, the owner of Nelly IX, often told me that he remembered the Evans setters well, and that all of the setters in the north were descended

from them. Jimmy Wright was gamekeeper to the
Earl of Castlestuart when Mr Robert Evans shot over
these estates, and remembers the Gortmerron setters,
and has frequently told me that the best setters in
Tyrone in the eighties of the last century were all descended from this strain.

" I have often tried to find out which, the red-and-
whites or the reds, were the older breed, and as far as I
can find out from the oldest breeders—viz., the late
John King, of Ballylin, the late Edward Evans, of
Gortmerron, and the late Mr Tom Hendrick, of
Kerdiffstown—the two breeds were distinct in their
time, but they all agree that in their early days the
reds were inclined to throw pups with white on face,
chest, and feet, and that some breeds were greater
offenders in this way than others.

" From the above we can deduce either that the
breeds were distinct and were sometimes crossed, or
that the original breed was red and white in no fixed
proportion of colour, some more red than white and
vice versa, and thus, breeding by selection from those
predominating in red, the red became fixed in time.
The latter deduction I am inclined to favour, especially as we know the setter evolved from the spaniel
and that white predominated in the early spaniels, and
that in parti-coloured animals one colour predomi-
nates. However, be that as it may, the red-and-white
was a beautiful dog, and, though a red-setter man, I
think a good specimen of the red-and-white was the
handsomer of the two, but I have not seen one for
more than thirty years, and, looking at our show setters

of the present day, I often think how superior was the red of the old red-and-white to the so-called red of many of the reds of to-day."

The present Earl of Rossmore has, I believe, still a very fine strain of the red-and-white variety at Rossmore Castle, in County Monaghan. It derives from a kennel established by one of his ancestors somewhere about the first quarter of the eighteenth century. Lord Rossmore is one of the few Irish peers who not only still keep their land, but who show first-class high pheasants, preserve game, and maintain the unstinted affection and loyalty of their tenants and people. He keeps up something of the old state of an Irish gentleman. The Rossmore setters are part of the picture.

I believe at one time, quite recently, they were sometimes known as Arran setters, merely from the fact that the family had moors in the Isle of Arran. Lord Rossmore considers that they are more easily broken and more tractable than the headstrong ' red dog.' Sherriff painted a picture in 1844 of a red dog with white markings and a red-and-white bitch, pleasantly called *The Rambles of Bob and Duchess*. It shows the present Lord Rossmore's grandfather with gillies and a shooting pony at the place which they had in Arran. I believe the picture is still at Rossmore Castle.

Now for what is reckoned to be the most authentic and oldest pedigree of Irish setters in existence. It is taken from the diary kept by a Sir Francis Loftus, of Mount Loftus, Kilkenny, and of its kind it is unique.

He was writing again of a red-and-white strain, similar to the Rossmore kennels. This is what he says:

" Mr Cooper made me a present of Quail in June 1817. She was then three months old, of his own true blood (he breeds in and in).

" She was red-and-white, the red not very deep, about the middle size, extremely handsome, and as good a bitch as ever hunted, never committed a fault in her life—but was too slow in roading in the potato-fields —was fast, stout, high-mettled, and extremely docile. She was the best rat-killer that could be, and fond of water.

" She was as good a brood bitch as ever was seen, often came to heat twice in one year, but never less than twice in three years. Generally had nine pups. She was an excellent nurse, but her puppies varied in size and colour, some being yellow-and-white, and some black-and-white. In general they were long and silky-coated, long sterns and very much feathered. She gave one that was as smooth as a pointer. All those she gave, which were trained, were as good as I could have wished them to be.

" Grouse and Dash, pupped in March 1820, were got by Major Irvine's famous old red dog Dick on Quail. As good dogs as ever hunted together. They were trained by Darby Ryan in 1821. Mr Cooper made Old Fan (the dam of Quail), a present to me in November 1820. I had her covered by a large red-and-white dog of Mr Davis's—the dog was of Mr Wallace's breed. She had pups on the 1st of January,

1821. She reared them, and then went mad and was killed.

" Fop and Rover were got by a dog of Mr Davis's on Old Fan, and were pupped January 1st, 1821, and were put under Darby Ryan's tuition in 1822. He did them no service. They were both large. Fop strong and handsome, but neither of them good in any respect. Parted with Fop July 22nd, 1826.

" Dick, Shot, and two bitches were pupped in 1821. They were got by a dog of Major Irvine's on Quail. I gave Shot to Major Irvine, and the two bitches to Mr Kennedy. I broke in Dick myself. He was a very fine dog, but a little too wild. He was killed in July 1825.

" Shot and Fan were pupped in 1822. They were got by a dog of Major Irvine's on Quail. I broke them in myself, and never saw two better dogs. In 1823 I gave them a little instruction; in 1824 I was in England, and they were idle. In 1825 I gave them practice, and had them well broken in by September 20th. They were two as good dogs as ever hunted.

" Romp and Jilt, by Major Irvine's dog on Quail, were pupped in 1823. Did not break Romp in until 1826. She took to her business the very first day, and in ten days become perfectly staunch, and as good a bitch as I ever met with.

" Began to break in Jilt about the 1st of August, 1826. At first she would not lay her mind to hunt, nor take the least notice of game. She has improved in beating and set a tame partridge. She has an excellent nose and showed very high mettle, which I did not expect.

"September 4th. Took Jilt out with the old dogs. She hunted beautifully, but sprung the birds.

"September 5th. Jilt by herself. She sets well.

"Began to break in Floss about the 1st of August. A beautiful beater, but too wild and high-mettled. She took great notice of game and set her birds well. Hunted well, but sprung the first covey, after which she took to road and set in the best manner possible. I caught a young partridge under her nose.

"September 6th. Took Jilt by herself. She hunted, set, and roaded in the most beautiful manner possible, has an uncommonly fine nose, and will be as nice a bitch as ever hunted. I caught a young partridge under her nose, which I hope to train the young dogs with.

"Ellen was got by a dog of Mr P. Hoare's, which was got by Mr Cooper's Flurry on a famous Castletown bitch. Ellen's dam was bred by Mr Sutton, and was got by a dog of his own.

"Rake was got by Buff, a dog of Major Cookman's. Buff was got by a dog of the Major's on a famous bitch bred by Colonel G. Eyre, of Galway. Sapho, the dam of Ellen, was out of a famous Castletown bitch. Ellen was brought to Mount Loftus by Redmond, the dog-teacher, about the 29th of July, 1826, and subsequently bought from him. Received some instructions the succeeding spring, and was again put into training in a week after she came to Mount Loftus. She made a good offer, though her feet were sore, and she was much out of condition. Redmond stayed a week at Mount Loftus and hunted Ellen and

Floss, and made Ellen quite perfect. She sets, roads, and hunts extremely well, and has an excellent nose. She is a very good poacher, and quite handy. She died in January 1828.

" Floss has been almost constantly hunted either by Redmond or myself since the 20th of July. She is high-mettled, a remarkably high goer, her nose not very good.

" September 19th. As yet she has not taken kindly to her business, though hunted daily on tame partridge. Floss being too high-mettled and her nose not very good, she was laid by and not hunted until the 1st of August, 1828. I then undertook to train her myself, which was difficult, as she was too wild and high-mettled, very disobedient, and would bear more work than three other dogs. However, by taking her out every day and working her for six or seven hours I by dint of perseverance had her broken in by the 20th September, 1828. I shot a great many birds over her that season. Though her nose is not very good, yet she is a good, steady bitch and a fine beater.

" Bride (first called China) was bought from Stokes, of Borris, about the 12th of September, 1828. Aged two years. Not broken in. I could not trace her pedigree. Scott, of Killedmind, undertook to break her in. About a week after I got her back. She set well after a few days when the season commenced. Her nose is good, and she beats well.

" Prices paid by Sir Francis Loftus for setters:

" 1817, I gave for Fox 6 guineas and my pointer Rap.

"For Rake I paid £7.

"For Roan I paid 3 guineas and Rake.

"For Grouse I paid 15 guineas.

"Got Quail a present from Mr Cooper, of Birch Grove.

"I gave for Fop £11 and my dog Ralph.

"I gave for Whack in 1816 £5 13s. 9d. and dog Juno.

"I gave for Rap in Dublin in 1816 £9 13s. 9d.

"Quail, the first setter bitch given to me by Mr Cooper, was out of his famous bitch Old Fan in 1817. . . . The setters at Mount Loftus in June 1840 were Quail, Fan, Wire, Signal, and Venus."

I like his notes about Quail. She must have been a grand bitch. If the modern woman had the same qualities life perhaps would be a little easier for the majority of mankind. Fortunately for the minority, there are still a few of the old type left. How, for example, do you not appreciate that description of "fast, stout, high-mettled, and extremely docile"?

On the more serious side of the matter I am enchanted to read that Quail was "the best rat-killer that could be, and fond of water." I wonder how many of these decorative, poor, pampered show-bench beauties of to-day could kill a rat or face water—and by water I do not mean the placid, slightly smelly waters of a brook, but let us say rather an outgoing tide in a coastal creek, when the wind bites, the mud is soft, the whole landscape looks level to the eye, and it is cold without and ten times colder in the water. But perhaps I demand too much of a mere setting dog.

The curly-coated retriever seems the more likely paragon to fill that exacting bill.

But there are points in this Loftus diary which are more than worth quoting. They are so full of complete common sense. I propose to burgle them, begging you to note that all these principles are applicable neatly to women. For example, " See that they are not on larks, but on game and nothing else." Then again, " Walk slowly." And, more particularly, " The whistle is preferable to the voice "—which surely means the kindly note in everyday behaviour, rather than loud-voiced dictation. As Sir Francis Loftus says of his dogs, " Creep the ditches; do not leap over them." You may make what more of his directions you wish. Here they are:

" A young sportsman has enough to do to manage one dog; when more experienced even two are enough, unless for a person who has had long experience, and has reduced dog-breaking to a science. Always beat to windward. Keep to the middle of the field, and when you wish the dog or one of the dogs to beat one way turn that way yourself and give him a slow motion with the hand, but no noise. The whistle is preferable to the voice.

" Walk slowly. Creep the ditches; do not leap over them. Never allow one dog to take the set from the dog which first found it, but force him to back to him. All this should be taught before the shooting season.

" When roading, make your dog stop occasionally until you come up to him. Never let him road faster than you can walk with convenience to yourself.

When you have a bird well marked follow him instantly. Do not suppose he will wait till you have found and killed other birds, and never allow your dogs to stir after you have fired until you bid them, though you have killed or wounded birds. When you miss a good dog from you look for him, but do not call or whistle; he may be at set at that moment.

" Do not feed with greasy or strong-smelling food; potatoes, meal, and milk well mixed make the best food with the exception only of bread and milk. Too much meal will not do.

" When your dog sets in potatoes, turnips, or stubbles, lift your feet very high in walking and lay them down lightly so as to make but little noise. Accustom your dogs to drop instantly at the word of command, and invariably to drop down when a shot is fired, and not to come galloping up to do mischief. Likewise use the young dogs to beat the same field over several times, and to come in the moment they are called to follow you into the next field, and never attempt to range again until you wish them to do so.

" When you suspect your dogs are on game make them drop down at once and creep up to the proper distance. Take care you do not blink them; also see that they are not on larks, but on game and nothing else.

" Never keep your dogs out long enough to tire them, and go home long before you can tire yourself. From the time you go out in the morning till you go home at night take every opportunity of saving yourself from unnecessary fatigue. You do not know what sport may be before you; therefore save yourself and your dogs as much as propriety will admit. Point towards the place you wish the dogs to hunt, and with the hand on that side."

There were at one time black setters in Ireland. Black-and-tan setters were used until comparatively recent times, and I dare say it would be possible to find specimens of them still knocking about in parts of the West. The late Edward Laverack always said that the finest type of Irish setter he had ever seen was a dog bred at Cockermouth Castle. This dog had a very thick, rich coat. His ears were tinged with black at the tips, and some of his stock worked out completely black. No one was ever able to break him, but he was apparently a good stock-getter. Laverack always used to say that one of the three best setters he had even seen, apart from this Cockermouth dog, was one belonging to John Wyndham, blood-red all over, but with a tinge of black on his ear-tips.

Mr A. McEnnery, a well-known Irish setter breeder, tells a story of the breed which is well worth repeating. I take it with acknowledgments from a letter which he wrote to Colonel Millner.

"Some years since we were on a shooting expedition. At the time I had the shooting on a large tract of the bog Allen, County Kildare, and in my employment had a gamekeeper of the name of Patrick Callaghan living at a village called Allan Wood, one of the best sportsmen and most reliable it has ever been my good fortune to meet. A partner that I had in Wicklow County had a ten-months-old Irish setter

MAJOR J. D. LLOYD'S ENGLISH SETTER FIELD TRIAL CHAMPION 'VINEYARD OF OTHAM'

Backed by 'Vision of Otham' at the Manor House, West Tofts, Brandon, Norfolk.

Photo Sport and General

THE KING'S KENNELMAN WITH A GROUP OF KING GEORGE V'S ENGLISH SPRINGER SPANIELS
BY A LAKE IN WINDSOR PARK

Photo Sport and General

puppy bitch that he reared in County Dublin and desired to have trained, one that had never been a mile from its kennel.

"I sent it down by the railway to Callaghan, who took her upon a car on to his place at Allan Wood, which is twenty-seven miles from Dublin. He kept her during the process of training, which was about four months.

"The first day of the grouse-shooting that year fell on a Monday, and our shooting party arranged to start for the mountains in County Wicklow on the Saturday, taking the train to Dunlavin from Dublin at Sallins, an intermediate station. Callaghan came up with a bitch, having driven over from Allan Wood, a distance of twelve miles. He handed her to the guard, and on arrival at Dunlavin we took her in charge with the other dogs and drove to our hotel at Donard, which is at the foot of the mountains, a distance of nine miles.

"Next day, Sunday, we took all the dogs, including the new arrival, out for exercise, and walked to a place called Davidstown, on the banks of the river Slaney, which was about four miles from our hotel. The day was exceedingly hot, and my three friends and I thought we should like to have a dip in the river, and there and then undraped on the banks, and I am ashamed to say in a very exposed situation, and where there was very shallow water. The shock of our nudity appeared to be too much for our young canine friend, as she took to her heels and bolted. We thought it most likely we should find her at the hotel on our return, but there was no account of her, whereupon we notified all the police-stations in the counties of

Kildare and Wicklow, but got no tidings from them, which distressed her owner greatly, as she was an extra-good one.

"On about the 16th of August I got a letter from Callaghan to say the bitch had just trotted into his cottage, footsore, weary, and starving. Allan Wood is thirty-nine miles from Davidstown, and to my mind a wonderful homing achievement for a fourteen-months-old puppy."

In 1885 the first real attempt was made to form a Red Setter Club. A meeting was held at No. 2 Morgan Place, Dublin, and a club was formed with a subscription of a guinea a year. The following were elected on the Committee: Mr Cecil Moore, Dr Gogarty, Mr L. F. Perrin, Mr D. Sullivan, Mr J. K. Millner, Mr J. Hamilton, Mr J. F. Dillon, Mr J. M. Barry, Mr W. Despard, and Mr J. J. Giltrap. The honorary treasurer was Dr Gogarty, and Mr Giltrap was elected honorary secretary.

This is the standard of points laid down by the club:

	Points
Head	10
Eyes	6
Ears	4
Neck	4
Body	20
Hind-legs and -feet	10
Fore-legs and -feet	10
Tail	4
Coat and feather	10
Colour	8
Size, style, and general appearance	14
Total	100

Well, there is a dull but useful catalogue for you. It is worth looking over whenever you come across a wild Irishman of to-day. For my own choice, as I said early on in this chapter, I would not have an Irish setter in the kennel as a one-man dog. But as a charming companion, a decoration, an occasional inspiration; as a light and lively element in the shooting landscape; as a racy addition to the humdrum world of everyday utility, I would have him every time. He is one of those people who add colour to life, grace to the scene, charm to everyday work, and that rare, ineluctable quality of the light-hearted cavalier to otherwise serious matters.

CHAPTER XI

OLD PARTRIDGE DAYS AND DOGS

Spanish Pointers—Fan, the Fat Spaniel, and Cheero, the Irishman—When King Charles churned the Cockerel—Shooting at
High Fen.

My MIND GOES BACK. An early morning in September, mist curling off the Fenland dykes, woolly about
the great thorn-hedges where the home paddocks
slope to the reedy fen. Hot black tea, in which you
could stand a spoon, stewing in a brown pot on the
wide, whitewashed hearth of the kitchen fire. The
clatter of hobnail boots on the square, light yellow
bricks which made its floor. A great, red-cheeked,
deep-bosomed kitchenmaid bustling about, cutting
thick slices of home-made bread, spreading yellow
butter from our own dairy, popping in great slabs of
cold fat boiled bacon, pickled pork, Suffolk ham.
Those were what they called 'thumb-pieces.' You put
a couple of such gargantuan sandwiches in your left-
hand shooting pocket—the right-hand pocket was
kept for cartridges—and you were ready for the day.

There was always the knowledge that a boy on a
pony or a farm labourer in a spring-cart would deliver
a 'brown hen' or two of home-brewed ale at this or
that focal point in the day's proceedings. That was the
ultimate goal of lunch-time—after the mists had
melted and been sucked up into the deep blue of over-
arching Fenland skies.

We began early in those days, for the Master—he

was my great-uncle—was a martinet in his fustian, country way. He demanded, and got, complete obedience. He worked by the clock. He ordered the little state of his own land, the little working army and population of his own people, by the definite rule of his own thumb. He stood no nonsense and gave none. But in fairness, in justice, in generosity, and in protectiveness there was no better master, none more loved.

Partridge-shooting on the First of September was a holy rite. It was a festival, talked of in the parish from one year's end to another. For on that whaleback of rich agricultural lands which thrust its blunt-nosed way into the black and steaming Fens there were only two sorts of shooting, partridges and wildfowl. In the whole 3800 acres of the parish there was less than ten acres of covert. Except for the bejewelled, long-legged, quick-hearing rajahs who ran in the reed-beds of the fen, there were no pheasants. Ten miles away at Newmarket and twenty miles farther on in Norfolk you could have a day at the best pheasants in the world. But here, in this individual, pig-headed, self-contained Fenland parish there was no pheasant-shooting of the orthodox kind.

But there were partridges, naturally bred, more or less unkeepered, strong on the wing, nurtured by the Spartan winds of the Fens. They flew fast and far. Like the hares, they were creatures of the elements, strong as the strong, rich soil which bred them. So you may guess that a day's partridge-shooting there was more like a field day with an army than one of

143

those comfortable, toddling days of easy peregrinations from one pocket-handkerchief field to another with which your Cockney squires divert themselves on the tenpenny fringes of London in the suburbanized counties of Surrey, Hertfordshire, Buckinghamshire, and the rest of the John Gilpin cluster which clings about the city's fringes.

So because we were vainglorious about our hardy Fen partridges, our hundred-acre fields, our flying of dykes and early morning starts when the mists were woolly and the tea was cooked in a kettle, barbarously —because of these things we had as an ally that vainglorious gallant the Irish red setter.

It was a fine mixed household of dogs. There was Black Bess, the Labrador, who knew more of snipe and duck, teal and widgeon, than any dog in Cambridgeshire, who had had her hair parted on the top of her skull by the spear-like thrust of a wounded bittern. There were Ponto and Tanto, the two great, solemn-eyed, double-nosed Spanish pointers who lurked in a dignified way about the house, a gentle gloom upon their countenances. They were grandchildren of the Spanish pointers owned by my great-grandfather, Robert Aspland, the little, old, dapper gentleman who wore black knee-breeches with stockings and silver-buckled shoes, who died at eighty-seven, and had a little white dog which, every day until his death, walked with him a steady four miles out from the house and back again.

I think those Spanish pointers knew that their day was done, that they were the last of their race—gone with the hand-sickle and the centuries of long September stubbles, where the partridges had sat like quails. And, indeed, in their day there *were* quails. I can hear them even now, down the dim alleys of childhood memory, whistling high and clear from the lush grass in the orchard at the bottom of the Weights —the big paddock at the back of the house where we trained Robert the Devil, where the rooks nested in the tall elms, where my uncle planted four walnut-trees in order that his sons might cut their own gun-stocks from their stems.

The pointers belonged to that passing day. They were of the time of George Morland, of Pope and Dryden. They belonged to the East Anglian age that had seen undying pictures painted by Constable and Crome, Cotman and Gainsborough. All that was of peace and beauty, age and dignity and the worth of a settled world, was in their quiet eyes. There are none of them now.

Then there was Togo, the big fox-terrier, bigger than most, who came from the Newmarket kennels of Felix Leach. He was a present to my father from Fred Archer, and as Fred Archer's memory will last in Derby history so the memory of Togo will endure as an early milestone in my own chapter of life. But his place belongs to another chapter.

There was Fan, the fat and bustling spaniel, busy about hedgerows, much occupied with fictitious scents, a creature of comfortable alarms and unalarming excursions. She was always there as a pincushion into which you might stick verbal pins. I never took her very seriously, merely as a busy, prematurely middle-aged old lady who could make any ditch-bottom pheasant's life a misery. When my brother and I tickled our youthful, romantic fancies by shooting with muzzle-loaders Fan was invaluable. She produced just the right blundering pheasant at the right short distance.

And when that skimming mandarin was duly blown up hinderways with an ounce and a quarter of No. 6 chilled Newcastle shot and a few flying fragments of *The Daily Mail*, which made most admirable wadding, Fan was the person who galloped fussily in, retrieved the disorganized corpse and brought it to hand. She trod the grass with splayed and feathered feet, a smug smile in her brown eyes, her old ears flopping. You almost felt as though it had been a *good* shot.

There was a Dalmatian who ran behind the dog-cart, a decorative creature, beloved by the ladies, scorned by us. After all, he looked like a pointer but had no uses. So why not scorn him? But for his spots, which challenge vividly on the retina of remembrance, he would not be worth recalling.

To crown them there was Cheero. Cheero was the wild Irishman. He was awake and stirring restlessly in his kennel before even that "Fen tiger" of a kitchenmaid had raked the peat ashes apart from the slumbering embers of last night's kitchen fire and poked in the slivered kindlings of her broken sticks to prepare her hellish brew. The other dogs slept, while the kitchen chimney smoked whitely into the whiter

woolly wilderness of the morning fog. But Cheero
paced his kennel like a wild red tiger.

As the guns roused themselves in slipper-baths of
cold, cold water, beneath squirming, shuddering
sponges, Cheero's excitement increased. I really believe that by some telepathic sense he was able to
follow the various stages of progress by which the
household of his lords and masters woke itself. There
was no pretence about a set breakfast. You gobbled
cold bacon and pickles and hot boiled eggs and black
tea in the kitchen. You used pewter spoons that were
soft to the fingers and thick cups. Bread was cut in
heavy slices on a walnut board that was part of the
very trunk of the walnut-tree from which the
stock of the Master's favourite gun had been
fashioned forty-eight years before, on his twenty-first
birthday.

Meanwhile there was a movement and stir in the
stables. The shooting cobs were being got out, thick-
set, sturdy ponies whom not even a 'five nine' would
have perturbed. The old brown-painted wagonette
was run out of the coach-house, grating on the gravel.
An almost too lively six-year-old was put to the shaft.
I always remember that horse. He was a hero in his
way. He once put my cousin Sidney, who considered
himself a little Fred Archer, straight over his head
into the stable-yard drain. The drain was full of
'pigs' juice,' mahogany brown and smelling like asa-
foetida. It was the concentrated, hyper-sweetened
essence of six months of stable-yard and pigsties. And
it lowered the masculine conceit of that young man,

blenched his cavalry moustaches with cataclysmic effect. The downfall was mighty.

I often wish I could put a few modern novelists of the Left Wing variety, a few intelligentsia of the six-penny international breed, and a few playwrights of the free-love type on to that six-year-old's back—with the drain wide open and welcome. After all, it would merely mean a return to the sewer.

Then we were off, gun barrels upright between our knees, the six-year-old spanking along the village street on the way to High Fen. A mile out, past Spinney Abbey on the left, grey among its thin, sheltering firs, the mist still curling off its fish-ponds, I thought suddenly of Henry Cromwell, Governor-General of Ireland, who in the days of his decline lived as a gentleman farmer in this monkish relict of a great house.

He thought he had found peace there, retirement from the garish bustle of the Restoration, freedom from the petty prancings of the Stuart Court, its whirl of women, whores, waste, and wilfulness. So the Puritan came back to this lonely abbey of the Fens, in the heart of the Ironside country that bred the Cromwell stock.

There he tilled his fields, fattened his stock, watched the wildfowl wing their way from Wicken Fen to Soham Mere, heard the geese clanging beneath the steely stars of winter, heard the nesting redshank trill their million bells beside his kingcup-bordered dykes in the gentle days of spring—and saw the enchantment of high summer spread above that flat and

level land of great bean-fields, broad cornfields that
slid gently down his hedgerow-bordered slopes into
the shining meres and tasselled reed-beds of the old
Fen. The bittern boomed deeply to him on the sunny
stillness of June afternoons, the wild duck waddled
ahead of their cohorts of young from the fish-pond in
his orchard. The swallows hawked flies about his barn
eaves, and the white owls snored noisily in his steading
roof-trees.

You might have thought that a fallen, forgotten ex-
Governor-General of Ireland would be safe in such a
peninsular retreat. But even kings discover forgotten
memories in unsuspected corners. So Charles II was
hunting the hare one day in the fields of Fordham,
near Newmarket. The hare took them by way of
Wicken to this Ultima Thule of the Fens. It was hot
and high noon. The King was thirsty and tired. He
asked where there might live a gentleman who would
give him a drink, a moment of shade, a chair to sit in,
a cool room to shade his eyes.

One of his suite told him that he knew of an honest
country gentleman living in yonder little grey abbey
who would be honoured to receive the King. They
clattered up the stony road to the abbey, their horses'
hoofs ringing. The courtier went ahead.

Presently he returned from the stockyard, walking
on foot, bearing aloft before him a muck crome. Behind him followed a buskined, embarrassed, bucolic
gentleman, ill at his ease.

"What is the meaning of this tomfoolery?" demanded the King.

"Sire, I bear before this gentleman, Mr Henry Cromwell, one-time Governor-General of Ireland, the present emblem of his agricultural pursuits, as I once bore before him another symbol of his dignity when I had the honour to serve him at Dublin," replied the courtier.

Charles soon put the wretched Cromwell at his ease, dismounted, took his drink, discoursed of hares and partridges, of fat stock and the wildfowl of the Fens. I like to think that he drank perhaps the thin sweet mead, the Saxon honey drink, light golden in colour, which they made in the village in my young days, even as they had made it for nine hundred years, since the days when Ethelred was Saxon King of England.

Those were the lands we used to shoot over with Ponto and Tanto, Black Bess and Fan, with Cheero, the wild Irishman, ranging ahead, head up and stern up, like a ship red-sailed, ploughing through the green ocean of glistening mangold leaves which winked back the morning dew like jewels.

The wagonette would grumble past Spinney Abbey, rumbling along on its way to High Fen, where the last farm of the Master's own little England stood white-walled, reed-thatched, amid its shivering poplars and shock-headed willows. Oddly enough, a farmer dwelt there called King Charles. He had a big beard, and he used to get drunk. Once he got so drunk that he chased a great Buff Orpington cockerel round the farmyard, caught it, stuffed it into the butter churn, and churned the wretched bird madly, whirling the handle with a red-cheeked frenzy. This, he announced, was done in order "to make the b—— lay eggs."

That was a lunch-time interlude on a partridge-shooting day when King Charles had looked too long on the sloe gin, drowned it too much in his own ale, and crowned it for too long with after-lunch port.

High Fen partridges were like no other partridges I have ever known. There were great, black, rich, peaty fields that ran on into a pearly horizon, bounded by the green upland of the Isle of Ely, where the white roof of the cathedral shone in the early morning sun, its soaring lantern and fairy pinnacles shining like the unreal minarets of an Arab mosque.

There were acres and acres of long stubbles, of green turnip-fields, of beans that were stacked black, of beans that scented enchantingly the air, of wheat and barley shocked in golden cascades. They were rimmed and bounded by shining dykes, where the kingcups in the spring shone brassily. Swallows twittered about the long friezes of marching willows which strode like files of shock-headed soldiery across the wide and level fen. On the left the flat Fen fields dropped to the green river washes of the Cam, where the pewits wept and wailed and the cattle stood, fly-flicking and heads down, on grassy river walls, the ancestors of Arnesby Brown pictures.

This was the country in all England of the wild Irishman. There were the spaces to roam, there were the partridges, strong and wild and cunning as any Irish grouse. There were the winds, unchecked by hedge or wood or copse, great streams of air to be sought by the questing nose of the galloping 'red dog.'

It was purgatory for the fat and bustling Fan, Paradise for the galloping, chasing Cheero.

And when the 'red dog' dropped to a covey, sat motionless, a vivid ruddy splash against the black earth and bleached stubble, the guns moved up. I can see it now. The covey burst like an opening flower. The sun glinted on the long barrels of the Master's old gun. His cheek dropped lightly to the stock that had been cut forty-eight years before from his father's — my great-grandfather's — walnut-tree — the tree that was planted on the day of his birth, to be cut and felled on his twenty-first year of coming to manhood.

The report rang out, heavy on the autumn sunshine. The bellying cloud of black powder smoke blew away on the breeze. A brace of birds dropped to the twin reports. That deliberate right and left was the old man's hall-mark. No fuss, no bother.

They made a good working partnership, the great six-foot, fine-headed old squire, with his plodding pointers as dignified, as steady, as immaculate as himself—and that added, enlivening quality of the rangy 'red dog' with his dash and go. They would keep going all day, man and dog, from six in the morning to six of a September evening.

They would take the Fen pastures back towards Spinney Abbey, walking in all Fodder Fen in a bold, ambitious sweep. They closed in over the dykes and under the elms, past the whispering poplars which stood silver-shivering in the wind, to the land which

Cromwell farmed, where Charles II hunted the hare.

And in the evening, when the duck whistled overhead on quick wings, there would be a laying out of the bag on the great stones of Spinney kitchen, a counting of hares and partridges, Englishmen on one side and Frenchmen on the other. There was always a grumble about the growing numbers of the red-legged Frenchmen—"damned skulking Napoleonic interlopers, only fit to spit and run." That was how he summed them up.

I can see him now, turning them over with a great ashplant, snorting softly at badly shot birds, pointing approvingly to those killed clean in the head, grunting disparagingly over a hare whose hind-leg has been broken by a first barrel.

He lingered lovingly over the two or three couple of teal that had been shot as they sprang gallantly from a dyke, scattering water drops which glistened in the sun as they fell. Their handsome green and blue heads shone like jewels against the kitchen flagstone. There was always a snipe or two, delicately pencilled, its beak probably still black with Fen mud. There were one or two redshank—we called them 'clews,' from their whistle, and still do so.

And there were corncrakes, or landrails if you like that name better. I am glad that the landrail is growing in his numbers in this last year or two. He is very much a bird of the old England, of those enchanted days. When I hear him creaking rustily I smell again the honey-sweet scent of bean-fields beyond hawthorn

153

hedges; remember the bending ocean of bowed and golden wheat; see again in my mind's eye the long stubbles in the windy corners of the fields where strong gusts had laid the wheat, and the reapers, perforce, had left such a length of stubble as they left behind in the hand-sickle days.

Cheero was death on landrails. He would scent them like an otter scenting fish, hunt them up dykesides, bustle them out of thistly hedgerows, set them in the long stubbles in those windy corners, retrieve them delicately, their long legs dangling mournfully from his rakish jaws.

I think the very elusiveness of their ventriloquial tricks challenged the particular qualities that made him what he was—a wild and undependable red ranger of those big fields. They were really much more his bird than was the humdrum partridge. But that was his pet secret, the weakness which peeped out.

CHAPTER XII

THE GAY AND GALLANT TERRIERS

Polecat in the Willow Holt—The Epic of Togo—The Last of
the " Fen Tigers "—The Otter Affair—And the Final Tragedy.

THE POPLARS RUSTLED IN THE WIND, turning
silver faces that shivered like sheeted ghosts. Thorn-
bushes were heavy with sweet blossom, sickly on the
air. Catkins hung furry, powdered with gold, from
slender willow branches, drooping perhaps with a sad
melancholy born of the recollection of their strewing
before the ass's feet as Christ rode into Jerusalem.

There were kingcups which glistened boldly along
the dyke-side where the spring grass marched like
young green spears down to the water's edge. Moorhens ran there, clucked busily. In the low branches of
one of the blackthorns a nest was building—a flat,
messy affair. They thought they were being clever
this year, getting out of the weasel's way. But he
would be up that foot of blackthorn-bush, when the
time came, in the twisting of a tail. Somewhere above
my head, high above the green mist of glistening,
sticky buds, of shooting leaves, of twigs with their in-
tangible aureole of spring, a wood-pigeon cooed
heavily—a feather-bed of song. It is odd that that
artful, cautious, case-hardened, shot-impregnable
warrior of the winter, defier of the gunner, should
lapse in these spring days into such a soft and sentimental moodiness of crooning.

155

High above him, in a patch of spring blue, hung a kestrel wing-quivering. I knew exactly where his mate was sitting on her rusty-mottled eggs. Just in that gaping hole in the straight, lightning-blistered stem of an ancient poplar across the corner of Treen's Meadow, just below the rook trees. Kestrels had nested there for years. It was their nursery, by age and right and usage.

For years we boys had taken the eggs. It was only the year before that I had got up that tree, come down with a cap full of addled eggs on my head, and had them squashed in a stinking mess into my hair, dribbling round my ears, by a boisterous outlaw who thought it remarkably funny. I stunk for days. My cap was uninhabitable, unwearable even to my barbaric senses. So I stuffed it down the lavatory at home. And because I smelt abominably to heaven, and would not or could not explain where my new school cap had gone, I was boxed on the ears, beaten on the bottom. Which seemed to me an injustice. So I torpedoed the outlaw with my head in his stomach, while Togo yapped at his heels. And he fell, like the walls of Jericho. We rampaged over his kicking body, Togo and I. Never again did he dare to squash a nest-full of kestrels' eggs under my cap.

We both thought lovingly of that little matter, Togo and I, as we sat there, in the ivied embrasure of ash roots, at the foot of a tree which mingled its misty green head with the misty green clouds of other trees on that spring morning when empires still stood and no Great War loomed like a thunder-cloud.

Togo was an Edwardian. He was born at New-market, a true fox-terrier, white all over but for his head, which was beautifully and evenly marked in black and tan. He had a cock-up tail, full of dash, the devil, and obstinacy. He was high before the eyes, flat between the ears, long in the snout, with jaws that could almost clip a rabbit in half, long, straight legs that would dig for hours, gallop a burst with any hedgerow rabbit, a deep chest with wind enough in it to swim any weed-encumbered lode in all the Fens.

And he had been bred by Fred Archer, the greatest jockey of all time, the " Flaming Tin-man," the darling of a duchess, the racecourse idol of the million. There was a rumour that King Edward VII had once patted him—Togo, not Fred Archer.

Togo was the dog of my dead father, the last of all the sporting breeds left from that dispersed and dissipated kennel. He was the friend of my rather lonely, buccaneering boyhood, companion on unlawful forays into other people's hedgerows, the terror of horned cattle—and therefore my protector, for I had always a haunting horror of cows, a nightmare of bulls, fruit of a fright from a calf-robbed cow when six years old—a cunning catcher of skulking moor-hens, and the hero of a berserk fight with a dog-otter.

There never was a dog like him, and there never will be. He had the gallantry of a great gentleman, the gaiety of a boy, the courage of a hero, the looks of all that his breeding had given him, and the companionship of a friend. He was frightened of nothing.

157

And when I sometimes beat him as I did with that brutality which is peculiar to small boys in their masculine possessiveness of the things they love he did not bite me as he should have done. He lay there, and looked at me with reproving eyes, with a dumb question of why this injustice should be. He might easily have bitten me. It would have served me right. And he could have bitten hard, and been off before there was any catching of him. But that is not in the quality of such creatures, whether they are women or dogs. They put up with it and still love one, God knows why.

Togo and I were waiting for a polecat. There had not been a polecat in those wild Fenland parts for ten years. But, oddly enough, a pair *did* turn up just about once in every ten years. Their periodicity of recurrence, as the Whitehall tapeworms would say, coincided with that of the sturgeon which once in a decade nosed their way up the brackish waters of the Great Ouse, following, by some blind inherited instinct, the ancient waterways which lured their spawning forbears in Palæolithic times, when the North Sea was no more than the confluence, amid swamps and low marshes, of the Elbe, the Weser, the Scheldt, the Thames, the Trent, and the Ouse.

Perhaps it was the same dim sort of instinct which brought the polecats to our stranded island of primeval fen, our little wilderness of swamp and reed. Two hundred years before they had been common, when all the Fens were vast and wild. A hundred years before they had been not uncommon. And in those boyhood days there still came, once in about every ten years, a pair of wandering, far-travelling polecats, journeying from no one knows where, to bed themselves in this lost echo of their family's past.

Such a pair had just arrived. No one in the village —except an old sedge-cutter, Jake Barton—knew of them. But Jake had been mowing sedge, footsole-deep in peaty golden water. He came to the root of a willow-tree. It was old, lichen-silvered. And it had a big hole in it. A furry, dark brown animal vanished into the hole. Jake stubbed the trunk with his great water-boot to drive it out. And it came out of that hole at him "like a flying cat," disappeared snakily through the reeds, vanished into this willow holt where Togo and I now sat waiting for it.

The afternoon faded into the sweet dusk of spring. Blackbirds, homing to their nests and mates, flung themselves into the blackthorn-bushes with a bullet-like *hooroosh*. The kestrel dropped to the dead poplar-tree. Rabbits hopped comfortably out of the hedge-rows, sat bunched up in the grass, scampered suddenly about. Togo pricked his ears. His eyes sought mine. A warning finger and he lay down.

Duck whistled over the holt, dropping to the reedy pools beyond the orchard in the next field. A heron squawked somewhere hoarsely. Little owls mewed one to the other from hollowed oak, apple-tree, and hedge-side elm. Reed-warblers started their thin, reeling song in the vast reed-beds of the bordering fen. Mists curled up like ghostly armies.

It grew chilly in the holt. The quick warmth of

159

spring was sucked up by the Fen mists. The violet of the dusk deepened to an almost opaque black. It was dark under the ash-tree, mysterious. The holt was full of creeping, pattering sounds. Mice ran about. Water-rats ran busily along the dyke bank, looking like miniature beavers. Once I could have sworn that the round bullet head of an otter came up for a moment in a huge oily dimple on the surface of the dyke.

Then suddenly an animal, heavier than any rat, pattered purposefully over the leaves and twigs beneath the blackthorns. We strained our eyes and ears. Togo stiffened. I dropped my hand gently to his collar. Faintly I could hear the unseen animal sniffing. There were no badgers in that part. We had seen only one in forty years. So the mysterious beast, coming nearer, must be the polecat.

Suddenly it stopped. Straining my eyes, I faintly made out a long, dark form, a bushy tail. It was as big as an otter. It listened intently. I caught the flat gleam of two green eyes. My hand slipped from Togo's collar.

With a plunge he was forward, on it. The most appalling stink I ever wish to smell smote my nose. It blotted out the sweet scents of the night in a cloud of skunk-like ferocity. It was penetrating, even clinging to one's clothes.

There came a surprised yelp from Togo. Either the smell or the creature's teeth had got him. Then they were off through the undergrowth, a fighting, snarling mass, a revolving ball of teeth and fur. I plunged through the bushes after them, scratching my face, tearing my hands, ripping my clothes.

Fifty yards on the animal went to ground at the root of a blown-down willow-tree. Togo was left scrapping furiously at the mouth of a hole. But it was too dark to see to dig. I had a rabbiting spade with me, so I filled in the hole, plugging it firmly with a bundle of sticks and then ramming down earth. Then we went home.

Next day I was down early, complete with mattocks, beetle and wedges, rabbiting spade, a gun, and Togo. For half an hour I dug, split roots, and excavated like a beaver. Then out of a widening hole, choked with dead leaves, there shot out a long, chestnut-coloured creature with a bushy tail, full of fight and fury. It cleared the dyke with a single bound. Togo chopped at it as he sprang, missed it. Then the 12-bore was up to the shoulder, a snapshot as it landed on the opposite bank, and it rolled over and over, kicking and clawing. It was a big buck polecat, in splendid condition and rich colouring. I have it now at home, the date 1906 testifying to that high adventure when one was very young.

Then there was the otter hunt down on Adventurers' Fen.

I think I was eleven then, and Togo was probably eight or nine—very near the limit of a working and fighting age for one who had fought hard and worked hard ever since he could run, without swaying, on the unbalanced legs of puppyhood.

We went off one afternoon, the two of us together,

on one of our many illicit expeditions into the vast wilderness of Adventurers' Fen. That was the reed-grown, dyke-seamed expanse of turf diggings, cattle marshes, and reed ground which stretched between Wicken Lode and Burwell Lode.

A few peat-diggers, the real old-fashioned type of Fenman, still worked there. Great, rough-handed, hairy-fisted fellows who wore round moleskin caps, shiny moleskin waistcoats which glinted bluely in the sun, rough pilot-cloth, double-breasted jackets and cord breeches which they gartered below the knee with twisted bands of sedge. Their job was the digging of peat from the half-drained fen. They cut long, shining trenches in the black soil, using sharp, long-bladed spades, rather like a ferreting spade, with a blade which projected at right angles. The turves were cut in oblong bricks, and set out in long, low walls to drain and dry in the sun and wind.

They had a hut down on the fen, a semi-subterranean affair dug two or three feet down into the earth and roofed over with a two-foot-thick, igloo-like roof, made of branches, over which were laid reeds, and then the turves. There was no window, and only a hole in the roof for the smoke to escape. The whole thing was overgrown with nettles and rough grass. Hawthorn-trees overshadowed it, dappled its roof with the sweet harvest of their sickly blossom.

Inside you stepped from a doorway, screened by a hurdle threaded with reeds, into a square chamber, perhaps twelve feet by twelve. A turf bank surrounded it on three sides. In the centre smouldered a turf fire,

ONE OF THE LAST OF THE OLD FENMEN DIGGING PEAT
ON BURWELL FEN

"Creatures of reed and water, turf-pit and sedge-cutting, they lived as near
the earth as man can very well live."

Photo Captain C. G. M. Hatfield

'SUPREME SELECT'

Mr C. H. Bishop's first-prize-winning smooth fox-terrier at the Kensington
Canine Society's Championship Show at the Crystal Palace in 1930.

Photo Sport and General.

163

never quite out. One or two dirty black billycans, empty cocoa tins, a screw of sugar in a knob of brown paper, fat thick bacon in a frying-pan, tea as black as your hat—that was their daily ration. They lived as near the earth as man can very well live.

Digging all day under blazing hot suns, reed-cutting in winter in biting winds, knee-deep in icy water, they were the hardiest, roughest, most honest set of men I have ever known.

They were, indeed, the direct descendants of that now almost extinct race the true Fenmen—the men who were so much creatures of reed and water, turf-pit and sedge-cutting, that many of them could neither turn their hands to plough nor sheepfold nor any of the gentler arts of the men on the high land.

Indeed, like the fishermen on the East Coast to-day, they openly despised the farm labourer. They considered themselves tougher men, more individual creatures.

And the farm-labourers were really rather afraid of them. They called them "Fen tigers," swore that they had spotted bellies, webbed feet, and would shoot their own mothers if they wore feathers.

A generation before the "Fen tiger" was indeed a lawless person. They even went so far as to have an illicit still at an old inn called Pout Hall, in Burwell Fen. It was a clearing-house for stolen sheep, for plundered corn, for pilfered chickens. Even fat bullocks had been slaughtered, cut up, and carried away more than once.

And when the first policeman ever came to our

village, the emblem of Sir Robert Peel's new reign of law and order, the "Fen tigers" hit him on the head, put the body on a turf barrow, wheeled it down to the fen, weighted it, and threw it into a fen pool. Troops and bloodhounds were out after them, but the murderers were never taken.

They sent a posse of dragoons to evict the sheep-stealers from Pout Hall, even pulled the old house down.

The king of the turf-diggers in my youth was one of the last of that lawless generation. He had been the biggest poacher, the hardest fighter, for miles round. And a muscular clergyman, Parson Thomas (incidentally the father of the present editor of *The Daily Mirror*), had reformed him. When I knew him he neither drank nor fought nor beat his wife. He was a great friend to me.

So when on this particular hot July afternoon of which I am talking we went, Togo and I, plunged, sweating, through the tall reeds to where the peat-diggers were hard at it, we were greeted with highly important news.

"There's a grut owd otter bin a-tomhossin' about in Norman's Dyke this last tew day, Master Wentworth," I was informed. "I reckon he's jest about the right mark for yew, an' our owd Togo there. Dew yew goo an' warm him up!" said John Butcher. John was "the cunnin'est owd masterpiece" when it came to fish and fowl, otters and hares.

So we set off. John loaned us—honour most royal— his twelve-foot-long fish-spear. He called it a dart. It had four-pronged tines set on a square metal cross-head, unlike the eel-spears or glaives, which had three, four, or five broad, leaf-shaped blades, each overlapping the others and slightly notched on the edges. No eel could wriggle off *them*.

We hunted that dyke from end to end for three-quarters of a mile, all through the hot, sweating, fly-bitten hours of that July afternoon. We stirred up the lily pads, thrashed out the reed-beds, peered, poked, and probed under the submerged trunks of Palæolithic bog-oaks. But no otter. We scared moorhens from their nests, startled the screaming redshank, disturbed a most dignified heron, sent the reed-warblers into chattering hysterics, and even scattered swallows from the black wooden draining-mill, as we thundered about inside seeking this momentous otter.

Evening drew on. The mists curled thinly. Mosquitoes and midges came out. Along the raised wall of the lode bank the figures of the peat-diggers passed home, a slow-moving, dignified frieze against the western sky. There was the donkey straining at the tow-rope, the boy urging the donkey, and then, gliding solemnly through the golden-brown peat-water, came the turf barge, stacked high with the black bricks dug from the fen. Young Bert Bailey, tall, dark, and Jutish-looking, stood in the bows, his dart poised ready for the first glancing of a jack or the dull silver swirl of a shoal of bream. The others sat and smoked, their red chokers making a gypsy splash of colour, their moleskin caps gleaming in the sunset light. You do not see that sort of picture nowadays.

"That's right—keep all on at him, master. If he ain't there now he will be time that's dark."

Thus encouraged we kept "all on." And it must have been three-quarters of an hour after that, when the moon came up, thin and silver, over the misty fen that, sitting motionless in the lee of a reed-stack, I heard the thin, high whistle of an otter, saw the black, bullet-shaped head cleaving a V-shaped wake down the dyke towards us.

We sat and waited. Not a breath, not a murmur. We were carved in stone. And the otter drew level with us. It was blowing a light beam wind, so he could not smell us. And as he drew level I launched the fish-spear—Togo plunged in.

That began the battle. The fish-spear struck the otter in the near hind-leg. Togo got him by the shoulder. The otter got Togo by the throat. The water was churned to an absolute cauldron. Terrier and otter thrashed round and round in the most Homeric battle I have ever seen between a dog and any other animal. At the first twist the otter shook free of the fish-spear. After that it was useless for me to try and use it. Dog and otter were mixed inextricably. To have thrown the spear would have meant getting one or probably both.

They fought up and down that dyke for twenty minutes. Once the otter got under a submerged bog-oak. I prodded him out with the spear. Togo was on him like a flash. And then the otter took Togo right under with him—and kept him under. So I jumped in too, prodding with the butt-end of the fish-spear, cheering frantically, my heart sick for my beloved dog. Up they both came again.

This time Togo was exhausted. I lifted him out on the bank, stabbed viciously where I thought the otter was. For a minute or two the old dog stood panting, his ribs going like bagpipes. Then he was in again. But the otter had vanished.

For another hour, with the enthusiasm of youth, we hunted that dyke from end to end. But no otter. We returned home, ignominious in mind, defeated in spirit. But somehow we knew that we had got him.

Two days later came the news by "Fen tigers'" telegraph—*i.e.*, by donkey-boy from the fen, by "our little girl" from the cottage to "the house"—that Uncle John had found Master Wentworth's big otter, dead, down on the fen by Lapwing.

It had lain two days in a hot sun. It was blown and flyblown. But it must have weighed a good 40 lb. Alas! it was useless to skin it—although our knives and our noses in those days were a match for any trophy, no matter how tough or high.

So the only thing to do was to let the maggots get at it, then bury it, dig it up a year later, boil what remained of the flesh off the bones, and keep the grinning skull—memorial of that most epic fight.

It was all done according to plan, religiously. But there must have been some wrong bearing on the cemetery in the stable-yard. For though we bored and dug, burrowed and excavated in the best Klondike manner, the skull was never found.

Eight years later I was a very young, very shy

soldier, newly joined under a wrong age. I had run away from home, enlisted as a private in the Dock Rats' Battalion—through a grotesque but happy clerical error of Whitehall—and I was home on my first leave, fresh from France. The War by then was almost a commonplace. I remember that my chief and most fervent wish was to get home to the old warrior Togo, then sixteen years of age.

When I arrived I was met by the long face, the gloomy blue eye, of Bob King, our eighty-four-year-old ex-coachman. Bob had worse news than wars or German victories over British armies. Togo was dead —murdered.

A fortnight before they had heard a shot at the bottom of the Weights, the great rabbit-haunted home paddocks which lay at the back of the house, full of old trees, owls, cuckoos, moorhens in the ditches, kestrels that hovered in the hot afternoons.

Those were the enchanted fields where Togo and I had caught our first rabbit, trapped our first moorhen, shot sparrows with a single-barrelled muzzle-loader, as they clustered in the bare hedgerows of November. All our adventures had sprung from the Weights, the Elysian fields. And that was where he was shot.

He crawled home, half an ounce of No. 6 in his ribs, reached the kitchen door, a pitiful, bloody mess, and died.

There were no witnesses, but there was a poaching, drunken lout, a small farmer who never farmed, who avoided me for years. He came from a near-by village. And Fen telegraphy—that whisper which runs from field to pub, from stackyard to the man who leads the horses—pieced it all together gradually.

The farmer left the district, the usual trinity of drink, women, and horses to blame. I was away for years. But he is still alive. One day we shall meet.

CHAPTER XIII

THE SWEET LITTLE MANCHESTER

" An active, graceful little dog "—The White English Terrier
—Billy and his Hundred Rats in less than Five Minutes—
" Stonehenge " on Colour and Points.

THE MANCHESTER, that sweetest of all little terriers, is one of the oldest. The old white English
terrier dates back to before 1800. But Edwards at that
time shows a black-and-tan which I should call a
Manchester. The Black-and-Tan Club was born in
1884, but you can find a true Manchester described by
Richardson in 1847. He calls it an English terrier,
" an active, graceful little dog," normally black-and-
tan in colour. And he writes this about it:

" The English terrier is, in combat, as game as the
Scotch, but less hardy in enduring cold or constant
immersion in water. It appears most probable that the
rough or Scotch breed was the primitive stock, and
that the smooth or English varieties are the result of
artificial culture. A small, well-marked English terrier, under 7 lb. weight, will, ' if as *good* as he looks,'
fetch from five to ten guineas. The celebrated dog
' Billy,' who killed the hundred rats in less than five
minutes, was a white English terrier, with a dark
patch on the side of his head."

Then in 1859 comes " Stonehenge." He, talking
about a Manchester-bred bitch called Lady, which belonged to the Hon. E. Lascelles, says:

" The English terrier is a, smooth-haired dog,

weighing from 6 to 10 lb. His nose is very long and tapering neatly off, the jaw being slightly overhung, with a high forehead, narrow, flat skull, strong, muscular jaw, and small, bright eyes well set in the head; ears when entire are short and slightly raised, but not absolutely pricked, turning over soon after they leave the head. When cropped they stand up in a point, and rise much higher than they naturally would. The neck is strong, but of a good length; body very symmetrical, with powerful, short loins, and chest deep rather than wide.

" Shoulders generally good, and very powerful, so as to enable the terrier to dig away at an earth for hours together without fatigue, but they must not be so wide as to prevent him from ' going to ground.' Forelegs straight and strong in muscle, but light in bone, and feet round and hare-like. Hind-legs straight but powerful. Tail fine, with a decided down carriage.

" The colour of these dogs should be black-and-tan, which is the only true colour; many are white, slightly marked with black, red, or sometimes, but very rarely, blue. The true fox-terrier was generally chosen with as much white as possible, so that he might be readily seen, either coming up after the pack or when in the fox's earth in almost complete darkness; but these were all crossed with the bulldog. Those which are now kept for general purposes are, however, most prized when of the black-and-tan colour, and the more complete the contrast—that is, the richer the black and tan respectively—the more highly the dog is valued, especially if without any white.

" In most cases there is a small patch of tan over each eye; the nose and palate should always be black. Such is the pure English terrier, a totally different animal from the short, thick-muzzled, spaniel-eyed, long-backed, cat-footed, curly-tailed abomination so prevalent in the present day. But he is a rank coward unless crossed with the bulldog."

And to continue these quotations from one other great authority—to wit, " Idstone "—he said, writing of them in 1872:

" The general formation of the black-and-tan is precisely similar to that of the white or other colour variety as to the shape of the head, size of eye, and general structure, but the coat should be more glossy and the skin finer. Absence of hair, however, is a great deterioration, especially on the skull and tail.

" The colours should be strongly contrasted—the black intense, the tan brilliant and rich, without any mixture of black or smuttiness. A pale or clay-coloured tan is a great fault. The redder, or, as artists call it, the ' warmer,' the better. Above each eye there should be a spot of this colour well defined; the larger the better. The forelegs should be tanned high up; the body black, with tan chest, neck, and throat; the cheeks, upper and lower, well tanned, and the nasal bone black; the inner thighs and the legs from hock to heel tanned; most judges agree that the outside of the hind-legs ought to be black; vent and lower part of tail tanned.

" Place this dog on short legs, do away with the fancy marks, leave his ears as nature made them, and he would be a very handsome, useful dog. As it is, he is an artificial creature, fit only to be led from show to show, to win cups and collars.

"The best specimens of late years of the larger breed, of 14 lb. and upwards, have been Mr Hodgson's Queen, Mr Lacy's Queen II, and his Staff and Baffles, and Mr S. Lang, of Clifton, has exhibited and possessed some of the finest specimens ever seen.

"Mr Handley, of Manchester, is one of the best judges of this class; and he has bred almost all the celebrated dogs of past days. It would be no more than the truth to state that he is at the present time one of the best authorities, and that his experience on the subject is almost unparalleled.

"I have never witnessed, nor do I expect to hear of, any feat of intelligence in the present exhibition terrier of this old English colour."

"Stonehenge" had a chapter on "terriers not being Skyes, dandies, fox, or toys," in his 1867 edition, and there he lays down the law as follows:

"It must be understood that we ignore in our present article anything approaching the toy terrier—requiring clothing, cushions, or a glass case. We are dealing with the vermin terrier, possessing courage, constitution or stamina, and hardihood, but still the terrier, without a trace of the old bulldog strain.

"White or black-and-tan are the best of all colours for a smooth terrier. Both colours are good, but on some accounts we prefer the white dog. Used for ratting, he is most easily distinguished; and he has the same advantage as to colour when his services are required for rabbit-hunting. But for a town we prefer the black-and-tan, provided that the tan cheeks, spots over the eyes, throat, and legs are brilliant in colour, and that the black is raven-black. In this case the dog should have no white about him—not even on his chest; and a white foot thoroughly destroys his quality.

"Whether black-and-tan or white, his coat should be smooth yet hard, and he should be perfectly free from the very least roughness, or anything approaching coarseness of coat about his muzzle, eyebrows, thighs, or any part of his profile.

"A smooth-haired dog may weigh from 6 lb. to 10 lb., or even 20 lb.; but, provided he is large enough for his calling, he cannot be too small. It is an advantage to keep down the size of certain dogs as much as possible, and to consider that two small terriers will do more than double the work of one large dog, whilst they consume no more.

"The muzzle must be fine, tapering, sharp, and fox-like; but the jaw must be muscular, the skull flat and narrow, the stop or indent between the eyes must be evident and ' pronounced.' The eye must be sparkling, bright, but not large. The ears round, flat to the head in repose, but raised, although falling over when the dog is roused. A tulip- or prick-ear is a great deformity, and betokens mongrel family."

Finally, the points as given by Walsh ("Stonehenge") in 1878 are worth setting out to-day. I have, I know, quoted Walsh extensively, but he was a man of great practical knowledge and infinite research, and his words are worth preserving to-day. His points are:

(1) MR J. R. BARLOW'S WIRE-HAIRED FOX-TERRIER
'CRACKLEY SURETHING'

Winner of the Kennel Club's 100-Guinea Cup for the best dog in the 1933 Crystal
Palace Show and many other prizes.

(2) FLAT RACING AT THE BELL MEAD KENNELS AT
HASLEMERE

A sharp sprint for "the Dogs' A.A.A. Championship."

Photos Sport and General

A 'RABBITY DAY' ON THE MARSHES

With a mixed lot of terriers and spaniels; marshmen attendant with guns of all bores and ages.

Photo Sport and General

175

ENGLISH TERRIER

POINTS OF BLACK-AND-TAN TERRIER

	Value		Value		Value
Head	5	Neck and shoulders	10	Coat	5
Jaws and teeth	5	Chest	10	Colour	25
Eyes	5	Loins	10	Tail	5
Ears	5	Legs and feet	10	Symmetry	5
	20		40		40

GRAND TOTAL, 100

1. The *head* (*value 5*) must be long and narrow, clean-cut, tight-skinned, with no bulging out at the cheeks; the skull flat and narrow.

2. The *jaws and teeth* (*value 5*). The muzzle should be long, lean, and tapering, with the teeth level, or the incisors of the upper jaw just closing over the under ones. The nose must be quite black.

3. The *eyes* (*value 5*) are black, bright, and small, neither sunk in the skull nor protruding.

4. The *ears* (*value 5*) are, for exhibition purposes, invariably cut, and much importance is attached to the result of this operation. It is required that the ears correspond exactly in shape and position with each other. They must be tapered to a point, stand quite erect, or slightly lean towards each other at the tip.

This is a practice I strongly deprecate, and never miss an opportunity of protesting against; I believe there is a general feeling arising against it; and among others who strongly condemn it is the best judge of the breed living, Mr S. Handley. The supporters of the practice cannot offer a single valid argument in its favour, whilst there are many strong reasons against it.

It is sheer nonsense to say the dogs look better cropped. It is not many years since people thought pugs looked better with their ears shorn off by the roots, but nobody thinks so now; and the practice as regards terriers could be

175

effectually stopped by a resolution of the Kennel Club to the effect that no dog with cut ears would be eligible to compete at any of their shows after 1879. There is this practical evil, too, in cropping, that it places the dog with naturally defective ears on an equality in competition with the dog born with perfect ears if they have been equally skilfully manipulated.

The natural ear is of three kinds : the button or drop ear, like the fox-terrier; the rose-ear—that is, half folded back, so that the interior of the ear can be partially seen— and the prick- or tulip-ear. But I have never seen the last-named kind, except in coarse specimens. The leather of the ear is thin, and generally finest in the best-bred dogs.

5. *Neck and shoulders* (*value* 10). The neck must be light and airy, well proportioned to the head, and gradually swelling towards the shoulders; there should be no loose skin or throatiness. The shoulders are not so muscular as in some breeds, but nicely sloping.

6. The *chest* (*value* 10) must be deep, but not wide; the latter would indicate a bull cross, which would also be shown in the head and other points. The body is short, the ribs rather deep than round, the back ones pretty well let down.

7. The *loins* (*value* 10) are strong and muscular, with this formation : there is an absence of the cut-up flank which the whippet and Italian greyhound crosses give.

8. *Legs and feet* (*value* 10). The former are straight, light of bone, clean as a racehorse, and the feet round, with the toes well arched and the claws jet-black.

9. The *coat* (*value* 5) must be short and close; it should look fine and glossy, but not soft in texture.

10. The *colour and markings* (*value* 25) are in this breed—which is now essentially a fancy dog—important. No other colour than black-and-tan or red is permissible; the least speck of white is fatal to winning chances, and it is in the richness, contrast, and correct distribution of these

176

that excellence consists. The black should be intense and jet-like; the tan a rich, warm mahogany; the two colours, in all points where they meet, being abruptly separated, not running into each other.

On the head the tan runs along each jaw, on the lower running down almost to the throat; a bright spot on the cheek, and another above the eye, each clearly surrounded with black, and well defined; the inside of the ears slightly tanned, spots of tan on each side of the breast, the forelegs tanned up to the knee; feet tanned, but the knuckles have a clear black line, called the ' pencil mark,' up their ridge; and in the centre of the tan, midway between the foot and the knee, there must be a black spot, called the ' thumb-mark,' and the denser the black, and the clearer in its out-line, the more it is valued.

The insides of the hind-legs are tanned, and also the under-side of the tail; but tan on the thighs and outside, where it often appears in a straggling way, producing the appearance called 'bronzed,' is very objectionable. The vent also has a tan spot, but it should be no larger than can be well covered by the tail when pressed down on it.

11. The *tail* (*value* 5) must be long, straight, thin, and tapering to a point. Its carriage should be low, and any curl over the back is a fatal defect.

12. The *symmetry* (*value* 5) of this dog is of great importance, as this point is developed to as great an extent as in any other breed, not even excepting the greyhound.

CHAPTER XIV

THE DOG IN LONDON SPORT

Hunting in Hyde Park—The Stag in the Edgware Road—The
Two Hounds in Piccadilly—Old London Race Meetings—Rat-
killing Records—A Dog-fighter of To-day.

I TAKE MY SUPPER at least two or three nights a week
in a venerable little supper club off St James's Street,
so old that no one seems quite sure when it was
founded. But there is a nice thought which says that
when an early Duke of Beaufort—I think it was the
fifth Duke—hunted all the country from Hyde Park
Corner to Berkeley Castle, on the Severn, and to Badminton, in Gloucestershire, he kept this little house in
St James's as a sort of dormitory for his roistering
squires up from the West Country. Some of them were
a little too noisy to be welcome in the Duchess's town
house. Moreover, they liked to smoke their pipes after
supper, to play backgammon and cribbage, as we still
do in that little club. And I think the Duke himself
liked it as an escape from the formalities of his great
mansion round the corner.

You can still sit and take your supper at the same
table where the Duke dined, still sit surrounded by
fox-hunting squires, by members of His Majesty's
Cabinet, by subalterns in the Brigade of Guards as
fiercely moustached as any ensign under the " Great
Duke." Neither the members nor the atmosphere have
changed much in a century.

And they still talk of hounds and dogs, of hunting and horses. But you can no longer step on a mounting-block at the door, mount your horse, and canter hollowly up St James's Street to a meet of hounds at Hyde Park Corner.

It has taken a long time for the march of the city to dislodge the dog from his place in London's sport. And as fast as you dislodge him in one sphere he returns with quadrupled popularity in another. There may no longer be stag-hunting with hounds in Hyde Park or bear- and bull-baiting with savage bull-terriers in Holborn or Seven Dials, and there is no longer a rat-pit off Cambridge Circus; but where those doubtful spectacles drew their hundreds greyhound racing to-day draws its tens of thousands.

I wonder how many people realize that in the time of Henry VII the whole of what is now London from the Palace of Westminster to Hampstead Heath was one great royal hunting-ground. Red deer, fallow deer, hares, partridges, and wildfowl abounded. So good was this royal hunting-ground that in 1536 a special game law was passed which forbade anyone to hunt with dogs or to hawk from Westminster Palace to St Giles's in the Fields, thence to Islington, to Our Lady of the Oak, to Highgate, to Hornsey, and to Hampstead Heath.

Elizabeth, Edward VI, and James I all hunted in Hyde Park. James I, who was a coarse, disgusting fellow, a heavy drinker who slobbered down his chin, thought more of his hounds and horses, of racing and hunting the hare, than he did of the government of his country. But we owe him at least two bows of gratitude across the grave. It was he who put New-market on the map, and it was he who made coursing a popular and noble pursuit. He put the hare upon a pedestal which succeeding generations of sportsmen, from the Duke of Norfolk to Lord Orford and General Critchley, have consolidated.

James had a hunting lodge in the middle of Hyde Park, somewhere near the bridge over the Serpentine, and there, after the day's hunting, they kennelled the hounds and drank till the stars reeled in their courses.

Actually almost the last stag-hunt in London was as late as 1796. A red stag swam the Thames from Bat-tersea Park, scrambled ashore on what is now Chelsea Embankment, and was hunted towards Cremorne House, where it doubled back along the river-bank. It went on past the church, then turned up Church Lane, which is now Church Street, with the pack in full cry, and bolted into a barn at the top of the lane.

Actually the last stag hunted in London was one which fled down Tottenham Court Road with the hounds in full cry behind it in the late eighties or early nineties. I cannot remember the exact year. This was a park stag hunted by a pack which in those days covered the country round Mill Hill. The Cox family, who produced the late Serjeant Cox and that well-known dog authority Major Harding Cox, lived then at Mote Mount, where they had a considerable estate and kept up a pack of hounds in the real style. They hunted all over Golders Green, Hendon, Mill Hill, and Hampstead Garden Suburb.

In fact, I remember hearing when I was a boy the story of a man who had a day's hunting with the old Serjeant's hounds. They killed late in the afternoon in a back garden somewhere near the top of the Edgware Road, and as the fox-hunter turned his horse's head for home he saw the unique sight of hounds being whipped off and taken home between the horse-buses, under the flickering gas-lamps of Edwardian London.

" I can't thank you enough for my day with your hounds," he wrote that night. " It was an experience which I don't suppose will ever be repeated, and I certainly never expect again to see hounds being taken home along a London street under the gas light.

" In fact, when I turned in at the Albany this evening I could almost have sworn that I saw a couple of your hounds upon the pavement in Piccadilly."

To which his host replied, " I think you must have been mistaken about those hounds you saw in Piccadilly last night. We were hunting the dog pack yesterday!"

There was a time not so long ago when the old Surrey and Burstow hounds were kennelled at Croydon on the very spot where the Grand Theatre now stands. Almost within living memory they hunted a hilly country of woods, bracken, and small farms which is now smothered by a red rash of bungalosis.

But as the foxhound declines within the perimeter of London so the greyhound and the dog-racing track take his place. The popularity of greyhound racing to-day, not only in London but in the large provincial cities, forces one to the inevitable comparison between the rise of the one pastime and the decline of its one-time rival, the suburban race-meeting.

It is remarkable when one surveys the sporting history of London to see the manner in which the race-meetings which were once one of the most prominent features of the sporting life of the Cockney have completely vanished.

James I introduced the first race-meeting to London. In his time there were meetings at Croydon and Enfield Chase. Then there was one at Hampstead, just behind Jack Straw's Castle, where the gravel pits are to-day. That meeting died out in 1732. A hundred years later the Kentish Town racecourse was every bit as popular as Epsom.

Then, in the year of Queen Victoria's succession, a Mr Whyte, a keen racing man with a lot of initiative, any amount of experience, and considerable honesty of purpose, started a racecourse on what was then known as the Bayswater Hippodrome. It covered the ground now occupied by Ladbroke Grove and the streets round about. The southern boundary was a pottery which stood in what is now called Potteries Lane, and I believe you can still see the old kiln standing. The eastern boundary was just beyond Portobello Road, and the course took in the present-day small recreation ground. The whole of the country round about, including Notting Hill and Notting Dale, was rural. There were a good many large mansions in the district, and a wealthy type of Londoner, the 'carriage classes,' lived in the neighbourhood. In fact, it seemed that Mr Whyte was on a certainty.

But alas for Mr Whyte and his hopes. The hamlet through which Potteries Lane ran was a nest of crooks. Mr Whyte and his race-meeting were heaven-sent gifts to them. Scarcely a person who attended that first meeting came away without having his pockets picked.

Furthermore, Mr Whyte had missed the fact that a right-of-way ran across the course. He could not stop the public from using this at the height of the racing. So the Bayswater meeting died a natural death. Bayswater originally took its name from the fact that a livery-stable keeper and coaching proprietor named Bays had his stables here on the main road out of London, with a large pond in front. There the coaches changed their teams and watered their horses. So naturally it became Bays' Watering.

Far worse than the Bayswater meeting was that held at Harrow. This had a very evil reputation. Pickpockets, thimble-riggers, three-card tricksters, roulette-table keepers, and every other form of thug and trickster turned it into a bear garden. The police did absolutely nothing. So it also died.

The Croydon meeting was definitely on a higher plane. Mr George Lambton was often seen in the saddle there. So were Arthur Yates and the late Bobby Ward. The fences were big, and the water jump was a twister. But Croydon has gone.

West Drayton, in Middlesex, which I remember before the War, was never much more than a pony meeting, a sort of flapping, catch-as-catch-can place. It was so badly run that on one occasion when two horses looked like dead-heating on the post the gang who had their money on one of them tipped the judge's box over with the judge inside it!

It is worth comparing these records of ill-management, rowdyism, and general thuggery with the decorum, law, and order which characterize the present-day greyhound race-meeting.

Apart from hunting, the main part which the dog seems to have played in London sport was in bull- and bear-baiting, rat-killing, and dog-fighting.

Bear-baiting and bull-baiting died long ago. Neither was an enlivening spectacle. The 'sport' merely consisted in tying up a bull or bear on a short chain and then setting dogs at him, usually a bull-terrier type.

Rat-killing went on at various rat-pits, and was as recognized a form of entertainment as cockfighting. The last of the old rat-pits in London was a dirty little underground place just off Cambridge Circus, hidden behind a shop where they sold pigs' trotters and sausages. It was going until just before the War. You went down a wooden sanded staircase and came into a large underground room, actually the cellars of two houses knocked into one. I have described it very fully in one of my previous books, *A Falcon on St Paul's*, which is a record of the sports and games of London.

The cellar was thick with smoke, and smelt of rats, dogs, dirty human beings, and stale beer. Flaring gas-jets lit up the centre, which was a boarded ring rather like a small circus arena. Rough wooden benches were built up in tiers all round this arena, almost to the ceiling. In the ring they had dog-fights, cockfights, and rat-killings. A hundred rats would be let out of a bag, and then there were great bets backwards and forwards on whose dog could kill the most in a minute. Billy, as I have mentioned elsewhere, the famous white English terrier, killed his hundred rats in less than five minutes—a snap, a shake, a toss, and it was all over. They said that more than once he had two dead rats in the air at a time.

A good rat-killer, who might be anything from a first-class bull-terrier to a mere mongrel, would kill fifteen rats a minute slickly and quickly. Think of it— a rat in every four seconds snapped up as he ran, tossed in the air, and another one caught probably before the first one hit the ground. There was a great dog called Jacko who was a record-breaker. He once killed twenty-five rats in one minute and twenty-eight seconds in 1861. On another occasion he polished off a hundred rats in five minutes and twenty-eight seconds, and a year after he went one better and clean killed two hundred rats in fourteen minutes and thirty-seven seconds. The stakes at these rat-killing matches some-times ran into several hundreds of pounds, and the bets were correspondingly heavy.

Dog-fighting was a sickening and beastly affair. Like cockfighting, it has long been illegal, but still goes on. I know of one small country squire near London, a man who ought to know better, who, on his own admission, has a private dog-pit where his own fighting bull-terriers, the true Staffordshire Bulls, are regularly fought against dogs from all over England.

A year or two ago, when I was editing a well-known

weekly sporting paper, I happened to write an article in one of the evening dailies upon the Staffordshire Bull. This tickled the dog-fighter's imagination, and he wrote to me to say that I was obviously one of the 'fancy,' and he considered that he possessed the only true fighting dogs in England. He ended his letter by remarking, " I could tell you how I got them, but———"

Suspecting the worst, I wrote a letter to draw him out. The result is enough to make any reasonably minded Englishman quite sick. It was this:

" I have noticed several letters in one of your daily contemporaries dealing with our breed—the Staffordshire bull-terrier—'bottomed to the last hair.' Now, sir, there has been a great deal of nonsense written and spoken about this fast dying breed. One individual compared them to a barge dog. (Mine simply blushed when they heard this—and went and hid.)

" This dog above is now—a month ago—dead. He went 23½ lb. fit, in his collar.

" He has killed an Alsatian dog in twelve minutes, and a hundred rats in nine minutes, forty seconds.

" They are bred simply and solely to fight—each other preferably, or any other dog—if so it happens. They are entirely useless for badgers as they almost invariably get an unsuitable hold and get killed. A true Staffordshire has no written pedigree, verbal only, never weighs over 25 lb., has a jaw like a shark, is never fawn or part white (these are nearly as soft as an ordinary show bull-terrier), a head relatively like a coal-scuttle—never, never squeaks and fights in silence. I doubt whether there are fifty in England.

"A six-month pup will never snarl and 'walk round' another dog. He will go straight in, with no warning. They are delightful with children, cats, and stock.

"Unreliable with horses—for they are liable at any time to 'snout' them—and it is not easy to get one off a milk-float horse either. He hangs in silence, and you can cut an inch off his tail with a chopper and he will still hang.

"They are from the Black Country. There are dozens up there for sale—of half-breed whippets—45–50 lb. But let anyone go and try to buy a 'reight red 'un' and see how he gets on. I am not a dealer, and I have none for sale."

A little further correspondence followed, and then came this:

"Thank you for your letter. Yes, this letter of mine will create a lot of controversy! I have pitted more bull-terriers than most people in England and abroad. We had a main here last week—and I saw a most curious thing that I have never seen before.

"I saw a *dead* dog win a fight. I set him up—and he crawled up to the white line, snarled, and died.

"The other had two hind-legs broke, and would not come to scratch. (They were in holds for just an hour.) The dead dog (mine), of course, got the decision. Most interesting.

"To get them fit one gets hold of a mongrel terrier, ties him up short, the far side of a really big fire in a very hot room. Tie up your dog on the other side with a long elastic rope just short enough not to allow him (be careful of the exact pull and stretch) to slash the other. Sick him to it; leave ten minutes. Next day twenty, etc. Don't go more than twenty minutes. And always eventually let him kill the mongrel each day. (They are easily found.)

"You can get a Staffordshire fit to bet £50 in a cottage kitchen if you go to work like this—if you keep him always in a pitch-dark room and feed on raw meat and blood. They go stale after a fortnight in the dark. About the eleventh day is usually when they come out like a tiger.

"About 1 per cent. of them are safe to turn loose, so road exercise is practically impossible. The elastic method is the only way."

The mentality of such a man is interesting. The family has produced two good lawyers, the leader-writer of a great London daily, another man notable for a famous breed of terriers, and the usual country squires. The breeding would suggest that the present-day representative would be a man of normal humanity. Instead we have an extraordinary throw-back to the worst type of sadistic eighteenth-century 'sportsman.' He is an air-pocket of mentality—as revolting a form of perversion as any of the miserable young men and unspeakable young women who to-day have made the perversion of sex almost fashionable. Both processes of mind are outside the law, and both should be killed by ridicule, disgust, and the law. The dog-fighter deserves the inside of Reading Gaol equally with Oscar Wilde.

CHAPTER XV

THE ORIGIN OF RETRIEVERS

Some Early Opinions and Definitions—" Stonehenge " on the
Ideal Retriever—" Idstone's " Views—Curlies, Flat-coats, Lab-
radors, and Goldens—Some History rediscovered.

IT IS PROBABLY SAFE TO SAY that retrievers as a
recognized breed of sporting dogs are, at the outside,
not over about eighty years old.

There seems little doubt that they started round
about the fifties as a cross between the Newfoundland
dog and the setter. "Craven," writing in 1859,
mentions such a cross. He also mentions what he calls
a retriever which was a cross between a bulldog and a
smooth terrier. It apparently retrieved a woodcock for
a bet, and thereby won its owner £17 10s. But we
need not take that very seriously when considering the
beginnings of the retriever type.

I should say that " Stonehenge," who wrote extensively on the breed in 1859, is the first real authority
who can be taken with any seriousness. He says:

" In speaking of the retriever it is generally understood that by the dog for recovering game on land is
meant the distinct kind known as the water-spaniel.
With regard to the propriety of using a separate dog
for retrieving in open or cover shooting, there is a
great difference of opinion, but . . . I shall confine myself to a description of the crosses used solely as retrievers, including the ordinary cross between the
Newfoundland and setter, and that between the terrier

189

and the water-spaniel, which is recommended by Mr Colquhoun, and which I have found specially serviceable.

" The qualities which are required in the regular retriever are: great delicacy of nose and power of stooping (which latter is often not possessed by the pointer); cleverness to follow out the windings of the wounded bird, which are frequently most intricate, and puzzle the intelligence as well as the nose to unravel them; love of approbation, to induce the dog to attend to the instructions of the master; and an amount of obedience which will be required to prevent his venturing to break out when game is before him. All these are doubtless found in the retriever. But they are coupled with a large, heavy frame, when he is to be conveyed from place to place. Hence, if a smaller dog can be found to do the work equally well, he should be preferred; and as I think he can I shall describe both.

" The large black retriever is known by his resemblance to the small Newfoundland and setter, between which two he is bred, and the forms of which he partakes of in nearly equal proportions. His head is that of a heavy setter, but with shorter ears, less clothed in hair. The body is altogether larger and heavier, the limbs stronger, and the feet less compact, while the loins are much more loose, and the gait more or less resembling in its peculiarities that of the Newfoundland.

" The colour is almost always black with very little white; indeed, most people would reject a retriever of this kind, if accidentally of any other colour. The coat is slightly curly but not very long, and the legs are not much feathered. The height is usually about 23 or 24 inches, sometimes slightly more or less. This dog can readily be made to set and back, and he will also hunt as well as a setter, but slowly, and lasting for a short time only.

" The terrier cross is either with the beagle or the pointer, the former being that which I have chiefly used with advantage, and the latter being recommended by Mr Colquhoun in his *Lochs and Moors*. He gives a portrait of one used by himself which, he says, was excellent in all respects; and from so good a source the recommendation is deserving of all credit. This dog was about 22 inches high with a little of the rough coat of the Scotch terrier, combined with the head and general shape of the pointer.

" The sort I have used is, I believe, descended from the smooth white English terrier, and the true old beagle; the nose and style of hunting proclaiming the hound descent, and the voice and appearance showing the preponderance of the terrier cross. These dogs are small, scarcely ever exceeding 10 lb. in weight, and with difficulty lifting a hare, so that they are not qualified to retrieve fur any great distance. They must therefore be followed when either a hare or pheasant is sought to be recovered.

" They are keen in questing and very quiet in their movements, readily keeping at heel and backing the pointers steadily while they are ' down charge ' for as as long a time as may be required; and when they go to their game they make no noise, as is too often done by the regular retriever.

"They do not carry so well as the larger dog, but in all other respects they are his equal or perhaps superior, and from their small size they are admissible to the house, and being constant companions are more easily kept under command: besides which they live on the scraps of the house, while the large retriever must be kept tied up at the keeper's, and costs a considerable sum to pay for his food."

Now this reference to the terrier cross is of immense interest. I wonder whether any dog approximating to that description is in existence to-day. Is it too fantastic to imagine that here and there a rough-looking spaniel of sorts may be the descendant of this terrier cross?

"Stonehenge's" reference to "the nose and style of hunting" proclaims the hound descent and fits one or two odd-looking village dogs which I have seen employed from time to time, and which were classified roughly as spaniels. And more than one of them has had a distinct resemblance to the note of a terrier in its voice.

Eight years later the same writer, who was, of course, editor of *The Field* at the height of its glory and prestige, says, speaking of "The Retriever Proper":

"No distinct recognized breed of retrievers exists, unless we make an exception in favour of the liver-coloured Irish water-spaniel, the rough Russian, and the deerhound. The Earl of Cardigan, Sir George Wombwell, Sir John Lister Kaye, and many well-

MR NIGEL HOLDER, THE WELL-KNOWN GUN-DOG TRAINER AND BREEDER, TAKING A BIRD FROM HIS GOLDEN RETRIEVER 'DUSTY'

A MAGNIFICENT HEAD STUDY OF A LABRADOR RETRIEVING
A GROUSE

Photo Guy B. Farrar, Hoylake

known sportsmen possess their own breed of dog, used for retrieving from land or water, but there is no established breed. Good retrievers are to be found of all breeds. Thirty years ago William Evans, now, we believe, head keeper to Lord Fitzwilliam, had a famous retriever, by a bloodhound of the late Lord Ducie's, out of a mastiff.

"An English retriever, whether smooth or curly-coated, should be black or black-and-tan, with tabby or brindle legs, the brindled legs being indicative of the Labrador origin. We give the preference from experience to the flat-coated or short-coated small St John's or Labrador breed. These breeds we believe to be identical. The small St John's has marvellous intelligence, a great aptitude for learning to carry, a soft mouth, great strength, and he is a good swimmer. If there is any cross at all in this breed it should be the setter cross."

Then he goes on to give the points which he considers necessary to the proper retriever. It is interesting to compare them with the show points laid down to-day or with the working points exhibited by any good-class dog which never sees the show-bench, but justifies its existence by work.

"He should have a long head, large eye, a capacious mouth, the ears small, close to his head, set low, and with short hair on them; his nose large, his neck long that he may stoop in his quest. We should give the points as follows: head, 10; nose, 10; ears, 2; neck, 8–30; shoulders, oblique and deep; chest, broad and powerful; shoulders, 6; chest, 4–10.

" His loins and back and hindquarters all of great importance; for although a hare will be the maximum of weight he will have to carry, he may be compelled to carry it a long distance, to get over a stone wall with it or to make his way through strong cover.

" Loins and back, 10; hindquarters, 10–20. His legs should be strong, straight, and muscular; his feet round and moderately large but compact, and the toes should be well arched. Feet, 6; legs, 6; hocks (large), 6; stifles, 2–20.

" If he is required for punt shooting his coat should be short and close; but for general purposes the texture should be black, shining and abundant. If black he should be all black, if black and tabby the black should not go far up the legs, and should be free from white. Colour and gloss of coat, 15; the stern should be well feathered, moderately short, and gaily carried. The feather should be decidedly heavy, but tapering to the point. Tail, 5."

To interrupt " Stonehenge's " discourse for a moment, I can imagine nothing more useless, uncomfortable, or troublesome than a retriever in a punt. I have tried it over a period of twenty years of punting, and my definite opinion is that a dog is a nuisance every time. They get into the mud, and bring it into the punt. They are swept away on the tides, and may have to be retrieved themselves. They shake water all over you, and then they lie and shiver for hours. They are a nuisance to the punter, and it is an unfair infliction on the dogs themselves. Any punter who knows his job should be able to pick a useful proportion of his useless birds with the aid of a shoulder gun and a landing net for divers. But to go on with " Stonehenge ":

" We have given no points for temper. No dog deserves the least consideration from a judge unless his temperament is evidently good at first glance. Temperament is the foundation of a good retriever. He should be about 24 inches at the shoulder, moderately long in his body, moderately short on his legs. He should be as clean-cut as a setter under the angle of his jaw. The setter cross is perhaps the best, but it certainly diminishes the liking for water, and in some instances the produce has a marked disinclination to quest in thick or tangled woodland.

" The remarks we have made as to the frame and temperament of the wavy-coated retriever apply to the curly-coated dog. The distinction between the two is simply one of texture.

" The origin of the curly dog is not well known, but it is supposed to be the result of a cross between the Irish water-spaniel and the Newfoundland. The face of a curly retriever should be clean; his hind-legs from the hock downward free from feather; the remainder of his body covered with short crisp curls.

" Windham, the property of Mr Gorse, is a good example of the wavy-coated dog; and Jet, in the possession of the same gentleman, is perhaps the best specimen of a curly-coated one ever exhibited. The flat-coated dog gained a first prize in Birmingham three years in succession, besides numerous first prizes at other shows. He has frequently been passed over for

195

Jet, or Jet has been put aside for him, but he held his own at Newcastle, Alexandra Park, Nottingham, and Leeds. His powers of scent are excellent, and we understand him to be broken well, but he is rather hard-mouthed, and this fault we hold to be hereditary.

"Jet, on the other hand, carries alive, and, having carried a live chicken for any length of time, will let it fly from his mouth at a given signal."

The reader will note that earlier on "Stonehenge" mentions the deerhound as presumably "a recognized breed of retriever." This apparently puzzling reference is explained by "Idstone," who, writing of "the Smooth or Hairy-coated Black Retriever," says:

"Deer-stalkers and deer-stealers have used a retriever for *their* game for centuries. No one ever thought of losing a crippled stag; and the monks of St Bernard always keep their fine Alpine mastiffs for the recovery of crippled human beings. But the handsome, intelligent, capable, highly disciplined black retriever is a comparatively modern institution.

"I recollect a black, flat-coated one a friend of mine purchased at a long price; but he was well worth the money, and a good deal cheaper than a shorthorn calf sold at a guinea an ounce because his mother was numbered the 12,489th, and his father belonged to Mr Somebody's herd.

"He was as black as a raven—blue-black—not a very large dog, but wide over the back and loins, with limbs like a lion, and thick, glossy, long, silky coat, which parted down the back, a long, sagacious head, full of character, and clean as a setter's in the matter of coat. His ears were small, and so close to his head that they were hidden in his feathered neck. His eye was neither more nor less than a human one. I never saw a bad expression in it.

"He was not over 25 inches in height, but he carried a hare with ease; and if he could not top a gate with one—which about one dog in two hundred does twice a year—he could get through the second or third spar, or push it through a gap before him in his mouth and never lose his hold.

"And then for water. He would trot into the launching-punt and coil himself up by the luncheon-basket to wait for his master as soon as he saw the usual preparations for a cruise. For this work he had too much coat, and brought a quantity of water into the boat; but for retrieving wildfowl he was excellent; and in the narrow watercourses and amongst the reeds and osiers his chase of a winged mallard was a thing to see. They seemed both to belong to one element; and he would dive like an otter for yards, sometimes coming up for breath, only to go down again for pleasure.

"But on a winged grouse, to see him swing and feather with his fine, bushy stern like a foxhound, and try the bits of ling and the grass and bog-myrtle, against which he suspected the bird had brushed, like an Indian on a trail, was most interesting; now and then hesitating at some suspicious clump, his tail more agitated and his eye kindling as he makes a dead point, and crashes through the brake. There is a flutter, and out he comes, his head covered with sand and splinters of the dead branches, with the poor cripple in his mouth. I saw this performance one sultry day when there was no scent.

"Subsequently, in the middle of an exceptionally dry September, when the turnip-leaves were yellow and orange-coloured and brown, and rattled like parchment, Snow picked up the birds with no trouble, distinguishing where they ran by a sort of instinct, in spite of the strong, rank smell of the roots and decayed foliage, dabbing for and retrieving them with marvellous precision.

"But the smooth-coated dog has a lighter eye—a pale hazel with an intensely black pupil, occasionally very like what is known as a 'china' or 'wall-eye.' Be that how it may, they are the best of all breeds for boating; they can stand all weathers, and though men unused to them call them butchers' dogs, I think them handsome, and know that they are sensible, and that the punt and shore men, living by adroit use of the long stauncheon gun and 'flat,' look upon them as part of their household, and in some cases—to quote the words of one old sporting farmer, to a duke who wanted to buy his horse—'No one has money enough to buy him!'

"Almost every preserver of game had his own favourite breed of retrievers, and dog-shows have brought out specimens of more than average beauty; still, only five dogs and two bitches were exhibited in the Birmingham Show of 1860.

"Mr Henry Brailsford won the first prize, of the magnificent value of £3, with a large black setter-headed dog, but decidedly a good one; and the same sum was given to a bad, liver-coloured, leggy bitch belonging to Lord A. Paget, which would not be noticed now, especially if compared with her companion in the class, a good, long, low, curly black, one of Mr Druce's. The Birmingham Show Committee was quite right to begin with low prizes, but the judges were at sea in their awards. Every one was young at these exhibitions, and even the disappointed exhibitor was unborn.

" In 1864 Birmingham divided the retriever classes into the curly and the smooth, or wavy-coated, breeds. They had already a cup and other prizes for Irish water-spaniels, and in 1866 a class was opened for retrievers " other than black," all which are continued to the present time. A champion class had been established in 1863, when Mr Hill's Windham, a smooth dog, was placed first, and a Mr Carver's Belle second, to the exclusion of five much better dogs; Mr Hill's Jet, subsequently purchased by Mr Gorse, and one of the most perfect retrievers ever seen; Mr Riley's Royal and his bitch Bess; Sir St George Gore's Dinah; and Mr Hill's Mab.

" The curly retriever follows, or ought to follow, the Labrador type in ear and head. He should have a clean face, an unfeathered stern, or at most very slightly feathered; a large, intelligent eye, and leg clean from hocks and knees to the feet, which should be close, firm, and rather large *to act as paddles*, and with respect to feathered stern Mr Gorse's first-prize dog Nelson, by Jet II, fails, but in other respects he is a worthy descendant of *old* Jet, the celebrated winner; better he could not be.

" Amongst the immense variety of dogs which I have seen, judged, and taken notice of, or even bred and broken, many pass from my recollection, but I don't think that I shall ever forget the original Jet. A photograph from an oil-painting, kindly forwarded to me by Mr Gorse, conveys a poor impression of him. His carriage was more sprightly, his head longer, and cleaner-cut under his jaw, and his stern was better placed and carried than the photograph represents. He was a mass of black, crisp, short curls, except his face and forehead, which were as smooth as the setter's, which he generally stood next to in the rank, with his champion card above him, barking a husky and, as I think, high-bred welcome to all who passed by."

Some years later, writing in 1877, " Stonehenge " gives a very useful tip for retriever-training which might well be used to-day.

" No retriever proper had so good a nose as the pointer or setter," he writes, " though there are some dogs of these latter breeds who seem incapable of trying for anything but a body scent—and they, of course, are useless as retrievers. Some years ago I endeavoured to devise a plan of trying retrievers in public, and in my experiments I used an old, worn-out pointer, which happened to be the only retrieving dog at hand.

" Constructing a trap on a tripod, which, on pulling a string, would drop a bird with its wing feathers cut

in a field of turnips or other covert, I found the old
dog invariably bring it to hand, although on one
occasion the bird had reached the next field, fully
three hundred yards from the trap; and as a result of
these private experiments I produced the machine at
Vaynol in 1871, in full confidence that it would serve
the purpose of the retriever trials. But there the retrievers proper could do nothing with a winged
partridge dropped on turnips exactly as I had done in
private, and if the bird happened to get away more
than fifty yards the scent was very seldom taken up,
and if found at all the success was owing to perseverance in seeking at random, and to accident, rather than
nose.

"Mr R. J. Lloyd Price's Devil, a curly, liver-
coloured dog, apparently a cross between the Irish
water-spaniel and the poodle, bred by Sir P. Nugent,
is the only dog I have ever seen perform in public
to my satisfaction, showing great perseverance in
hunting, with a good nose, but not coming up to the
level of the old pointer above alluded to. With this
exception, the best private retrieving I have ever seen
has been with crosses of the terrier and beagle; for
with one of these little dogs I never yet lost either fur
or feather, though, of course, he could not carry a hare
across a brook or over a gate. Still, we must take the
world as we find it, *and the world of* 1877 *demands
a retriever proper*, black by preference, and either
wavy-coated or curly."

"Stonehenge" goes on to say:

"The wavy-coated breed is generally supposed to

be a cross between the Labrador dog, or the small St John's Newfoundland, and the setter; but in the present day the most successful on the show-bench, as above remarked, have been apparently, and often admittedly, pure. In the belief that the nose of the pure Labrador is inferior to that of the setter I certainly should advise the cross-bred dog for use; but to be successful on the show-bench, under such judges as Dr Bond Boore, Mr Handley, and Mr Lort, the competitor should display as little as possible of the setter. In all other respects Major Allison's Victor was perfect, his symmetry being one of the most beautiful order; but Dr Bond Moore could not forgive his setter-like ears, and his fiat was against him."

Then, speaking of the " black curly-coated," he says:

" Little or nothing seems to be known of the history of this dog, now so extensively bred throughout the United Kingdom. At all events, there is no getting at the exact source of the breed, and on that account I am led to think that some non-sporting dog, such as the poodle, has been used. Possibly successful breeders do not like to give information which may lead to a repetition of their success in other hands; but my experience does not lead me to place much reliance on this interpretation of their secrecy.

" It is admitted that the curly-coated dog is remarkably sagacious, and more 'tricky' than the smooth, and this confirms the above suspicion; but I confess that I have no proof whatever to allege in its support, and my theory must be taken for what it is worth as such. The general belief is that the water-spaniel and the small Newfoundland have been used in establishing the breed, and there is little doubt of the truth of this theory.

" This variety of dog has certainly not increased in numbers of late years, or improved in symmetry, *and has notably gone off in the shape of the head, which is now too narrow by far.*[1] The falling off numerically is probably due to the fact that the public have pronounced in favour of the Labrador, which has been largely imported by ' Idstone ' and others, as well as extensively bred by Dr Bond Moore and Mr Shirley, who have, with Mr Lort and Mr Handley, composed the goodly company of judges in this department. From whatever cause, however, the curly-coated dogs of the present day are not exhibited in such large and good classes as they were about ten years ago, and they are notably deficient in those indications of good temper which should always be looked for in the retriever."

To come to the present day, it is fairly safe to say that we owe the perfect status of the Labrador retriever, first of all, to the Hon. A. Holland Hibbert, who in 1909 began to show some of his famous Munden kennel at various shows, and thereby brought the breed to the notice of the general public. The Duke of Buccleuch, the Earl of Malmesbury, Mr N. Portal, whose famous dog Flapper is almost among the immortals, and, finally, Mrs Quintin Dick, now Lorna, Countess Howe, all contributed a very great

[1] The italics are mine, and the words are applicable to-day.—J. W. D.

share to the perfection and popularity of the breed. Lady Howe has probably done more than anyone, and her Banchory champions are outstanding milestones in the development of the breed.

One of the highest prices ever got for a Labrador was the £500 which Mr Scott McComb paid for Horton Max, bred by Mr Allen Shuter.

Lord Lonsdale threw a minor bombshell into the Labrador world when, on the 31st of March, 1926, he wrote to *The Daily Mail*, stating that no Labrador cross had ever been used in the development of the Labrador, but that it sprang from the Chesapeake. But, as will be seen from the chapter on the Chesapeake dog, this diversion is surely not of great importance, as it seems fairly certain that the Chesapeake began as part of a Labrador cross.

The general appearance of the Labrador should be that of a strongly built, short-coupled, very active dog. Compared with the wavy or flat-coated retriever, he should be wider in the head, wider through the chest and ribs, wider and stronger over the loins and hindquarters. The coat should be close, short, dense, and free from feather.

Head. The skull should be wide, giving brainroom; there should be a slight 'stop'—that is, the brow should be slightly pronounced, so that the skull is not absolutely in a straight line with the nose. The head should be clean-cut and free from fleshy cheeks. The jaws should be long and powerful, and quite free from snipiness or exaggeration in length; the nose should be wide and the nostrils well developed.

The ears should hang moderately close to the head, rather far back, should be set somewhat low and not be large and heavy. The eyes should be of a medium size, expressing great intelligence and good temper, and can be brown, yellow, or black.

Neck and Chest. The neck should be long and powerful, and the shoulders long and sloping.

The chest must be of a good width and depth, the ribs well sprung, and the loins wide and strong, stifles well turned, and the hindquarters well developed and of great power.

Legs and Feet. The legs must be straight from the shoulder to the ground, and the feet compact, with toes well arched and pads well developed; the hocks should be well bent, and the dog must neither be cow-hocked nor move too wide behind; in fact, he must stand and move true all round on legs and feet.

Tail. The tail is a distinctive feature of the breed; it should be very thick towards the base, gradually tapering towards the tip, of medium length, should be practically free from any feathering, but should be clothed thickly all round with the Labrador's short, thick, dense coat, thus giving that peculiar 'rounded' appearance which has been described as the 'otter' tail. The tail may be carried gaily, but should not curl too far over the back.

Coat. The coat is another very distinctive feature; it should be short, very dense, and without wave, and should give a fairly hard feeling to the hand.

Colour. The colour is generally black, free from any rustiness and any white marking, except possibly a small spot on the chest. Other whole colours are permissible.

The flat-coated retrievers, then known as wavys, first appeared on the show-bench at the Ashburnham Hall in Chelsea in April 1864. We owe the development of the breed very largely to Mr Thorpe Bartram, a grand old sportsman, still alive and kicking in his nineties, whom I visited in 1937; to the late Colonel Legh, Major Harding Cox, Mr H. R. Cooke, Mr Allen Shuter, Mr Percy Heaton, and especially the late Mr E. T. Shirley, the founder of the Kennel Club.

It is always said that Mr Shirley was the first man to breed this type, which he did at Ettington Park, in Warwickshire, where he was supposed to have crossed a setter with a Labrador. Many authorities consider him the founder of the breed.

The golden retriever appears to have sprung from some very good-looking cream-coloured dogs which the Hon. Dudley Marjoribanks discovered in a circus at Brighton. This was some time after the Crimean War, and they were supposed to have come from Russia. Mr Marjoribanks was so impressed with their brains and good looks that he bought the lot and took them up to Guisachan, his deer forest in Inverness-shire, which, as Lord Tweedmouth, he later sold to the Earl of Portsmouth. They were used up there for following deer, and trained as retrievers to feather.

Since those days Mrs Charlesworth, Lady Harris, the Hon. Mrs Grigg, Captain Hardy, and others have done an immense amount of work to make the breed popular. I am, as I said before, not greatly enamoured of them, but perhaps that is because, as a wildfowler, I expect too much of them, and have perhaps tried them too highly under exceptionally arduous conditions. They are handsome, likeable dogs, charming companions, good performers in the field, but I have yet to be convinced that they have the hardihood of either the curly-coat or the Labrador. That, however, by the way.

I am going to wind up this chapter with one story which has gone the rounds of the gunrooms for years. It appeared in *The Gentlewoman* some years ago, and is too good to be missed.

" My father-in-law," said the correspondent of *The Gentlewoman*, who, I suspect, must have been a lady, " once owned a dog which was something of a politician. She was a handsome retriever with a handsome pedigree behind her. The stableboy had to go every morning to the station for the newspaper, and so this intelligent boy trained the dog to go, instead of him, every morning, in order that he might indulge in half an hour's longer sleep.

" Mat never failed to bring the paper back to him, but one day she appeared without it, and, the stableboy hurrying to inquire the reason, the stationmaster told him that he was short of *The Times* newspaper, and had presented a *Telegraph* to the dog instead, who would have nothing to do with it, but laid it down on the floor and came home without it.

" The boy told his master, who naturally was disinclined to believe the story. The stationmaster, however, assured him it was true, and, to prove it, a week later my father-in-law rose betimes and hid himself in the station.

"Sure enough, the dog arrived, and on being presented with the *Telegraph* laid it down on the floor and protested by barking. Then the stationmaster gave him a *Times*, and the dog trotted off with his parcel.

"We supposed that the reason was that the two papers were of different weight, and that the ink or paper tasted wrong to the sagacious animal. Mat continued to fetch our daily paper for some years, and she even tried to teach one of her sons, with some success, but I regret to say that after her death her son could not be depended on."

And there I think we may justifiably draw a decent veil on the retriever.

CHAPTER XVI

THE MASCULINE RETRIEVER

Black Bess and the First Pheasant—Nell, the Adder-catcher of
Langenhoe—Bruno, the Curly-coat of Salcott—Tide-line and
Snipe Fen.

H E STANDS ON THE HORIZON of youth as the one
dog which is an all-round man. There is nothing
feminine about a retriever. He is utterly masculine,
whether he is the old English curly-coat, the toughest
of them all; the flat-coat, who loves water like an
otter; the Labrador, who has the stern qualities of
that grim coastline whence he takes his name; or even
the golden retriever, present-day descendant of the
breed which Lord Tweedmouth first made famous at
Guisachan. I love them all. Of the four I would
thank you least for the golden. He, by dint of show-
bench, soft living, and too many women owners, is
becoming a handsome, flighty fellow, full of charm,
but too apt to throw up the sponge.

Once I remember writing an article in an evening
newspaper about this breed. I said that every time I
saw one I was reminded, rather maliciously, of the
old squire who, when he tried one for a season, wound
up explosively, "Damn it, the thing's just like a
ginger biscuit—hard in the mouth and breaks up in
water!"

The result was that a most ferocious female, clad in
breeches and a cutaway coat with brass buttons, armed,
so I was assured, with a dog-whip, descended upon the

editorial citadel, demanding, if not my head upon a charger, a more nursery form of punishment. Fortunately I was not there. But I believe the editor was very frightened.

So you see that the golden, at any rate, has the rare quality of stimulating loyalty.

But Black Bess is the first milestone of them all. She was my father's dog, a magnificent flat-coat who shone in the sun like a raven's wing, who walked the grass with the gait of a queen. She was all good looks, good breeding, and good heart.

That was a long time ago. Edward VII was King. The great houses and the great manors of England were not yet despoiled or split up at the bidding of a short-sighted democracy which has discovered for itself the astonishing oological fact that if you kill the goose he will, for some odd reason, cease to lay golden eggs.

We lived then near Newmarket in a funny little house which had a surprised face and tall chimney-stacks which stuck up at either end. It was exactly like a rabbit cocking his ears under the edge of the wood to test the scents and sounds of the evening.

And, indeed, it stood under the edge of a great wood with a green dell behind it where the rabbits *did* hop and *did* cock their ears at the house with its questioning chimneys. A little stream ran through that dell, and farther back in the wood there was a green and quaking marsh, full of pink cuckoo-flowers, with yellow irises set flauntingly about its edges and great white water-lilies that mocked the moon. Here and there in this decorative garden were bits of Roman brickwork, sunken remains of a great Roman bath which some proconsul with a pretty sense of Pan-like beauty had set in this green hollow of the big woods beneath the high heath of Newmarket.

They called the house the Marsh House, and there I was born. It was an odd precursor of the fact that the rest of my leisure in life should be spent, so far as was possible, on marshes and wild places where water gleams and winds blow freely.

Now this little house of ours was set about by one or two other and greater houses. One of them shared a garden wall with us. The garden gate was always open. The man who had that house next to us was a Prince Radziwill, one of that family which has made its mark on the histories of Austria, Poland, Hungary, and Russia. Prince Radziwill and my father were friends. They shared horses and guns, dogs and fishing. They talked each other's language. And the one thing my father had which Radziwill coveted was Black Bess.

That, indeed, is almost my earliest recollection. For there was the day when our two nursemaids wheeled the two prams of the two houses side by side in the kitchen garden. They left them for a few moments, in the shade of an apple-tree, the other small boy and myself.

I do not know whether it was the natural insularity of the Englishman or merely the feeling that here was a foreigner trespassing in our garden, so, as there was no brick handy to throw at him, I might as well hit him. We went at it hammer and tongs. I boarded his pram in the best Nelson manner and fetched him a terrific clip which nearly landed both of us on the gravel. The battle then proceeded in great style, the pram rocking on its springs like a small boat in a short sea.

And then, my innocent eyes still suffused by the barbaric light of battle, I was suddenly conscious of two grown-up faces bending over us, my father's voice remonstrating. We were told to desist. We did, sat back panting. I glared at the small olive face with its black, blazing eyes opposite.

And then I distinctly remember hearing this said in that slightly foreign accent which Radziwill never quite lost: "No, no, Jimmy! Let them fight it out. Come on, I'll give you six to four on the Englishman —no, I won't! I'll lay you a monkey to your Black Bess that your boy wins."

Now the concatenation of a monkey with my Black Bess and the dim feeling that the fate of that beloved animal might possibly hinge on the outcome of our fisticuffs filled me with no little dismay. All the fight evaporated. I wanted to see the monkey. And what would Black Bess do with it when she got it? Or was the monkey going to fight Black Bess? They roared with laughter. Not unnaturally, I was hurt. And there the memory fades.

But there was another memory, a much more serious affair, my first poaching. We went out one Sunday, Black Bess and I, into Lord Durham's woods at Harraton House. They had been shooting the day before. George, the gardener, told me that the King had been there, exhibited two empty royal cartridge-cases which he had got from a loader in the village pub the night before. They were most important cartridge-cases. George was going to put them on his sitting-room mantelpiece and point them out to his grandchildren—the cartridge-cases which had actually been handled and fired by King Edward VII himself.

I thought about those cartridge-cases for quite twenty minutes that Saturday night before I fell asleep under the whitewashed wavy ceiling of the old nursery with its sloping roof. Obviously the thing to do was to get out early before any of them were about, take Black Bess, who knew everything—almost *more* than everything—and with my determination and her superhuman nose we were bound to find some royal cartridge-cases.

So I was up and dressed and out, five years old and full of fearful joy. Nanny was still asleep. The house was wrapped in the quiet of a Sunday morning. Somewhere in the kitchen regions Albert, the houseboy, clattered about. Blue smoke went up straight into a pale blue sky from one of the chimneys. That meant breakfast. And I was very hungry. But great faith knows no belly-worship, so I sneaked a couple of apples from the dining-room sideboard, slipped out of the garden door, pattered round to the kennels, and let Black Bess out of her run. She frisked and jumped, clattered her tin bowl. The pointers were excited, the spaniels fussed about importantly, and both the terriers yapped until I could have killed them. At any moment the noise might discover us.

And then we were off, running under the shadow of the currant-bushes, bent double. Once through the garden wall and we were away for the woods, safe from anything but the most determined pursuit.

I do not know how many miles we walked, but I do know that we found a great many cartridge-cases, all smelling acridly, excitedly, of burned powder. But how on earth was one to know which had belonged to the King? That was the trouble. Evidently George had some secret source of information denied me. Surely Black Bess ought to know.

Almost as an answer to the question Black Bess was suddenly off, nose down, sniffing excitedly, purpose expressed in every wriggle of her body. She was running. I ran. It was all I could do to keep up.

Up the ride we went, turned sharply off through a mass of thick bushes, scratching ourselves horribly, plunged down through the twisted roots of a great beech-tree into a sandy pit where rabbits scuttled, climbed the opposite bank, frightened a pheasant out of the undergrowth who got up with a most terrifying clatter, and then fairly raced across a bit of open grass.

What on earth had the King been up to to take such a crazy course through the heart of the wood?

Down another bank into a wet marshy bit where the stream bubbled under a quaking carpet of green. I went ankle-deep at every step. There was going to be an even bigger row when I got home.

And here Black Bess threw up her head, paused irresolutely, quested back and forth. Something had gone wrong. I wondered, fantastically, if the King had sunk. Then Black Bess solved the problem. She was off again.

Up the opposite bank and through a perfect *cheveux de frise* of brambles, and suddenly she was head and shoulders down a big sandy rabbit-hole, scrabbling furiously, uttering excited little grunts. She was far too well bred to bark like a spaniel or yap like a terrier. But, for a great lady, I have never in my life seen anyone of her degree in such a state.

Clearly there was something which was beyond her. This was where a man was needed. So I caught her by the collar, braced my heels, and fairly flung her away from the hole. She plunged at it again. But I was ahead of her, the whole length of my arm and shoulder down the hole, fingers groping.

I felt feathers, live feathers, frighteningly alive.

It needed a bit of courage to grope about with that urgent, unseen body scuffling determinedly in the blackness of that rabbit-hole. It might bite, peck, or scratch. It might be almost anything—even a Jabberwock or a dragon or something that flew about on creaking wings of the night and lived in rabbit-holes out of the sight of the sun. Suppose it had hooks on the end of its wings. I almost fell out of the hole at the sudden fearful picture.

But I daren't with Black Bess looking on. Black Bess was frightened of nothing. She would only laugh at me. And when you are five you can't bear to be laughed at by the people you like. Anyway, one thing was certain; it was *not* the King.

But it was something most certainly even more exciting than the King. So I groped again, grabbed a scaly foot, something with great claws which gripped me most horribly. And it had a spur, sharp and strong,-just like those on one of Father's fighting cocks —the clipped game-cocks that for some reason we kept shut up very secretly. No one was allowed to talk about them.

Here was the moment for action, for resolution. I grabbed the foot harder, pulled—hauled on it. And out of the hole came a terrific, flapping, fighting, squawking body, all red and brown, with a crimson eye and great wings which beat me about the head. I almost let go.

Then Bess plunged at it, had it in her mouth. Relieved, I *did* let go.

It was a cock pheasant—a winged bird left over from yesterday. Any young fool might have known that. Dragons—Jabberwocks—hooky-winged things! What a fool I had been! Anyway, Black Bess could not possibly *know* that I had thought such things. Or did she? You never quite knew how much she knew. I gave her a sidelong look. But she was busy with the pheasant, putting one paw on it, getting a fresh grip so that it could not flap its wings.

Then she looked up, the bird neatly packed in her jaws, its head moving snakily from side to side. Of course, what she really said was, " Well, now we've got it, so we'd better go home."

WAITING FOR FLIGHT

A curly-coat, the hardiest of all the retrievers and a born water-dog, waiting
with his master for the evening duck flight.

Photo Alex. B. Beattie, Huntley

WILL LEAVETT OF TOLLESBURY

One of the best fowlers on the East Coast waiting for the flight with his golden retriever.

Photo Sport and General

And off we went. How far we walked back I can't
say, but it was long past breakfast-time, and they had
almost called out the cavalry to look for us. There was
a bit of a row, but not as much as I expected. 'She'
was very upset, so relieved to find us safe that she
wanted to spank me. 'He' was amused, I thought
rather pleased, wanted the full story. He grunted
dreadful things about Sunday poaching, "tearing
through Durham's woods upsetting the birds," "bad
for the dog," and ended up with "You'll get the stick
if this happens again."

But I seem to remember that that afternoon, latish,
he took me down to the dell, on the edge of the butter-
cup marsh, with a little rifle, and, excitingly, taught
me how to stalk rabbits, shot one, made Black Bess lie
down, although she was aching to be after it; then,
like a god, waved her on, told her to fetch it, without
uttering a word. So I think that early morning raid
must have shown him that the young idea was set fair
for the future.

I said that the retriever was all masculine. So he is.
He has none of the lap-dog qualities of the spaniel,
the readiness of the terrier to adapt himself to house-
life. The retriever always gives you the impression
that the house, even if he is allowed in it, is merely a
place wherein to eat and sleep. Even in fireside dreams
he twitches in ghostly hunting.

Yet all the retrievers I have known which really
stand out in memory were bitches. There have, of
course, been dogs, great, grim, doughty fellows. But
somehow the bitches linger in memory as wise, lovable

creatures of infinite sympathy, of great heart and wisdom, with courage undefeatable.

There was Nell of Langenhoe. Langenhoe, which is the old Danish for "the Long Creek," is a desolate and lovely marsh in Essex. It is a peninsula of windy cattle-marsh and sunken fresh marsh, lying between the northern end of Mersea Island and the mainland parish of Fingringhoe. I had it for four years. Never was there a more enchanting place.

Great fleets cut the green marsh like shining swords. The tides gurgled in the crab-holes on the salts, brimmed against the sea-walls. The clouds marched in endless procession like blown galleons across a vast skyline. There was a smell of the sea in the wind, the strong tang of bared mud-flats. There were redshank on the marsh in summer, duck, coots, and moorhens that nested within the reeds, gulls which quarrelled in great congregations on the saltings, like chattering choristers in white.

Herds of half-wild cattle roamed the upland fields, for there was a ridge-back, which ran from east to west, dropping on either side to the marsh. It was a derelict place. The Hall was half lived in. The church was shuttered, its door nailed up, its grey square tower a parliament house of jackdaws and snoring owls.

In a clump of wind-twisted trees in the middle of the ridge-back stood a great, forlorn, empty Essex farmhouse, wild vines scrambling over its eyeless windows, leaves drifted against its doorway. Its roof was red and warm in the sun. Its walls were yellow, stained with the endless rains of uncounted winters. But no man or woman dwelt therein.

Across the marsh stood two empty cottages, their roof-trees bared, their rafters bleached as bones.

And farther still, on the very end of the ridge-back where the high land swept into the misty prairie of the cattle-marsh, stood a little black, weatherboarded cottage of four rooms, a duck-pond in front of it, a ruined bakehouse behind it. There was no glass in its windows. This was the "Found Out," for, said Ted Allen, my marsh-keeper, who had been born and bred on Langenhoe, "When the Lord God made Langenhoe this was the last place He found out—and the old Davvle was a-livin' here then."

Now Ted, who, as I said, had been born and bred on this wild, enchanted marsh estate, to whom its sixteen hundred acres were his own especial kingdom, bred the finest race of marsh retrievers I have ever known. They may not have been in the book, had no kennel names, and boasted no great lineage, but they were superb. And Nell was the mother of them all.

I know nothing of her breeding, and I rather fancy she came from, as Ted put it, "some lord that used to shute here when Rimington Wilson had it." Ted always referred to Rimington Wilson's tenancy of the marsh as the golden days. There never had been such a shot, such a walker, such an employer, such a sportsman, and there never would be again. Nell was the visible memorial of those days.

She was the only dog I have ever known that could both point and catch an adder. The sea-walls were full of them. In the first warm days of May and June they wriggled sluggishly from great cracks in the baked earth, squirmed through the grass, lay about in dozens. There was one field called the Adder Piece, so thick with them that from May to September we dared put neither horses nor cattle in it. It was only sixteen acres of marsh pasture, but I will swear that it held between two and three hundred snakes.

Allen would go on his rounds in the morning, carrying his gun, his big canvas side-bag, and a forked stick. Nell trotted behind. On the sight or smell of an adder she would point, like a pointer pointing a partridge, stand immovable for a second, then plunge forward. The adder was snapped up in the flash of an eye, whirled about her head until she seemed a very hydra-headed dog, a windmill of snakes.

When she dropped it, it was dead—a few twitches, but no active energy left whatever.

Time and again she had been bitten. Allen " reckoned that the owd bitch was full o' pison," but it made no difference to her. She must have become immune at an early age. Late on in life her hearing went a little, and she was stiff in her joints. Allen put it down to the accumulation of adder poison. I doubt that. It was just as likely—indeed, more likely—to have been the accumulated result of winter after winter of cold water, icy immersion, shivering waits. That dog lived a life which would have killed half the golden retrievers in England.

She was a great fox-dog too. The marsh swarmed with foxes. Hounds never came there. It was an impossible country to hunt, being full of concealed ditches, rills, pot-holes, bottomless dykes, and neck-breaking traps of every sort. So the foxes swarmed. I remember we once wrote to the Master of the local pack, telling him that their numbers were really getting beyond a joke, that it was high time we either reduced them or caught them up and sent them to him in bags. His reply was illuminating and perfectly above suspicion. " I want no bagged foxes."

So we had a few fox-shoots. Nell was the great fox-catcher on these occasions. She would wind a fox nearly half a mile away, work up to him with a sly look on her face, until finally, having located him in a reed-bed, she would flop on her belly, squirm over the marsh, using her legs like a swimmer, splayed out on either side, and then, on the edge of the reed-bed, suddenly stand bolt upright.

For a second or two she would remain at a perfect point, turning her head once to make sure that the gun had worked up behind her.

The moment everything was ready, in she went with a plunge, out shot the fox, bang went the gun, and that was that.

If I recollect rightly the record bag was sixteen foxes in a fortnight.

Years later Allen put the decline in her scenting powers down to " that there fox-shutin'."

But the most magnificent performance I ever saw her put up was on a curlew one bitter afternoon in January. At the top of the tide there was a regular curlew flight right across the marsh from the Pyefleet

Channel to the north Geeton Creek. They came over in hundreds, usually obliging enough to move in small bunches. So one got some very pretty shooting. But sometimes they were exceptionally high.

The apple of my eye was an enormous double-barrelled hammer 8-bore, built by old Joe Lang, weighing 16¾ lb. and shooting a 4¼ inch brass case loaded with two and a half ounces of shot. It was a formidable weapon, capable of death-dealing at great heights.

One afternoon I took it out for the curlews. A big bunch came over—at least ninety to a hundred yards high. Here was a chance to try the big gun. I let them have both barrels. A shattering roar, a great cloud of black powder smoke swirling away on the wind, and the herd broke up in skirling confusion. But one was hit. He turned right back in his tracks, and with wings outspread planed down over the Pyefleet, hit the mud opposite nearly half a mile away, picked up his long legs, and ran like a process-server. Within sixty seconds of hitting the mud he had vanished in the sea lavender on the saltings.

Even while the curlew was planing low down over the water Nell, her eyes fixed on the bird, was galloping along the top of the sea-wall.

The tide was running out at a good four knots, icy-cold, full of thin fragments of half-melted ice-floes which swirled and jostled. It was more than any dog could swim in. Nell stood for one second on the sea-wall before she ran down the mud. I saw her eye taking in the speed of the drifting icebergs. A moment's judgment and she had raced up the wall, galloped down the mud, plunged into the water at a point where the tide would sweep her level to the spot where the bird vanished.

She was gone for half an hour. At the end of that time she reappeared over the saltings. I was watching her through the glasses. She had the bird, evidently still a strong runner, in her mouth.

For a moment she stood taking her bearings. Then, with a flick of her tail, as much as to say, " I've got it all weighed up now," she trotted composedly up the bank for about a hundred yards, took to the water, and swam strongly across until the tide landed her at my feet.

Later, at dead-low water, we took the gunning punt across the fleet, landed, traced her footsteps over the saltings, down the mud into another creek, up the opposite bank, over more saltings, across another and wider creek, until finally we picked up the spot where she had run into her bird. I reckon that out and back she had travelled a good mile, swimming one very broad creek and two sizable ones, in all of which the tide was running out strongly.

Then there was Bruno, the curly-coat. Bruno came to me from Sudbourne Hall, in Suffolk, that grand sporting estate which, when Kenneth Clarke had it, ran to 11,200 acres and comprised a bit of everything—first-class pheasant-shooting, magnificent partridge manors, grand duck marshes, tidal creeks, woodcock covers, and, most precious of all, two of the finest duck decoys in England, the Iken Pond and the Chillesford Pond. The Iken Pond was the place where Frank Greenfield and one or two others have more than once killed over a hundred duck apiece on a morning flight.

I am glad to say that, instead of being scattered to the wind as so many good sporting properties have been, Sudbourne has been almost entirely reassembled by Sir Bernard Greenwell, who nowadays lives at Butley Abbey, on the south side of the property.

So Bruno came to me with a first-class background. He was a good-looker from nose to tail. He stood well and moved well. He would face any tide and sniffed at the cold. I remember sitting for three and a half hours one winter afternoon in a sunken barrel by the side of the fleet on a marsh at Salcott, snow falling and a north-easterly half a gale blowing. Bruno scarcely moved the whole time, and never whimpered.

Yet when you dropped a bird he would go and pick it up, run round in rings with it in his mouth, and then roll on it. Once he ate a curlew in front of my eyes.

The crowning insult came when I shot a moorhen. Bruno, brought up on one of the best sporting properties in Suffolk, very properly considered that moorhen-shooting was schoolboy stuff, beneath contempt. But he need not have shown it so pointedly. He swam the fleet, brought the moorhen to my feet, dropped it, looked up at me—then calmly raised his leg and baptized the moorhen!

That finished Bruno with me and me with Bruno.

CHAPTER XVII

THE MERRY SPANIELS

The Old Sussex Squire and his Rabbiting Pack—The Master
of Shooting Spaniels—Charlie Crisp of Upware and his
'Village Dog'—The Spaniel who was going to be put on
Skates—Salt-marsh Dawn—The Looker and the Bull—Ernest
Parr and his Jess.

I USED TO READ, when I was a boy, a nice story about
an old Sussex squire who had a lot of spaniels. He
lived somewhere on the Downs at the back of East-
bourne. I cannot recollect his name, and I fear that I
cannot even remember the name of the parish that he
lived in. That is a pity, for one loses a vast amount of
good local history by not knowing such small, essential
things.

But the main point about this lost, unknown Sussex
squire was that he was a man who believed in preserving the native dog of his own country. He bred
and kept the Sussex spaniel. Now that is a rather
heavy sort of spaniel, with a nice, shining coat, bred
to hunt rabbits out of those vast beds of gorse which
cover the Sussex Downs with a golden sheet. They
look out over the Channel to the incoming mariner
with a warm promise of England.

The Sussex gorse covers do more than merely hold
foxes. They hold the warmth of the soil, the sharp
strength of the chalk, the sudden, imprisoned glow of
endless summer suns. They are England's answer to
the garish colours of the South of France. But naturally, since they are native, we are inclined to disregard

P   225

them. That is the peculiar snobbery of the English. Call Miss Helen Boot Elena Butsova, and she immediately becomes a glamorous operatic star. Offer a Sussex gorse covert to the outgoing tourist as a form of beauty and he will sniff at it. Produce the same gorse covert in Brittany or its equivalent in another and more foreign form of herbage on the South Coast of France, and he will, with the joyful snobbism of the middle classes, pay three times as much for the pleasure of dwelling, even temporarily, within sight of it. It is illuminating, not so very new, and extremely silly.

But we are wandering a little from our Sussex squire who had a squad, or posse, if you like, or, better still, a pack, of Sussex spaniels. He trained them to hunt the South Down rabbit, just as that other Sussex squire I have talked of hunted them with his beagles. They had collars about their necks and bells hung on them. And this gallant squire would take his pack of spaniels from one side of the county to the other in pursuit of the humble but always gallant rabbit. He was a sort of travelling Master of Shooting Spaniels. He was a perpetual harrier of Brer Rabbit.

Wherever he went he was remarkably popular. He and his spaniels were given the best of the seed-cake, the largest glass of light wood port, the free run of the house, the quickest smiles from the best-looking daughters, always an invitation to dine and sleep, and invariably—after his departure—the pleasant compliment of its being said that " Old So-and-so was here with his muddling spaniels, and, do you know, it was a most amusing week-end."

Now that, I think, is a triumph of the individual. Here was a man who toddled about with his slow-footed spaniels, all trained to hunt thick covert, whether gorse or rhododendron, all answerable to their master's voice or whistle, all part and parcel of the little feudal household which travelled with them —and, mark you, all out and organized to provide sport and fun for those whom they visited.

It was a small, individual part of that pleasant England which meant so much in the make-up of our national life before the awful urge of industrialism swept over the land like a blighting finger-print. Suburbanism gropes dumbly, semi-consciously, for these old lost echoes. The people who live in towns wish to see them on films. Thwarted men who gather in bars talk of these things regretfully, listen to second-hand versions on the wireless endlessly. It is an unblottable shame on the copybook of our national development that we should have let such small, simple things slide.

That old squire is dead. His spaniels are forgotten. No rabbit mourns him or them. The country houses which sheltered him for jocular week-ends are either shut up, deserted by their owners, turned into tinny road-houses, or hired off at high rents—at whose magnitude the rural mind mocks secretly—to week-ending stockbrokers, to the modern version of the 'City gent,' whom Surtees lampooned for all time.

It is a curious, oddly pathetic, changing picture. But the spaniel remains. In his own sloppy, sentimental way he hangs on. No other dog has quite the same appeal to man and to woman. The spaniel bridges the gulf between the two. He can be a very useful gun-dog and a most intolerably nonsensical lap-dog. He will lie on his back, ask for his stomach to be tickled, wag his ridiculous paws, weep crocodile tears from liquid eyes, and spill sentiment by the bucketful. He will pad sycophantically from one silk-clad knee to another, lick up all the chocolate cream that stupid young women like to offer him. As an inspector of good-looking knees I envy him. But as a gun-dog in such surroundings he deserves a charge of shot.

But take this lickspittling, carpet-bagging courtier to the country, train him severely under the masculine eye, and the spaniel—I speak of the whole lachry-matory, wide-eyed family with their paddling feet and indiscriminately wagging sterns—you will find, sur-prisingly, can be turned into quite a respectable dog. He has nose and heart. He has guts and go. He has feet and energy.

He is the sworn enemy of the rabbit. He is good on the hedgerow pheasant. He will even find and retrieve the brook-side duck. In gorse and in rhododendron the spaniel is without a peer. He worms his sinuous, wag-ging way into any bush, bramble, or brake that a rabbit can penetrate. And he can be very good in water.

Two spaniels spring to my mind—two and a half to be precise, for one is a ghost. The ghost is the old liver-and-white field spaniel that I used to find squat-ting at the foot of Charlie Crisp, our champion skater, snipe-shooter, and beer-drinker, the King of the Fens, the unconquerable pride of Upware. At that ridiculous little kingdom of sixty or seventy souls, stranded on the banks of the Cam, midway between Cambridge and Ely, Charlie and his spaniel were the heart and soul of the hamlet. If any evil work of a roisterous nature was afoot you might be sure they were in it. Nothing missed them. That old spaniel once trailed a wounded hare a mile and a quarter across snow-clad fields, found it in a ditch, and dragged it painfully back for fully half a mile before Charlie, his little round legs going like peg-tops, his twinkling old red face shining like a winter sun, met her. That was an epic in itself.

That old spaniel was a marvel on snipe. I have seen her wind them upwind and at, I swear, two hundred yards' range, work up to them, nostrils twitching, tail going like mad, jumping peat-diggings, wallowing through water, thrusting her way through reeds and sedge, until finally she would stop dead, one eye over her shoulder, to see if Charlie with his double-barrelled 14-bore pinfire was near enough for the shot.

As soon as that rotund little form, with its brass-buttoned waistcoat winking in the winter sun like a heliograph station, was within range in she went.

"Scape, scape!" *Bang, bang!* Three of them are up, flickering white and grey against the bleak sedges. And two are down. That was usually the case. Spend a long day with Charlie on the fen, and if there were ten couple of snipe in the bag at the end of it you might rely on it that six and a half were his.

Now I like that honest fustian sort of village sportsman. I doubt if Charlie ever had more than forty shillings a week to call his own during the whole of his life. He had a nice little four-roomed cottage, with a nice sister-in-law who bore the provocative name of Mrs Gotobed. He had an acre or two of garden and small holding, a cow or two, a few pigs, and a couple of goats which grazed on the river bank under the whispering willows where the swallows played in summer.

He had no wife, but he had his dog, his gun, his pipe, and his glass. He had, too, his long leather water-boots, his fourteen-foot Fen jumping-pole, with which he flew over ditches like a harlequin—and, to top the lot, his long bone 'Fen-runners.' They were probably the last pair of bone skates used within living memory. Fashioned out of sheep's shin-bones, they were pointed to blunt ends, shaved smooth on the under-side, and secured to the boot by leathern thongs passed through holes bored fore and aft. The actual surface which rested on the ice was probably a quarter of an inch broad. That was the old traditional skate, such as they used in Elizabethan England, long before iron and steel came in to corrupt the values of mankind, to add new hardnesses to the hardness of life.

Charlie always swore that he was going to put the old spaniel on skates.

" I count the owd bitch 'ud goo like a bloody steamingin, 'specially if the wind got in 'er tail," said he.

Charlie and the spaniel are both dead. I mourn them as lovable, robust memories. There are not many of that sort nowadays in the villages. Board-

230

A GROUP OF MUSSETTS

They "have always had good dogs, good guns, been good shots and good sailors, grand wildfowlers and fearless fishermen." Douglas Mussett (left) is youngest of a family group whose ages total nearly three hundred years.

Photo Douglas Went, Brightlingsea

'JESS'

"The liver-and-white, lion-hearted little Fen spaniel" retrieving a duck to
the author on his fen in Cambridgeshire. Ernest Parr, "a Fen man of the
old school," is on the left of the picture.

Photo Sport and General

school education, mass-produced thought, and the lure of a stinking rag in the nearest garage are whittling all that rich material down to the basest of base metal.

But, oddly enough, spaniels bring to my mind two other splendid village sportsmen who tread in the footsteps of Charlie Crisp, the skating, shooting, drinking champion whom neither of them ever knew. One is young Douglas Mussett, of Mersea Island, in Essex. The other is Ernest Parr, of Reach, the lost city of seven great churches in Cambridgeshire, now declined to a dreaming hamlet of whitewashed cottages, speared like an oyster on the end of the great green ancient British dyke which there thrusts its nose almost to the very edge of the drowned Fens.

But first of all the spaniel of Douglas Mussett. I cannot even remember her name. But I remember her performances. Mussetts have always had good dogs, just as they have always had good guns, been good shots and good sailors, grand wildfowlers, and fearless fishermen. There have been Mussetts on Mersea Island since the first De Musset was chased out of France by that Louis who hounded out the Huguenots to his own country's detriment and our enrichment.

There is good blood in that family. Look at any Mussett you like—there are a score of them—and you will see the signs of fine breeding, the noble lines of good blood. They were there long before the cackling invasion of young women in trousers with synthetic hair, of Cockney yachtsmen who moan perpetually at the bar.

231

Once upon a time I had a shoot, a great, wide, windy expanse of marsh and upland fields, near Mersea. You got to it by sailing up a windy creek, through flat mudflats that bared like silver and shone like broadswords when the tide went down. There were duck on it and clouds of wheeling teal, and redshank which rang their mocking bells. There were curlew who cried mournfully, whistled derisively. There were bargeese—the shelduck of the books—with their haunting dead man's laugh. And there were rabbits by the million. The hedgerows were so thick with them that if you poked your nose in one it stunk of rabbits. The ground crumbled beneath one's feet. It was suicide to ride a horse.

One year we killed over 6000 rabbits on that 700 acres. We shot, ferreted, trapped, and netted. And still the rabbits flourished.

Those were grand mornings when we set off from my fowling cottage, long before the first crack of dawn, fumbling our way down through the orchard, past sleeping cows, over the saltings to the oyster-shell 'hard' where the gun punt lay long and narrow, a black cigar-shape on the mud. And as you ran her down the mud she took the water with a silken swish. A million glittering blue points of phosphorescent fire leaped into sudden light.

Down the creek we glided smoothly, the chill wind-before-dawn stirring the cordage on anchored smacks, cold on our cheeks. At the village 'hard' a long-booted, blue-jerseyed, peak-capped figure was waiting with two guns under his arm, a wicker jar of beer, a canvas bag of bread and cheese, bully beef, and onions. That was Albert Lovechild Greenleaf, my man. He had the food, the beer, and the ferrets. Albert stepped aboard gingerly. The punt sank until, with the three of us, there was little more than three inches of free-board. Then we were off again.

Lights gleamed in a building ashore. The Cockney swizzlers were still at it.

" I see the're still all a-gooin on up at the Never-Never," grunted Albert.

" Why do you call it the Never-Never?" I asked.

" Never was a gennelman among 'em, an' never will be," he explained. " That's what us fishin' chaps call 'em."

" Any other names?" I inquired.

" Oh, Number Forty."

" Number Forty?"

" Yis, yis. Forty bloody thieves, and all the hull lot on 'em drownded in a barrel o' beer."

So much for the unvarnished Essex version of some of its purse-proud, self-complacent London week-enders. I wonder how often the townsman gets the real rustic truth about himself?

We drifted up the Channel under a rag of sail, a gliding, ghostly form in the starlight. Curlew sprang from the mud, vociferous. Somewhere out on the Naas End brent geese cronked. Wings whispered overhead. A black-backed gull, over on Old Hall Marshes, set up a melancholy wail.

" Ghostses a-walkin' on that there mush," vouch-safed Albert. " Count there ought to be several on 'em

233

there the way they slit up them Revenoo men's throats in Pennyhole a hund'ed year ago. Twenty-tu on 'em, all dead as pigs in the boat, awashin' backards and forards on the tide. Cold as pork when they found 'em, and nobody never knows who done it. I reckon some o' yu Mussetts was in that lot "—with a sly glance at Douglas.

" There ain't nothin' writ about it if we was," said Douglas firmly.

" A cut-throatin' old gang, the best on 'em," observed Albert blandly to the declining dawn edge of the moon.

A puff filled the sail. We drifted on, a ghostly shape moving silkenly on sliding, dark waters that gurgled seaward.

Now this, you will observe, was a lawful expedition. But, being of a lawless nature, we chose to surround it with the careful plans, the illicit joys, of some desperate expedition into which no right or usage of the law should enter. There was to be a sneaking up the creek, snakily, into the saltings. There was to be a careful, splayed-out advance over the sea-wall, guns cocked, on to the fleet, a fusillade of shots as the duck that had rested there all night rose vociferously on urgent wings.

And then there was to be ferreting in hidden ditch-bottoms, quiet purse-netting jobs carried out with fantastic secrecy.

Why? It was my own place. But there was a marsh-looker who was death on poaching, a man who revelled in alarums. So we were going to give him one. As it happened he gave us the best one of our lives.

We topped the sea-wall. The fleet shone silver against the black velvet background of the marsh, where wind-stirred bent grass moved whitely. A sudden hoarse quack of alarm, a scuttering on the water, and fifteen, sixteen, eighteen—twenty or more dark shapes shot skyward, catapulted from the sleeping water. It was just light enough in that ghostly twilight to see them silhouetted against the eastern edge of the sky, the sea horizon where the first faintest apple-green showed shyly. Six shots rang out. I got one old mallard as he climbed fast, cut him down handsomely, and missed another.

At the shots others got up, four or five of them. Duck jumped from other pools in farther, blacker recesses of the marsh. The whole wild expanse of salting and creek behind us burst into a clamour of curlew. Redshank shrieked. Shoveller grunted as they whistled past. Bargeese cackled. A rush of wings overhead, and just as I had reloaded I got one—heaven knows what it was—against the moon. It came down in the mud with a *sock* like a bottle falling. That one was dead enough, anyway.

A busy ten minutes picking up the slain. There was a pochard here, floating black and blob-like on the surface of the fleet. There was a winged mallard who gave the spaniel a short chase over the grass. Meanwhile I was out on the mud, groping for my very dead one. I found him, a beautiful cock pintail. The silver-grey of his plumage showed up like the shine of a sword in the gentle moonlight. He was very handsome with his pencilled feathers, shapely, snaky head and neck, his long, proud tail. We did not get many pintail there. They were birds of the outer sea. We saw them more often from the smacks over on the Black Grounds. Almost I regretted that hasty shot against the moon.

There were a couple of widgeon to be gathered, and that was the tale of it all. Five duck, four different species. That is the sort of wildfowl shoot I like. I remember one evening, when four or five of us bagged forty-four head, and there were eleven species among them—mallard, pochard, widgeon, shoveller, shelduck, redshank, merganser, teal, tufted duck, curlew, and coot.

After that there was not much to do but wait for the dawn. No more duck would come in, and the only chance of a stray shot would be a bang or two at an odd curlew or a plover—the latter protected by law, but we never bothered about that. What nonsense in any case! The green plover is well able to take care of himself, and the only danger from man that he has to fear is the taking of his eggs.

But far away on the other side of the marsh was the widgeon pond. It was an old decoy pond, a star-shaped, green depression in the marsh, surrounded by grassy hillocks, mute mementoes of the days when the iron hoops were bent above the pipes, when the netting stretched tapering above them, and the old decoy man from the tiny red-brick cottage high up on the marsh took his hundreds of widgeon and 'dun-buds' every week. There was always a foot or eighteen inches of water in the widgeon pond. I used to feed it with maize, and there were usually a few duck of some sort or other upon it. Now it was just possible they might not have been disturbed by our shots, three-quarters of a mile away, with the wind blowing from them to us.

So off I set, crunching through the frosty grass in long boots, a couple of ferrets wriggling in a canvas bag in my left-hand pocket. For I had decided that this was to be a one-man job, and that I would join them under the hedge for beer and bread and cheese round about nine o'clock. The spaniel followed. But I did not notice that at the time. I had gone a good fifty yards before the padding of those feathery feet in the crisp hoar-frost drew my eyes backward. I might have sent him back, but sheer selfishness urged me to keep him from his master.

We plodded across the ghostly marsh, going by that sailor-like instinct which guides one on such places when you happen to know them. Every rill, every gut, every reedy dyke, every isolated, cattle-polished post, was familiar to me. The walk across it in the semi-dark was like turning the pages of a book ten times read.

Away over on the right, where the cornlands met the marsh, tall, bare elm-trees, their leafless tops spidery against the twinkling sky, stood cloudlike. Beneath them, black and many-angled, were the roof trees of the farmhouse, red and Caroline, the straggling eaves of barns and cowsheds, the sharp cock of the hay-loft against the sky, the lowlier line of the cottage where the looker dwelt.

I pictured him, stirring in his bed, cursing "them Maldoners," the hardy puntsmen from Maldon who were his sworn enemies. For he would be sure to lay our shots at their door. They were his particular bugbear. And, from what I have heard, they had more than once fired their guns from the deck of a passing smack at dead of night in order to fetch him out hastily, oilskin pulled on over nightshirt, long boots clammy on naked legs.

I had presented him with an old Verey-light pistol, a relic of the War, with which to frighten off such raiders. It was the darling of his eye. At first it had been more than efficacious. But now the prowling punters, the longshore gunners, knew his screaming rockets for no more than the pyrotechnics of an elderly and choleric man who could neither run nor fight.

A low grumble rumbled across the marsh from the farm buildings. That was the bull. They had a nasty shorthorn up there, just over three years old, into the dangerous age. He was kept on a short chain in the little barn.

The tumps and hillocks of the widgeon pond showed ahead like miniature mountains. I worked carefully round until the wind was blowing straight in my face, crept crouching up to the edge of the pond, peered over one of those ramparts. Six black forms swam in the moonlight. Two or three others dotted the edge in the careless, lazy attitudes of feeding and preening.

The gun came slowly to the shoulder, a careful aim, a deliberate double-shot, one trigger pressed immediately after the other—and two were dead, floating paddles uppermost, while two wounded birds scrambled madly for the shore. Others shot upward on whistling wings.

We had an exciting time getting those two birds. Both were winged, and both were strong runners. We were quite a quarter of an hour about it, and the second one had just been pulled out of a reedy dyke and I was biting his head when a snort, a cloud of blown silver on the frosty air, made me look up. There was the bull!

At a quick guess he was ten yards off. How he had got so far without being heard I shall never know. But he stood there, glowering. My heart froze. Marsh bulls are no joke. Only a year before an old labourer, seventy-three years old, had been caught by a young bull over at Abbot's Hall, tossed over a hedge on to a half-cut haystack, left there with a hole in his ribs into which you could have poked your fist.

Down he went on his knees, groaning, tossing the earth. The next move would be the charge.

I let one barrel go at the ground in front of his head, jumped the dyke like a greyhound, and was off across the marsh towards the sea-wall two hundred yards away as fast as a double-barrelled 10-bore and a pair of rubber thigh-boots would let me travel.

The bull must have cleared that dyke an instant after—for I heard him thundering behind. Half a glance back, and there he was, tail up like a poker, travelling with terrifying directness. I have never been so frightened in my life.

239

And then the miracle happened. The ground in front of him suddenly erupted a noisy, barking, hairy animal which leaped at his hocks, snapped, snapped again, was kicked a yard, rebounded to the charge like a football, snapping and snarling. It was a four-legged fury. And it brought that bull to a standstill. He wheeled, lowered his head, roared, tossing his horns from side to side, stood irresolute. His back-end was towards me. Never was there a better, more enchanting target for an ounce and three-quarters of shot. He got it. And I do not believe that bull touched earth between jumping-off place and the farm buildings half a mile away.

Later, when we met under the hedge and the looker had unglued his lips from the wicker jar, he remarked slyly, " Well, bor, ef thet *hed* a'bin them Maldoners, *that* would ha' onsettled 'em. Time I heered them shots o' yourn a-bungin off I reckoned I'd louse the bull and let him see the b——s orf the mush. Carn't blame me, can ye ! "

" But," he added, with reluctant admiration, " yu haint harf scarified his owd rib. Thet charge o' shot laid a furrer open what you cud lay a· rubbin'-stone in."

Which is why I shall always have a tender spot for the long-legged, bulldog-hearted village spaniel of doubtful degree.

And the third village dog in my happy recollections is Jess, the liver-and-white, lion-hearted little Fen spaniel whom Ernest Parr, keeper on my wild fen in Cambridgeshire, produced one day. Ernest, who is a

Fen man of the old school, the youngest-looking man of forty I know, alert of mind, unresponsive to strangers, with a boyish love of birds, Fen waters, the whisper of reeds, and the feel of a gun, is a good dog-man—but no sentimentalist.

He produced her deprecatingly. He held that she was handy in the punt, "a tidy little dog," but nothing to shout about.

Jess came out with me on early mornings when the duck whispered in on fog-heavy wings through the Fen 'dag '—there is a good Saxon word for you, for it means 'mist'—when the bittern lumped overhead on heavy, owl-like pinions, when the starlings rose up in the magic half-hour after dawn on a million wing-beats, like the waves of the sea.

It was pure enchantment to sit there, in the stern of the punt, seated barely an inch from the water, the mist glistening in beads on the gun-barrels, reed-warblers twittering confidentially from the bulrush stems not a foot from one's ear, redshank running in the shallows like ballet dancers.

There was a heron who stood silver-grey, slender and solemn, boding and beautiful—a cross between a virgin and a parson—contemplating whether he should fish or not, knee-deep in tiny pink flowers which starred the sleeping water. There were two green plover who dropped in on heavy, rounded wings, flirted almost with my hat, slipped sideways in the air, either from fright or disdain, and landed delicately in precisely three-quarters of an inch of water. They knew how to judge it *so* beautifully.

And there, white-waistcoated, their crests delicately curved upward like feathered scimitars, they walked back and forth, pecking. There was no question of gobbling or gross feeding. They pecked. They were selective, esoteric feeders. They were almost affected. But they had the air of knowledgeable connoisseurs. So one could forgive them that slight affectation of gait, that knowing sideways cock of the head, the bright, beady-eyed approbation of animalculæ.

I sat and watched it all, too fascinated to move, too interested to shoot. And suddenly I realized that I was not alone in this dawn-before-sunlight picture. Some one else was taking notice too.

There sat Jess, eyes bright and alight, head moving questioningly, ears cocked, not a thing unnoticed. She was not only looking, but thinking, and I will swear that she realized that this was no moment for shooting, but rather a time of beauty.

She glanced sharply at the reed-warblers, followed their quick, mouse-like movements, observed their confidence. Then she looked at me, full-eyed. It said as plain as plain, " Too small to shoot—not snipe, but I rather like them."

She took a long look at the heron. He impressed her. She rather wondered whether one ought to shoot such a very parsonical person. I do not think she altogether fancied the possibility of retrieving him. This time a rather quick, disconcerted glance at me as much as to say, " If you want him for a glass case—of course —but . . ."

The redshank fascinated. Their quick dancer movement lit a new light in her eyes. They were young, gay. So was she, under all the discipline of training. They kindled almost a light of lawlessness in her eyes. I could see it quite plainly.

But the plover annoyed her. She had had too many doses of them already—one month mobbing her, flocking and screaming about her ears, in open field; another month pretending to be broken-winged when they weren't, making a perfect unforgettable fool of oneself—and then, again, when one was shot, they put up a very poor show. They could not run as fast as you expected, and when you collared one it had neither the heart to twist like a duck nor the spirit to fight and scratch like a cock-pheasant. Oh, no! Plainly it was sheer foolishness to allow these pirouetting manikins to prance about in such precious preciosity within gunshot. Give them a barrel and settle their nonsense! Her eyes said it. But, of course, I didn't.

I liked Jess. She was as near human as a little dog might be. She was quite tireless. Defeated neither by sedge nor reed, by icy water nor deep black, peaty mud. She would swim and plough, snuffle and snort, until she had found her bird.

And then one day Parr got rid of her. Why? I asked him. He thought she was hard in the mouth. I told you he was no sentimentalist. Probably he was right. She was his dog, in any case, to do with as he wished. But I mourn her. My enchantments in the punt without her are the less enchanted.

243

CHAPTER XVIII

THE GENTLEMANLY POINTER

A Declining Aristocrat—Old Days in Norfolk—Pointers at
Killarney—The Pointer who went Home in Disgust—And the
other one who pointed the Weather—With a Note on the
Pointer who pointed a Partridge in a Pike in a Pool—And the
Pointing Pig just to finish the Story.

I DO NOT KNOW MUCH ABOUT POINTERS. Few of us
have the chance to-day when stubbles are shaved to
their shortest, when the Gordon setter seems to have
ousted the pointer on most Scottish moors. But I have
a few memories, and they are early ones. There were
those great double-nosed Spanish pointers of my
great-uncle at home, finely built creatures with large
eyes, the carriage of aristocrats.

They were part of that unfading scene of childhood which has faded for ever from actuality. They
are part of the picture in which there are russet apples,
brown-gold stubbles, quail whistling in the orchard,
dogcarts that rattled on stony roads, a pair-horse shooting brake which used to start for Newmarket at an un-
earthly hour in the morning so that one got there, to
the shooting place, in time for breakfast.

They are one with the musty, friendly smell of
plush in the family brougham of the de Greys which
took one from Watton Station to Merton—surely the
last family brougham which ever rumbled over West
Norfolk roads. There were pointers in that picture,
the picture which holds the swing and bump of the
old carriage, that lights for a moment the bright red

waistcoat of that prince of head keepers—John Buckle.

They belong to the picture of the more leisurely, perhaps better-ordered day, in which there was more time to enjoy the sun of life, less cut-throat hustle.

And there was a beauty only last year, a big liver-and-white old dog snoring comfortably in a smelly corner of the deer-shed at Kenmare House, a very echo of the past, as I watched Dan Donahue, the greatest stalker in all Ireland, cutting up the stags we had shot that day on the hill.

And it was Dan who produced that immemorial, oft-repeated story which every man claims as his own —and has done for the last hundred years.

" Is there another one in the kennels, Dan?"

" Sure, sorr—and a foine wan too. But ye cannot let the pair of them out together. I tell ye they fight bitther and natural—just like man and wife."

On those wild hills, so wild and lovely that you would not believe them to be of heaven or earth, the pointers still point the grouse in the good old style. And there are a number of moors in Scotland where they add beauty to the scene, charm and workmanship to the field.

The pointer, in fact, is one of the oldest of sporting dogs. You can if you like credit him with a classic origin, for Xenophon, speaking of the manner in which various dogs find their game, says that some will " go a long round in a circle till they reach it, and whenever they light on the scratch follow uncertain in-dications; and when they do sight the hare in advance, tremble, and do not proceed until they see him make a move."

That might be any sort of a gun-dog; but the pointer fans have taken it unto themselves.

Mr Arkwright in his magnificent monograph on the breed claims, and probably quite rightly, that the word 'pointer' originated from the Spanish *de punta*—the pointing dog.

He claims that there were references to the pointer in the thirteenth century, but so far as English is concerned he was fairly well established in this country about 1720. The Duke of Kingston, who bred black pointers which earned considerable fame, was shown with a pointer in a portrait painted of him in 1725.

This Duke of Kingston was, after the style of Colonel Hawker, quite unscrupulous when it came to poaching on his neighbour's land.

Taplin, writing of him, says:

"It is no more than thirty or forty years since the breed of pointers were nearly white or mostly variegated with liver-coloured spots: except the celebrated stock of the then Duke of Kingston, whose breeds of blacks were considered superior to all in the kingdom, and sold for immense sums after his death."

Taplin, speaking of the Duke's *penchant* for poaching, tells the following story:

"The three brace of birds previously killed having nearly filled the net, it was unavoidably necessary to dislodge a cock to make room for the full-grown cock-pheasant just brought to hand. In the act of kneeling to make room for one, by the removal of part of the

other—and this in the most awful, still, and seques-
tered wood—a gentle tap or two upon the shoulder of
the writer was not productive of the most pleasing sen-
sation; little doubt can be entertained but the shock,
acting with a degree of electric vibrations, occasioned

> each particular hair to stand on end,
> Like quills upon the fretful porcupine,

particularly when accompanied with the very emphatic
exclamation of 'Who are you?'—a question at that
moment not to be so readily answered. Upon a sort of
half-recovery from the palpitations the writer hastily
(and not without a considerable portion of alarm) inquired from the lad, as it proved to be, why he asked.
From whom he received the following answer: that
the writer had got into the heart of Mr B.'s game preserve, where even his uncle never shot off a gun.

"'Indeed. Why, who is your uncle?'

"'The gamekeeper.'

"'The devil he is! And where is he?"

"'In bed with a fever here in the cottage just the
other side of the copse fence—and, hearing a gun
fired, he sent me to see who it was and to inquire your
name.'

"'Oh, he did! Aye! That's very right—my name
—oh, aye—very true—there, there's a shilling for
you—you may tell him my name is Johnson—Captain
Johnson.'"

With which information the lad withdrew and the
newly yclept Captain made a most expeditious exit.

Edwardes, in his work dated 1800, gives three
examples of pointers, a chocolate-brown dog, a white

one marked with yellow brown, and the double-nosed dog which I knew in my youth, except that the head of him looks much more like that of an old sheep-dog. His story is that a Portuguese merchant was the first to bring the Spanish pointer to this country "at a very modern period, and [it] was first used by an old reduced Baron of the name of Bichell who lived in Norfolk and could shoot flying."

He refers several times to a very rough-coated, tough-looking pointer of the period, apparently a cross between some sort of water-dog and a Spanish pointer. This, Edwardes says, was so striking in constitution that it preferred lying up in cover to sleeping in kennel.

There was about that time an animal known as an Italian pointer or lady's pointer. It stood only about twelve inches high, a graceful little creature quite useless for sport, and apparently evolved for decorative, drawing-room purposes, much in the same fashion as the Italian greyhound. We need not bother about it.

Towards the beginning of the nineteenth century the slow-footed Spanish pointer was crossed and recrossed with the foxhound in order to give him more speed. The result on the whole was satisfactory, although some critics maintain that the foxhound cross produced a dog which ran with its head too low, and sometimes overran the scent altogether.

General Hutchinson, who lived about that time, and wrote a very good book called *Dog-breeding*, well worth picking up second-hand, said:

"My proposed dogs must have as united a gallop as

a good hunter, and have small, hard, round feet. This, I hope, will be a more certain test of endurance in the field than any other point that you could make. Rest assured that the worst-loined dogs with good feet are capable of more fatigue in stubble or heather than the most muscular and best-loined with fleshy 'understandings.' The most enduring pointers I have ever seen were more or less of the strain of the foxhound; but doubtless they are harder to break, for their hereditary bias on one side of the house must have given them an inclination to chase and carry their heads low."

Richardson, writing on the pointer in 1847, says:

"The English pointer is remarkable for his extraordinary stamina. Pluto and Juno, property of the celebrated Colonel Thornton, *stood for an hour and a quarter in the act of pointing*, without moving during the whole of that time, while they were being drawn and painted by the late eminent artist Mr Gilpin.

"A well-trained pointer is very valuable, and will fetch a high price. A fine pointer, also belonging to Colonel Thornton, was sold for £160 worth of champagne and burgundy, one hogshead of claret, an elegant gun, and another pointer, with the proviso that if any accident should at any time disable the dog, he was to be returned to the Colonel, at the price of £50."

"Idstone," however, had a different version of this bargain, for, speaking of one, whom he described as "liver-and-white, a long-necked wiry animal of good form and with undeniable shoulders, back, and hindquarters," he says that he "was purchased by Sir R. Hills for one hundred and twenty guineas and a cask of Madeira wine, subject to the stipulation that the dog should be returned for fifty guineas when rendered unfit for work. The first season he broke his leg, and was returned according to agreement."

Richardson has a beautiful story, which I am resolutely determined to believe, of a pointer who so abhorred bad shooting that after one or two misses he would go home. He says:

"A pointer hates a bad shot. My old friend Captain Brown related the following capital anecdote. A gentleman, having requested the loan of a pointer dog from a friend, was informed by him that the dog would behave very well so long as he could kill his birds; but if he frequently missed them the dog would run home and leave him.

"The pointer was accordingly sent, and the following day went out for trial, but unfortunately his new master happened to be a remarkably bad shot. Bird after bird rose and was fired at, but still pursued its flight untouched, till at last the dog became furious and often missed his point. As if seemingly willing, however, to give one chance more, he made a dead stop at a fern-bush, with his nose pointing downwards and forefoot bent and the tail straight and stiff. In this position he remained firm till the sportsman approached with both barrels cocked. Then, moving steadily forward a few paces, he at last stood still near a bunch of heather, the tail expressing the anxiety of the mind by moving regularly backwards and forwards.

"At last out sprang a fine old black cock. *Bang, bang*, went both barrels—but the bird escaped unhurt. The patience of the dog was now quite exhausted, and instead of dropping to charge he turned boldly round, placed his tail between his legs, gave one long howl, and set off as fast as he could for his own home."

There are numerous stories told of pointers which have gone out on their own, found game, then returned home, and by wagging their tails and by an air of general excitement have told their masters that it was time to get the gun and go out on business.

But the best pointer story of the lot is that of the pointer who pointed a pike in a pool. He stayed there for an hour or more immovable. So they sent for a fishing rod and a live bait, caught the pike, and cut it open. Inside was a partridge!

But you can cap that one with the story of Mr Richard Toomer, a gentleman who lived in the New Forest and trained a black pig to point any sort of game that was about. Mr Toomer strongly objected to paying taxes on sporting dogs. Hence the pig.

He was a blood-brother in spirit of Mr James Hirst, of Rawcliffe, who so hated the thought of paying a tax on horses that he used to ride a bull out hunting!

To get back to the foxhound cross, "Idstone" has some interesting notes on this. He says:

"That the old type was too slow, he quartered his ground; he carried a high head, and this brilliant style gave him the command of wide parallel, whilst his exquisite power of scent served him instead of speed to such an extent that, only give him the wind, and he would crawl up to his game in a direct line, and there stand for as many as *twelve* hours! But in long days he fagged, stood still, rolled in the sun, or, wagging his short tail, followed panting at his master's heels."

I am enchanted to think that "Idstone" considered that a point of twelve hours scarcely constituted a long day. He goes on:

"To counteract this it was found absolutely necessary to cross him with some lighter frame, even at the peril of injuring his haunch, for all confessed, in the days of old Colonel Thornton, that they would put up with the tedious old sort no longer."

And then he proceeds later on:

"The Spanish pointer was, I believe, a liver-and-white dog with a great preponderance of liver colour. He was very seldom thick or flecked on his white, and bore a close resemblance to the well-known picture of the breed by Reinagel, in which he is represented with a very heavy head and jowl, deep flews, sunken large eyes, and tremendous bone and muscle. This picture hands him down to us as rough in coat, though the profile of his body is not obscured by it, with hackle on his white collar a blaze of white, as are also the inner margin of his legs and arms and the end of his tail, which has been shortened by about a third of its length."

He goes on to say:

"I am by no means sure that the foxhound was the only cross used to give pace and fire to the well-known English breed, but I am sure that a pointer's staunch-ness has not been injured. Fresh colours have been produced, all having their adherents and admirers, and these various colours have been the outward marks that the sportsmen have established as their own breed. These have been gradually introduced, and now we have self-coloured dogs, and now we have white, black, liver-coloured, sandy, lemon, and black-and-tan. Besides these we have the pied or blotched dogs, which are any of the above colours mixed more or less with white. Sometimes the white is flecked with the same colour as the dark, and occasionally the dark blotches are shot or powdered with white specks. This is more frequently the case with liver or black dogs than any others; and in my opinion it has a very nice appearance.

"How long ago it was discovered that a dog would back the point of his kennel companions it would be hard to say, but at the present time no dog is considered thoroughly broken unless he will acknowledge the point of his fellow-worker and become cataleptic directly the other dog draws up to game. I recollect seeing, at an exhibition of celebrated pictures in town, a large oil-painting by a celebrated artist of eight or nine pointers pointing and backing, and this work of art must have been from eighty to a hundred years old.

"When this talent has been thoroughly drilled into a dog it enables him to help in the day's sport without coming into collision with his companions; and when dogs are good backers their master can take out as many as he likes together provided they cross each other in hunting and do not run in couples. In other words, provided each dog not only backs but has an *independent range.* All modern breakers profess to teach this, but many are too idle or ignorant to do it, and the result is mischief and disappointment.

" One of them, Old Jesse, a chance dog, which was purchased off a deserter in Yorkshire, was a fine example. As he was of an unascertained pedigree, Mr Meir, his owner, would not breed from him, but he was a fine specimen of the Yorkshire dog; he was liver-and-white and large. If I missed him on driving off to my snipe ground he would track my little white French pony and gig like a snoop hound; and many a time I have found him close at my heels when I have looked back for him in vain for several miles.

" One bright winter morning I sat on a gate waiting for my companion, a Captain Hall, and looking up a long stretch of road, when I spied Old Jesse coming along with a young dog which he had evidently invited to join the fun; and as I let the young dog work for snipe—game he never was on before—it was a sight to see how Old Jesse tried to teach him the trail.

" I had two pieces of snipe bog two miles apart, and one bad scenting day he missed my track and went to the wrong piece, so that it was past one o'clock when I reached the piece to which he had gone. On getting to my second piece, which I generally shot first, I saw Old Jesse standing stiffly on a mound. How long he had been pointing I cannot say.

" Frequently as I walked up to his point I had snipe and shot them before I reached him, but this made no difference to him, nor did it interfere with his steadi-

ness. Once on this occasion he snarled at the youngster for flushing a jack, and when he repeated the fault
he went up and *severely worried* him.

"As two of us shot together he got into the habit
of coming up to my room in the morning to see if I
were dressed for shooting, and if I were not he would
go to my companion's chambers and accompany him
or track him through the streets if he had gone on. I
do not remember that he ever failed to find him.

"Julie, a liver-and-white pointer bitch, was
another of my pointers which showed a great sagacity
and firmness. We have frequently lost her for a considerable time in high cover on a celebrated piece of
ground called Keysworth, in Dorsetshire, belonging to
my friend Mr Drax, and at last we have seen the sting
of her fine stern above the rushes—for she always
wore it higher than her head. She was one of the
most intelligent dogs I ever possessed, and would retrieve any game alive. Though only in her second
season, she was the animal always sent out with young
hounds, and if they ran to pick up their game she
would bark at them reproachfully. I never had a
pointer before that seemed so keenly to enter into the
sport or to appreciate as she did the real and proper
style of beating for game.

"Belle, out of the famous Queen, was another of
my pointers, a dark liver-and-white with a streak down
her forehead, and a spot in the centre of her skull. She
nearly broke herself, and the least hint of what was
required was sufficient for her. Unfortunately I never
got but one litter from her, and I lost the breed, for

no doubt I should have kept as many pointers as a setter. In her old age she was a martyr to rheumatism and became a house pet, often assisting in the killing of as much game as a pointer of her own age and leading my team of young setters for six or seven seasons.

"Her death was the occasion of deep gloom in my family for a long time. Even my cook, whom she tormented out of her life, said, as old Weller said of his wife, that 'On the whole she was sorry she was gone.'"

Those anecdotes of great pointers of the past are a fit, and in the main true, memorial to a graceful, gallant, but, alas! diminishing breed. It is sincerely to be hoped that this magnificent sporting dog will never be allowed entirely to die out.

As a tailpiece let me tell two stories. First there is that of the pointers, quoted from an issue of the old *Sporting Magazine*, which accompanied a gentleman to a shooting party in October 1811 near Lewes:

"His dog stood, the covey rose, and he discharged both barrels, bringing down his bird to the right and left; finding his dogs still *stationary* in the high stubble from which the birds had risen, he reloaded, but found that by his *first fire* he had not only shot the *partridges* quite dead, but his two *pointers* also! This sporting casualty was occasioned by the dogs standing on a small eminence and the birds going off very close to the low ground, immediately in a line with them."

The chronicler of this very tall story does not add, as he might have done, had he been true to the spirit

THE DUKE OF MONTROSE

Working one of his pointers on his Brodick Castle moors in the
Isle of Arran.

Photo Sport and General

THE BEST DOG OUT OF IRELAND FOR THE ALL-ROUND
SHOOTING MAN

The Irish water spaniel is one of the finest water-dogs in the world. Here is
Mr Trench O'Rorke's champion 'Breifny Chieftain.'

Photo Sport and General

of his age, that the dogs stood there stiff but immovable for twelve hours!

America caps the lot with the story of a pointer from South Carolina which was such a good weather prophet that, as his master said:

"Whenever I observed him prick up his ears to a listening posture, scratching the earth and rearing himself up to look to the windward, where he would eagerly sniff up the breeze, though it was the finest of weathers I was assured of the succeeding tempest. This animal was grown so useful to us that whenever we perceived the fit was upon him, we immediately *reefed our sails* and took in our spare canvas to prepare for the worst."

CHAPTER XIX

THE LAST WILD RED DEER OF IRELAND

Stalking in the Fairy Glens of the Castlerosse Country—
Deerhound Country—Old Dan Donahue, the Best Stalker in
Ireland—The Place of the Druid and the Fairy—The Hags'
Glen.

In a house which was once a stables, with a courtyard like a French *château*, lives a man who is a strange mixture. His father is an Irish earl, with gypsy blood in his veins. His mother is a Baring, of the banking house. His name is Castlerosse, once a sailor, educated in a monastery, a guardsman, a stockbroker, till eventually he became a journalist—the highest-paid one in England. An odd fellow who prefers reading to writing, a philosopher of a kind, though he is not always kind.

Now I will tell you what happened to me when I visited him. For years we have been friends. Once we worked on the same newspaper together, and that is a bond which those outside the craft cannot value truly.

Drink and conversation flow freely in Kenmare House. Of a night the great gusts of the westerly wind are punctuated with equal gusts of laughter, sometimes on unlikely subjects such as, for instance, whether the Jews were polygamous when laying down their marriage laws, or whether Irish deerhounds existed, as some say, in the first century B.C.

However, enough of that. The dawn has broken—

breakfast has been eaten. The rifles and glasses are in the car. I cast a backward glimpse at that almost too perfect, park-like vision of green meadow-land, with a scattered spinney or two of tall, brooding trees—beyond them the belt of a yellow barley stubble, beyond that the fantastic blue of the lake the poets wrote and dreamed of, and, beyond again, the shifting light and changing shadows on Tomies, the Great Mountain. It was the world of a hundred years ago brought to life.

Women were moving along the road, shawled and shuffling. They had bright eyes and lined faces, the old ones. The young ones were positively beautiful. And, mercifully, they had learned nothing from the cinema, and were the lovelier because of it. A jaunting car passed, its horse *clip-clopping* on the hard road. Indeed, all that road to the mountain was horse and donkey. They passed in little sidecars and ass-carts, bearing turf from the bogs and farmers from the market. It was all of a dirty gentleness, a grubby, earthy serenity. The bordering trees that leaned serenely over the demesne wall; the green pastures which ran raggedly up the hillsides; the straggling stone walls, the whitewashed cabins; and the people in their shawls on their ass-carts, all alike—trees, fields, walls, men, and asses—smelt of the gentle rain, æons of unending rains; of turf smoke; of wet leaves, of peat-water whisky, of everything Irish, untidy, undesirable, and completely irresistible.

So we drove for ten miles through a country that had changed not a jot nor a tittle since the year of

259

Waterloo. It was green, rich, alluring, and lovely. It was untidy, and it was wasted. It would have made a Scot knit his brows in economic disapproval, and an Englishman reach for a theodolite. It was all rich, lovely, and wasted.

It made one understand the greed of Elizabeth; the harsh dominance of Cromwell; the bitter resistance of the Irish people, a spirit romantic in its instinctive root, murderous in its Corsican vendetta-fury. The rain and the wet, the moving mists and the shining lakes; the dripping cabin eaves—women under shawls and long, lean men with burning, purposeless eyes—here were the edges of a drama whose motives have moved the inner strings of an empire as the fingers of a tempestuous woman might play suddenly, heartbrokenly upon the strings of an enormous harp in the cathedral of the world.

Then suddenly we came out of this lowland, more or less understandable, conflicting countryside into a mountain land like nothing I had seen. The hills ran up from the sides of the road like the bosoms of a wild and lovely woman. They were not cold, hard, and clipped like the mountains of Western Scotland. There was none of the dour majesty of Ben Loyal, the cold, towering beauty of Schiehallion or the sheer, house-top, challenging starkness of Scurr-Ruach, in Ross, where the ridge-backs stand out into the western sea like sprawling fingers of granite.

Here the mountains surged away on either hand, brown with bracken, gold with gorse, clad for half their tawny heights with old and marching woods of scrub oak, of birch, that strode up their sides. The valleys broke away in broad, noble panoramas.

Those great lakes which a railway company, turned suddenly lyrical, has described as "the Reflex of Heaven" lay, a thousand feet beneath one's eye, in unbelievable, beautiful confusion. They were wild and shining, like crooked swords thrust broad-bladed into the bosom of the hills. The mists moved above them. The sun shone brokenly upon them. The colours moved and changed. And I suddenly realized that there was more than poetic licence in that poet who wrote "the long light shakes across the lakes," for here the long light shook like wavering lances on the hillsides, and across the wild lakes that had neither house upon their banks nor sail upon their waters.

The car stopped at "Old Road." Two men stood there, telescopes slung over their shoulders, long hill sticks in their hands. They were old Dan Donahue and young Dan Donahue. Old Dan is seventy-eight, but I will back him to walk the mountain against any man of forty I know. He will climb a precipice with the businesslike nonchalance of a fly. He cuts across the sheer face of sloping rocks as though he were walking a broad pavement. These Donahues have an instinct for deer. They spend their weekdays stalking deer and their Sundays watching them. They have the eyes of hawks and the instinct of foxes. I have seen young Dan spot a deer with the naked eye a mile and a half away across the bare shoulder of a mountain. He picked up and pointed out the tips of his horns, just showing through the Finaun—which is

Irish for long grass—as casually as though he had
been drawing one's attention to a passer-by on the
other side of the road. They have the steady, un-
wavering eye, father and son, which you find in all
mountainy men.

They tell a grand story at Kenmare House showing
the difference between the Irishman and the Scot.
Some years ago the Earl of Kenmare killed a fourteen-
pointer and a fifteen-pointer with a right and left. Old
Dan Donahue took off his cap at the spot where the
deer fell, dropped on his knee, and thanked God aloud
that he had seen the day when his chieftain, the Earl,
could do such a deed.

That was the Irishman at his emotional height. But
Davidson, then the head stalker, a cold-blooded Scot,
merely remarked drily, " It would be about here that
I am thinking I lost a bone collar-stud two weeks ago.
I'll be looking for it."

And down on his knees he went in the heather,
looked for the bone collar-stud, and, may the fairies
and Lord Castlerosse be my witnesses, he found it!

There are two more nice stories about this forest of
Poulagower, where, by the way, I stalked and shot
the best stag I have ever killed, a grand wild nine-
pointer who went twenty stone clean. He was an old
royal who had gone back.

Some years ago young Lord Revelstoke, who was
then only twenty-one, shot a sixteen-pointer which
scaled thirty stone on Ullauns, which lies over to the
right side.

Next day he went up the hill without a rifle, but

with a mason and a chisel. In the rock he chipped out this inscription: "The happiest day a man has spent for a hundred years. 20th September, 1932."

Stalking is the whole business on these Irish hills. It is all long sight, long patience, and long crawls. There are no long shots and scarcely ever any wounded deer. But when you do kill a stag he makes Scotland look silly. Mr Henry Longhurst, the golfer, came out with me one day. I doubt if he had ever seen a stag outside Richmond Park. But old Dan took him in hand. At the end of the day Henry Longhurst knew almost as much about stalking as he does about golf. And he finished the day by killing a royal and an eleven-pointer with a right and a left. I rather fancy he still thinks stalking is an easy business. But old Dan knows.

There are grand heads in the estate office at Kenmare—wild, branching fourteen- and fifteen-pointers, great, fine beasts that beat anything I have ever seen in a Highland lodge. They are eloquent of the mountains and the lakes of this, the loveliest place in the British Isles, a place made by nature for sport.

The fishing is some of the best in the British Isles. The golf-course which is being planned on the shores of the lake should enchant even the average golfer. The duck-shooting is first-class, and the woodcock-shooting has no equal. They think sixty couple a day of 'cock pretty good, but nothing to write about.

But I have taken you a long way from the moment when we met old Dan and young Dan standing by the roadside, telescopes slung over their shoulders, long hill sticks gripped in their hands, the "Old Road" beckoning.

We were out of the car, squelching across a boggy patch, and then climbing up the "Old Road"—they call it that, for it was a mountain farm road a hundred years ago, when there were little lost, poor farms in the hollows of those wild hills. We were climbing up the "Old Road," over green moss and slipping stones, through an Arthur Rackham wood of old bent trees, all bent one way like scrawling witch-fingers, hung with foot-long beards of silver moss, climbing up the hill where the deer walked like lordly frescoes against the mountain-edge.

We left the lakes and the view, the scarce-breathed breath of Victorian poets almost audible, the world of Edwardian Ireland understandable. We left all this for a wood and a world of mountain and deer, of badger and fairy, where time had stood still for a thousand years.

The raven croaked as we climbed. The badger shuffled in the rocks beneath those ancient bearded trees. The Japanese bucks whistled shrilly as they scampered, titupping, through the fantastic, silvery trunks. A peregrine swung in a wild and airy beat, and a cock-grouse crowed with a shrill defiance.

It was suddenly borne in upon one that here we trod in a world unknown by the Cockney sportsman, the effulgent city gentleman. Here we were on a deer forest older than history itself, unquoted in the annual dreary commercial catalogues of those estate agents who cater each year for Throgmorton Street and the

Stock Exchange. No weary professional scribes of the consciously charming, would-be rural pen had climbed these mountains.

Here was a wild place, untouched, unmoved, uninterpreted except by her own poets, and perhaps even by that fierce instinct of her own mountainy men which has led them alike to fight bloodily for the British Empire and bloodily against it. It was a world of the Druid and the fairy, of the glancing buck and the stately moving stag, a world where the ancient bearded tree stood like a gnome, where the raven croaked and the salmon splashed in the pools.

There are quiet places on these hills where the snipe spring suddenly. You may stand at the head of a glen as I did, while my host, Lord Castlerosse, that man of the poetic spirit and the mountainous body, said, spreading out his arms, " There is the Hags' Glen!"

I forebore immediate remembrances of London restaurants, any of which might well deserve that name. I remembered, instead, suddenly captured, grateful memories of Victorian novels about such mountainy places, such long, spreading lakes, such shifting mists where hags of an undoubted authenticity had dwelt. There were their rocky caves. Their bleary eyes had gazed in crooked witchery above the winding lakes. The wild winds took them with unbelievable velocity on village grocer's broomsticks on pagan eves. They were of the age that saw a white wild goat shot with a silver bullet, that knew a witched hare pursued by the fairy greyhound of a vanished queen.

We went up through the old, wild wood. The trees

leaned upward to the hills. Long, ragged beards of moss hung from their scarred, silver trunks. I think those old trees must have stood there for a hundred years. They were unreal, but entirely sure of themselves. I walked in a world unreal. The iron nails in my stalking shoes slipped on moss-covered stones. Their sudden clatter rang with a mechanical insult upon the thousand-year silence of the wood.

A raven slipped off a tree. He went through the wood on soft, sliding wings, a thing of awful tradition. There flew the bird of Odin. There went, through the silent Irish woods, the echo of forgotten battles. On the hillside, far beyond the wood, over and beyond a rusty mile of reddened bracken, he lifted like a Valkyrian shadow against the clear horizon of a mountain-side that had seen his kind since the birth of history.

It was strange, coming from London as we did. I think we should have walked that " Old Road " with pencils in our hands, with notepads poised. We should have gone off in the proper spirit of eighteenth-century note-takers—or even twentieth-century gossip-writers.

Instead, we walked in the old style, with the studs in our shoes striking sparks, rifles in our hands, the stalker with the glass ahead, our bellows pumping, and our host leading the van, an Irish chieftain with his incredibly light foot (in spite of his eighteen stone) set upon the turf of his native heath.

The woodcock went before us. They sprang from the bracken like gnomes. Japanese deer leaped up on all sides like hares. There are 3000 of them, even perhaps 5000, on this 30,000-acre demesne of the Earls of Kenmare, of which Lord Castlerosse is hereditary Lord to-day. A hundred years ago his great-grandfather put down two does and a buck. The result is this rabbit-like increase. Politicians may trace their parallel in democratic representation.

The aristocrats, the red stags, are the biggest in the British Isles. Their weight in body and spread in head is bigger than anything in Scotland. They are the last of the authentic wild deer of Ireland, and by that token and that heritage, the best that we have in our British Isles. Their carriage is magnificent, their gait a thing of beauty, their spread of horn something almost out of the forgotten ages. They move on the mountains like true creatures of the mountain. They have not been harried, chased, and shot at by fifty years of city sportsmen paying their miserable cheques in order to kill a head that might conceivably adorn a Putney villa. These are noble, unforgettable animals.

They say there are fifteen hundred of them on the hills. They walk those wild ridges where the O'Donaghue of the Glen still rides above the long Lake of Killarney on a white horse in the thunder-born moment of a legend which says that he comes out of the hillside in a clap of light, rides the waters, sorts his books at that fantastic " Library "—do you know that little, lonely, uninhabited isle in the Lake where the rocks, jagged but marvellously alike, look like gigantic books piled one upon the other?—and then goes over through the gap in the hill line above

Rosse Castle, borne on a trail of fire. If you don't believe it, the boatman will tell you about it.

And when I asked Lord Castlerosse who was this magnificent man, this knight of the Irish past, this banner-bearer of history who rode up all the wild and lonely lakes, from the Pass of Dunloe to the ruined castle where he took to his wings and flew over the hill—when I asked, "Who is the O'Donaghue?" he replied, "*I* am the O'Donaghue!"

And the boatman said, in a quiet echo off the water, "Of the Glen and the Lakes—his Lordship."

That is South-west Ireland. And they produce a local newspaper called *The Kerry Champion*. Do you wonder? I do not.

CHAPTER XX

THE IRISH WOLFHOUND

A Breed which claims 1800 Years of History!—Early Records
of a Noble Hound—A Pirate, his Daughter, and his " Dirty
Grey Dog "—The Dog which could smell Royal Blood—Lord
Caledon's Pure Stock—The Founding of the Irish Wolfhound
Club—Points to look for—The Breed To-day.

I WROTE IN THE LAST CHAPTER of the last really
wild forest in Ireland where the native red deer of
that country roam and live at their own free will. I
regard Kenmare as a truly wild open forest, the last
great home of the Irish red deer, for although Glen-
veagh is described as a deer forest, and still, I believe,
carries a considerable head of deer, all or most of it
was enclosed by miles of fencing for many years, and,
I believe, still is.

It is difficult to determine with accuracy the earliest
history of the Irish wolfhound, to my mind one of the
oldest and noblest breeds of sporting dog in these islands.

Ossian records that when the children of Uisnech
were forced to flee from Northern Ireland to Scotland
in the first century they took a shipload of greyhounds
with them, 150 or more. He tells us that Mesroda,
King of Leinster, possessed a great greyhound named
Ailbé, so savage, so ferocious, and so faithful that it
defended the whole kingdom of Leinster against the
King's enemies, more fiercely and savagely than an
army might have done. Both the kings of Connaught
and of Ulster wished to buy this ferocious hound.

They offered 6000 head of cattle, lands, slaves, and weapons for him. But Mesroda refused to sell. So war broke out. It was the undoing of the gallant Ailbé, for, deserting the King of Leinster, he joined himself with Ulster and attacked the chariot of the King of Connaught. He seized the axle and hung on while they hacked at him with swords. The result was that his head was cut off. But even in death this deathless hound refused to let go. The chariot rumbled off with the jaws of the hound still firmly fixed to the axle, the dripping head still grimly clinging on.

Ossian is full of references to greyhounds which hunted the deer, which made the mountains magical with their savage music, which were mighty in war and great in defence of the castle. Bran, the hound of Fingal, is immortal.

I like that story in *Tales of the Irish*, which was published in 1892, of "the Thieving Monster and Most Hideous Pirate, . . . a son of mishap who lived on the black rocks out in the sea," with a daughter who was a match for 300 men, and a great, shaggy-haired grey dog which was accounted equal for another 300 men at least.

Cælite, a member of the household of King Cormac, determined to break up this thieving gang. So he waited one morning, under the rocks on the shore, with his sword, his spear, his bow, and his hand full of darts. Early in the dawn, as the first shafts of a red sun covered the waves with blood, he saw a curragh driving inshore, a thing of hides and wooden ribs. At the oars was the pirate, a great, black, shaggy monster of a man, a sight to strike terror at the heart of any normal human being. Opposite him sat his daughter, "A great lump of a wench, bald and swart, that from a distance loomed like some jutting point of rock." Cælite heard the pirate order his daughter to unloose the dog, "a shag-haired dog of a dirty grey that round his neck wore a rude iron chain."

"Let the dog eat the man yonder on the rocks," said the pirate.

Thereupon Cælite, murmuring "My Creator and my Tailchann both I put forth against you three," threw a dart, with a clear eye and a steady hand—for there had been no mead the night before—and very neatly got the hound in the throat as he lifted his head, skewering both jaws together.

Now I do not know whether we can regard this shag-haired dog of a dirty grey as a forerunner of the Irish wolfhound whom we know to-day, who frequently is both shag-haired and of a dirty grey, but to step from the misty legends of Ossian to the more erudite, and possibly reliable, *Cynegeticon*, which was "Englished and Illustrated by Christopher Wase, Gent," in 1654, we find there definite, clear-cut references to a breed of Irish wolfhounds which were so powerful, swift, and well bred that foreign potentates, including the King of Poland, sent ships especially for them and paid long prices.

There are numerous references all through the literature of the dog from the earliest days to the possibilities of wolf crosses, and there seems no valid reason why such crosses should not have occurred from time to time. I could quote data in support of this theory to a monotonous degree, but it is scarcely worth while, other than to bolster up an academic argument.

The interesting point, though, is that I can find no record of a wolf cross ever having been used in the Irish wolfhound. Howel the Good, who published his Laws of Wales in A.D. 930—they were printed in Welsh and Latin in 1730—refers to what he calls *Gell-gi*, which were Irish dogs, and *Bleidd-gi*, which were wolf-dogs. If the Irish dog came from the kennels of a king he was worth 240 pence trained, and half that sum untrained. A nine-days-old puppy was worth fifteenpence, and one between six and twelve months sixty pence.

And he adds, "An Irish greyhound belonging to a noble is worth half the king."

There was great sense in those old laws, for in Paragraph 17 we find this:

"But a shepherd's dog, who is kept to guard the flock and leads out the flock in the morning, and at evening brings it home, will be worth the best animal in the flock which it guards."

There are then these references to Irish hounds, which I think worth extracting from the schedule of rules laid down with regard to hounds and dogs in general, since they show clearly the great value which was attached to the Irish hound more than a century before the time of William the Conqueror, and, moreover, prove clearly that the Irish hound was a definite and highly valued breed:

(1) MR I. W. EVERETT'S IRISH WOLFHOUND 'FELIXSTOWE
KELCULLY'

A magnificent specimen of this noble-looking breed.

(2) TWO OF MRS DUNLOP-HILL'S PRIZE-WINNING SCOTCH
DEERHOUNDS

Champion ' Carron of Chattan' and ' Spey of Chattan.'

Photos Sport and General

A TYPICAL FIELD TRIAL

Dr T. W. Stanton's 'Folkingham Sand' retrieving a hare at the International
Gun-dog League's Retriever Society's Working Trials at Hatfield House, Herts.

Photo Sport and General

273

" 22. The puppy of a royal Irish hound before it begins to see is worth 24 pence.

" 23. In the kennel with its mother, 48 pence.

" 24. In the palace, 96 pence.

" 25. While it is learning to hunt, half a pound.

" 26. When it is trained, one pound.

" 27. A royal greyhound will always be worth half the value of an Irish royal hound at the corresponding age.

" 28. Whoever damages the eye of a royal Irish greyhound, or cuts off its tail, shall pay 4 pence for every cow the dog is worth.

" 29. A dog on the same day may be worth from 4 pence to a pound.

" An Irish greyhound is the only animal whose value can increase on the same day from 4 pence to one pound; for if in the morning it belongs to a villein it will be worth 4 pence, and if on the same day it be presented to the King it will be worth a pound.

" 30. A greyhound without a *collar* loses its status.

" A stallion feeding in a field and a greyhound without a collar lose their status.

" 31. A nobleman's Irish hunting hound and a royal greyhound shall have the same value.

" 32. A nobleman's Irish hunting hound from birth till it be full grown shall be worth half the value of a nobleman's Irish hunting horse of the same age."

Just to give extra point to this canine snobbery Jesse tells the lovely story of an Irish wolfhound which had so keen a nose that it could pick out a descendant of an

s   273

Irish king in a crowd of people! I suspect that some of the Southern Ireland loyalists might have a great deal of fun to-day at any meeting of the Dail with such a hound.

Jesse's story is as follows:

" A gentleman of an ancient family with a name unnecessary to mention, he having been engaged in the troubles which agitated Ireland some forty years before," was breakfasting in a coffee-room of a Dublin hotel, his dog at his feet. It was a magnificent specimen of the old Irish wolfhound, then almost extinct.

One other person entered the coffee-room. The hound immediately went up to him and made a great fuss of him—a little embarrassing with an animal the size of a calf. But the stranger, instead of being frightened, or in the least nervous, patted the dog and made a great fuss of it. The owner, however, begged him to leave it alone, warning him that it was a savage beast and might easily attack him. The stranger bowed and sat down to his bacon and eggs.

But the wolfhound returned to him immediately, thrust its head in his lap, and plainly asked to be taken notice of. This so astonished its owner that, addressing the stranger a little stiffly, he said, " You are the only person whom the dog would ever allow to touch it without showing resentment. May I beg the favour of your name?"

The stranger bowed and gave his name, one which was part of the royal history of Ireland. He was clearly of the line of Irish kings.

" I do not wonder then at the homage this animal

274

has paid you," said its owner. " It recognizes in you the descendant of one of our most ancient race of gentlemen, to whom this breed of dog most exclusively belonged, and the peculiar instinct he possesses has now been shown in a manner which cannot be mistaken by me when so well acquainted with the ferocity this dog has hitherto shown to all strangers."

No wonder *Punch* said that anybody who could swallow this story could " bolt the whole book of Jesse without blinking."

That was in 1846. In 1859 " Stonehenge " was saying that the breed was extinct. He admitted though that " There are still some gentlemen who maintain that they possess the breed in all its pristine purity of blood." The Irish wolfhounds of that day were reckoned to stand about 38 inches high, were generally fawn in colour, very like a deerhound in appearance, but much taller.

Then in 1885 came the foundation of the Irish Wolfhound Club, from whose efforts spring the splendid examples of the breed which we see to-day.

I think it would be unfair to suggest that the present-day specimens are 'manufactured.' It is more than likely that true examples of the pristine breed remained lost and forgotten in old castles in the far West, in villages tucked away in the mountains, in desolate bog dwellings, and in old deer forests such as Killarney. The present Earl of Caledon has told me more than once that his grandfather kept the pure Irish wolfhound at Caledon Park—a lovely, wild demesne still full of deer—that they were there in 1860, and that there was no reason to doubt that they were the genuine stock.

Ten years before that time some of the true breed were supposed to be in existence at Drogmore. Lord Derby is supposed to have owned some at that time. In the seventies Mr Frank Adcock, of Shevington Hall, Wigan, announced in an American sporting newspaper that he had a kennel of pure Irish wolfhounds, "blackish grey and grizzle in colour with stiff, wiry coats, like deerhounds in shape, but more slightly made." Then came the Irish Wolfhound Club in 1885:

"A club to 'promote the more complete recovery of this grand dog, and to fairly establish the race, by endeavouring to make the qualities and type of the breed better known,' has lately been formed, with officers as follows: President, Lord Arthur Cecil; Committee, Messrs. J. Davies, B. Olive, G. W. S. Lennox, B. Clifton, A. Russell, A. F. Laloe, M. L. H. Kennedy, and Lieut.-Colonel Garnier; Hon. Secretary and Treasurer, Captain Graham, Rednock, Dursley; Hon. Secretary for Ireland, Mr R. Clifton, Usher Street, Dublin. The annual subscription to the club is two guineas, and honorary members at the reduced rate of one guinea; already twenty-three members have been made, and prospects for the future success of the club are bright.

"The following description or standard, by which the Irish Wolfhound is in future to be judged, has already been drawn up:

"1. *General Appearance.* The Irish wolfhound should not be quite so heavy or massive as the Great Dane, but more so than the deerhound, which in general type he should otherwise resemble. Of great size and commanding appearance, very muscular, strong though gracefully built, movements easy and active; head and neck carried high; the tail carried with an upward sweep with a slight curve towards the extremity.

"The minimum height and weight of dogs should be 31 inches and 120 lb.: of bitches 28 inches and 90 lb. Anything below this should be debarred from competition. Great size, including height at shoulder and proportionate length of body, is the desideratum to be aimed at, and it is desired to firmly establish a race that shall average from 32 inches to 34 inches in dogs, showing the requisite power, activity, courage, and symmetry.

" 2. *Head*. Long, the frontal bones of the forehead very slightly raised, and very little indentation between the eyes. Skull not too broad. Muzzle long and moderately pointed. Ears small and greyhound-like in carriage.

" 3. *Neck*. Rather long, very strong and muscular, well arched, without dewlap or loose skin about the throat.

" 4. *Chest*. Very deep. Breast wide.

" 5. *Back*. Rather long than short. Loins arched.

" 6. *Tail*. Long and slightly curved, of moderate thickness, and well covered with hair.

" 7. *Belly*. Well drawn up.

" 8. *Forequarters*. Shoulders muscular, giving breadth of chest, set sloping. Elbows well under, neither turned inwards nor outwards. Legs, forearm, muscular, and the whole leg strong and quite straight.

" 9. *Hindquarters*. Muscular thighs, and second thigh long and strong as in the greyhound, and hocks well let down and turning neither inwards nor outwards.

" 10. *Feet*. Moderately large and round, neither turned inwards nor outwards. Toes well arched and closed. Nails very strong and curved.

" 11. *Hair.* Rough and hard on body, legs, and head; especially wiry and long over eyes and under jaw.

" 12. *Colour and Markings.* The recognized colours are grey, brindle, red, black, pure white, fawn, or any colour that appears in the deerhound.

" 13. *Faults.* Too light or heavy a head, too highly arched frontal bone, large ears, and hanging flat to the face; short neck; full dewlap; too narrow or too broad a chest; sunken or hollow or quite straight back; bent forelegs, over bent fetlocks, twisted feet, spreading toes; too curly a tail; weak hindquarters and a general want of muscle; too short in body."

The Kennel Club gave the breed a class in 1886, and although there were no entries there were nine the following year, and fifteen the year after that.

Since then the breed has gone on from strength to strength, the subject of endless controversy, reams of letters in *The Field*, and a great deal of hard hitting. We will leave that to the experts.

For those who are interested, without acrimony or unduly pedantic criticism, the breed as it exists to-day is worthy of both ownership and admiration. The modern wolfhound is a commanding animal, deep-chested, easy in movement, muscular, and active. The usual colours are white, fawn, brindle, black, red, and, more usually, grey. A dog should weigh not less than 120 lb. and a bitch 90 lb. The bitch stands at about 28 inches and the dog at 36 inches—possibly a little more. I should say that the finest kennels in the country are those of Mr J. V. Rank at Ouborough, near Godstone, in Surrey.

CHAPTER XXI

THE SCOTCH DEERHOUND

The Hounds who saved a Knight's Head—Early Types and
Stories—Deer Drives and Deer-coursing—Scrope's Story of
Tarff and Derig—Queen Victoria's Support of the Breed—
Prince Albert's Bran—The Breed To-day.

PENTLAND MOOR IF YOUR HOUNDS hold her, and
your head is off if they lose her." That was the ulti-
matum of the Bruce to Sir William St Clair. They
were hunting deer on Pentland Moor. Sir William
boasted that his two hounds, Help and Hold, would
take any stag roused. And, as would happen on such a
day, they roused the magic white deer, the deer whom
no living hound might hold.

Off went the deer, the hounds in hot pursuit, the
King blazing with excitement, Sir William, we may
assume, slightly sick with apprehension. It was not the
sort of bet that a medieval Ladbroke could afford to
smile at. The stag reached the edge of March Burn,
plunged in, swam strongly for the other side. Had he
reached it Sir William's head would have been off.
But Help and Hold plunged into the Burn, followed
the stag, bayed it, and held it. Up came the forester
with his knife—and the white stag's day was done, Sir
William's head safe, and the whole of Pentland Moor
his own.

That is the sort of story which runs through the
history of the deerhound in Scotland.

Like all Gaelic history, it has no apparent beginning

279

or ending and a great deal of middle. You can read a
vast amount, believe as much as you like, and find great
pleasure in delving.

Boethius talks of a hunting dog used by the Picts,
presumably before the days of the Romans. They
hunted deer with them, but the Scots apparently had a
faster, better breed, able to pull down the stag without
the aid of an arrow. So the Picts demanded that some
of these hounds should be given them. These they
got. But to make sure of their bargain they stole another, the swiftest hound of the lot. The result was a
tribal battle in which " sixty Scott gentlemen " were
killed, and over a hundred Picts.

Whether this fast hound was an original deerhound
or not no one may say, but by the middle of the six-
teenth century Scottish greyhounds were spoken of in
the chronicles of the period. They were described as
being swift, fierce, and true. By 1728 Robert Lindsay
in his *Chronicles of Scotland* speaks of an order by the
king, who " warned all gentleman that had good dogs
to bring them, that he might hunt in the said country,
as he pleased, the whilk, the Earl of Argyle, the Earl
of Huntley, the Earl of Athole, and so all the rest of
the gentlemen of the Highlands did and brought their
hounds in like manner, to hunt with the king as he
pleased."

I do not think we may take this as a definitely authentic reference to the deerhound, but by the middle
of the eighteenth century the great Highland chieftains, the Earl of Mar and others, were using greyhounds in the great organized deer-hunts which have

been handed down in history. Scores of deer were killed at these hunts, whole herds being driven helter-skelter from the hillside at full gallop through certain corries where they were shot.

Tennant, who was at Gordon Castle in 1769, says he saw "a true Scottish greyhound . . . of large size, strong, deep-chested, and covered with very long, rough hair." Dr Johnson after his visit to Skye spoke of "a race of brindle greyhounds, larger and stronger than those with which we course hares."

Then in 1838 came Scrope's great work, a book always worth buying. In it Mr Archbold Macneile, of Colonsay, the island whence the Earl de Folcoville obtained his celebrated strain in 1842, wrote a chapter, and gave full details of the breed.

He speaks of Buskar, the finest dog of the time, 28 inches high, 32 inches round the chest, and 85 lb. in weight, quick and keen for work.

"This dog," he said, "is a pale yellow, and appears to be remarkably pure in its breed, not only from his shape and colour, but from the wiry elasticity of his hair, which by Highlanders is thought to be a criterion of breeding."

There were grey dogs, yellow dogs, and dark dogs at that period, but Macneile does not seem to have thought much of the grey dog, for he says that they seem to be "less lively, and did not exhibit such a development of muscle, particularly on the back and loins, and have a tendency to cat hams."

He says very rightly that once a stock is allowed to deteriorate it will be more than difficult to recreate it properly. Scrope says the same thing too. Indeed, at that time there was a serious risk of the breed dying out altogether. However, a few Highland gentlemen hung on to their last remaining specimens, refused easy crosses, and bred carefully. The result was that by 1842 the breed had increased materially, was of good quality and not uncommon. A good dog would fetch up to two or three guineas.

Their day of usefulness, however, had declined, for stalking was coming into fashion, and few lairds, if any, cared to course the deer. It upset the forest too much, moved the deer, and discouraged the first beginnings of that tide of English money which was shortly to flow into Scots pockets in the shape of rentals for deer forests. But the deerhound still had a use in following and baying wounded deer. Many stories are told of their courage in facing an angry, wounded, dangerous stag.

Scrope tells the comparatively well-known story of Tarff and Derig, who followed a wounded stag.

" The stag stood on a narrow, projecting ridge of rock within a cleft, in the mid-course of a mountain cataract, of which the upper falls plunged down behind him, coursing through his legs, dashed into spray and mist around him, then leaped down into the abyss with that rush only water knows."

As the stalkers came up they saw the two dogs on the edge of the cleft, baying the stag, holding him at the peril of their lives.

" Whenever the deer turned his antlers aside to gore Tarff, Derig seized the moment to fly at his throat.

The stag at length, maddened at these attacks, made a desperate stab at Derig, and in avoiding it the poor dog lost his footing—his hind-legs passed over the ledge of rock, only his forelegs bore upon the ledge, and he scraped and strove with them to the utmost; but in the position of a drowning man who attempts to get into a boat.

"In struggling with his forelegs he appeared to advance a little, and then to slip back again, gasping painfully in the exertion; at length he probably found some slight bearing for the claws of his hind-feet, and, to the inexpressible relief of every one, he once more recovered his footing and sprang forward at the deer as rash and wrathful as ever."

"Stonehenge" in 1859 says that there was then little practical difference between the Scotch deer-hound and what he describes as the rough greyhound, the only distinctive difference being that the deerhound when running carries its head higher.

There is no doubt that the breed was very scarce in his day and in danger of extinction. Even Sir Walter Scott, who should have known better, failed to procure one. His famous Maida was supposed to be a cross with a Pyrenean wolf-dog.

But a Mr Chaworth Musters, of Kirk Langton, kept a kennel pure and untouched. Queen Victoria liked the breed, and took an interest in it. Her keeper Cole had several good ones. One or two Highland landowners also possessed specimens.

By 1860 it had come into general popularity, partly no doubt owing to the Queen's interest. The Birmingham

283

Dog-show had a class for them, and though the entry was not particularly good it was good enough for Leeds to have a class a year later. But only one dog was entered. However, by 1870 the breed was well on the way. The Duke of Sutherland, the Earl of Breadalbane, Lord Henry Bentinck, Mr Spencer Lucy, Sir St George Gore, Cameron of Lochiel, Graham of Durnock, and others were all breeding and exhibiting. A Mr Menzies, who lived on the shores of Loch Tay, not far from Taymouth Castle, was supposed then to possess a strain which had been in his family's possession for a century, but they were terribly inbred.

Prince Albert's well-known Bran was bred by Mr Morrison, who sent it to Macniele of Colonsay, who gave it to the Prince. That was enough to start the interest for the general public. The deerhound became a necessary adjunct to almost any picture of that Highland life to which the Queen's interest had given a romantic popular appeal.

The breed to-day is well established in what we may perhaps safely regard as popularity. I will not go into a wearisome description of points. It is enough to say that a dog should stand at least 30 inches, a bitch not less than 28 inches; a dog should weigh from 85 to 100 lb., and a bitch from 65 to 80 lb. The head should be long, broad between the ears, with a flat skull, no stop, and a black nose. Narrow chests should be avoided, and the hindquarters should be drooping but powerful. A little white on the chest or toes need not be bothered about. The coat should be harsh and about three inches long, the action of the dog powerful and full of dignity.

There may be no forests to-day where the hunting of deer with deerhounds would be welcome, but as a grand sporting dog who has kept his pride and grace of place the deerhound deserves to endure.

CHAPTER XXII

THE SUPER-SPORTING SEALYHAM

Sir Jocelyn Lucas and his Pack—The Origin of the Breed—
The Pembrokeshire Terrier—Game for Badger, Polecat, Otter,
and Rabbit—Real Hound-work—Some Points to look for.

Mr LILLEY, if we are to believe John Aubrey, said
he saw a fairy which vanished with a most melodious
twang. Now, I believe I saw a fairy, hunting a pack
of bouncing cloudlets—all white and fussy, all of
them hard on the heels of a rabbit. Obviously the
rabbit was only laughing at them. He could go *so*
much faster.

But the white cloudlets bounced into the bracken,
poured through the brambles. The fairy, who was in
green, tall, remarkably muscular for such a melodious
twang, twanged again and sprang valiantly into the
thorns. The hunt was up.

The whole woodland sang with it. Tall, winter-
whitened elms, in whose bare branches sang the sea
wind, rang with the music. The valley which sloped
to the sea was alive with a shrill clamour. Here was
no bell-mouthed anthem of the foxhound, no deep-
throated dirge of the bloodhound, no melodious under-
note of harrier or chiming of the beagle, but a shrill,
yapping *crescendo*, a terrier-like cacophony.

Clearly they had bought the place—or, as I prefer
to think, had owned it for a great many years. It was
very businesslike, a little noisy perhaps—but a businesslike noise. After a moment or two I changed my

mind about the chances of that rabbit. And the fairy, who by now, I saw, was no fairy at all, but had a bristling black moustache, a very sharp eye, and a command of most biting language—spoken, mark you, in an almost apologetically gentle voice—sprang about, twanging melodiously—but, as I observed, with a deathly intentness on the encompassing of that individual rabbit.

In fine, he was *hunting hounds*. And they were behaving like hounds. There was no panoply of pink coats, no thrusting for places at gates or gaps, very few —but there *were* a few—camera-conscious young women; no horses with their supercilious ascendancy, and certainly by no means any suspicion of a stockbroker. Indeed, there was a not altogether lamentable absence of that tinselled, week-ending squirearchy who lend so much colour, grace, conscious glamour, carefully cultivated phraseology—in fact, *all* the tricks— to a meet of hounds; or, equally, to most pheasant shoots, some partridge shoots, and even, alas! a few wildfowl shoots.

Oddly enough, this particular day's hunting was like nothing I had ever seen before. I have not seen a great deal of orthodox hunting, in any case—but a great deal of unorthodox hunting. And this was the most orthodox unorthodox hunting I have ever dreamed of—let alone seen.

But they killed their rabbit. They killed half a dozen in the course of a day. And they gave us a very good run—several good runs. They went chiming down through the woods towards the Roman River, where the sea trout leapt with a splash before some modern improvement polluted the stream. They made the whole deep green valley below Fingringhoe ring with their music. They brought hard-bitten, hard-riding Essex farmers out of their stack-yards and stock-yards to gaze with admiration, to voice naïve praise. They even frightened a hare so badly that I do not think it stopped running until it had swum the Colne to Wivenhoe.

Now this phenomenon was an occasion of the meet of the Sealyham pack which is owned and mastered by my friend, Sir Jocelyn Lucas, Bart. I doubt severely whether he will appreciate my description of him as a fairy—but, after all, if you are clad in green and hunt a pack, if you are remarkably active, if you spring about in a wood twanging a horn, and if John Aubrey's lines come instantly to the mind, small blame to the writer.

His is the only pack of hunting Sealyhams in the country. During the winter months they travel all over England, packed comfortably in their hound van, ready for sport of a humble sort wherever it may be offered them. They provide a lot of fun for a great many people, and in their own way they provide some quite amusing studies in miniature hound-work.

The Sealyham, as most people know, was originated by Captain Edwardes, who owned the estate of Sealyham, in South Wales. He began the breed about 1860 with the object of providing a stout, game, plucky terrier, all white in colour, short in the leg and strong in the jaw, for the purpose of badger-digging. In order to get the best he used to run them on a drag which led to a pit in which there was a live polecat. If the terrier went straight in without hesitation and tackled the polecat he was reckoned a worker fit to breed from. If he faltered or merely stood and barked he was thrown out.

The Sealyham is, in fact, the English version, from the utility point of view, of the dachshund—that is to say, he was bred and designed solely for badger-digging.

There used to be a form of badger-hunting years ago which was entirely different, and in which the Sealyham took no part. That was the hunting of badgers at night. Badgers lie up and sleep during the day, but soon after dusk they leave their setts and take to the woods in search of young rabbits or wild honey, roots, and their other forms of food. The old idea was to stop up the badger's earth, post watchers to signal his whereabouts with a lantern, and then hunt him with a pack of either terriers or beagles. But the dog for such hunting had to be fairly fast, for the badger can travel from ten to twelve miles an hour. I happen to know their speed accurately, for Captain Bill Fawcett and I dug two badgers out of the grounds of the Convent of the Sacred Heart at Roehampton, where they were undermining the Calvary. We put them in a bag, took them off by car down to Claygate, in Surrey, shook them out of the bag, and then timed them with a speedometer, running beside them as they went for the woods. They managed well over ten miles an hour over about a quarter of a mile of good grass going. Now that is more than the Sealyham could deal with.

I dare say a big Sealyham, long in the leg, might be able to hunt a badger above ground, but there are several other breeds of terrier that could do it better.

But they are excellent for rabbiting, very game, will stand up to any amount of work, thorns, bushes, and cold. They have strong jaws, and when they do fight they hang on like death.

Sir Jocelyn Lucas, who owns one of the leading kennels in the country, told me that when a pair of his Sealyhams get a grip he merely lifts them up and hangs them either over a door or a wall! They have to let go then. He very rightly says that to beat fighting dogs is useless. It merely means that you hurt them unnecessarily, and seldom or never succeed in parting them. Indeed, what usually happens is that the beating encourages other dogs to have a go as well.

He considers that the Sealyham when small and active makes a first-class badger-dog for the badger-digger. But they should not be too big, as the badger can dig himself underground at the rate of about a foot a minute in loose earth, and a long-legged Sealyham cannot keep up with him and get him out. The breed is becoming more and more popular every day, and nowadays fetch big prices. Puppies go for about three guineas, older dogs for anything up to £50. Two of Sir Jocelyn Lucas's champions, Hagley Hustle and Bantam, can be seen in the South Kensington Natural History Museum, where they are rather badly set up. Hagley Hustle fetched £300, and was an inter-

THE SEALYHAM PACK

Major Sir Jocelyn Lucas, Bart., M.H. (second from left), with his pack at a meet at Aldenham House, near Elstree. They hunt rabbit all over Southern England, and show excellent sport.

MRS BOYD'S FRENCH POODLE 'FUDGE OF PIPERSCROFT'

At the Associated Sheep, Police, and Army Dog Society's Show at Tattersall's
in 1937—a good-looking specimen.

Photo Sport and General

national champion and a rare dog on polecats, rats, and rabbits.

Another champion from his kennel, Hagley Hood-wink, fetched £450 from an American breeder, which is by no means a world record price for the breed, as Champion Ivo Caradoc went to Mr Ross Proctor, of New York, for £850 before the War, and Champion Delf Discriminate fetched £1000 after the War.

Sir Jocelyn Lucas tells me that they make excellent mothers, are remarkably hardy, need little exercise, and take good care of themselves. The average number in a litter is about five, but ten and eleven have been recorded. Sir Jocelyn says that you should pick a long-bodied bitch if you want a big litter. A good brood bitch will fetch about twenty-five guineas, and a good dog ten guineas more, but moderate-quality dogs are less expensive than moderate bitches.

On the whole it is a good-tempered breed, very friendly and affectionate without being sloppy, quite intelligent and adaptable to most forms of sport.

In fact, Captain Edwardes, who started the breed, used them as adjuncts to his pack of otter-hounds. He used to hunt the rivers Sealy and Cleddau and various other streams in Pembrokeshire. Some authorities place the beginning of the breed as far back as 1848, but it does not seem that they attracted any general notice until about 1860. That branch of the Edwardes family is now extinct, so it is practically impossible to find out how and when Captain Edwardes evolved the breed.

The first show class was at the Kennel Club Show

in 1910, from which it will be seen that the breed was practically neglected by the dog world for fifty years. Mr Freeman Lloyd, who came from Haverfordwest, not far from Sealyham, was exceptionally active in bringing it to the notice of the general public, and I believe he was the man responsible for the formation of a club in 1908 which interested itself in what they then called "the Pembrokeshire terrier."

Since then it has become largely a pet, and has suffered accordingly. Sir Jocelyn Lucas has done more than anyone to restore a sense of self-respect to the Sealyham by giving it the chance to justify itself as a real, working, sporting terrier, which is what it was bred for and what it is supposed to be.

Most of the show-bench dogs of to-day are heavy, clumsy, big-boned, and obviously unfit for active work either on badgers or rabbits.

On the other hand, the very short-legged specimens are more than a nuisance, for they pick up a lot of dirt, and cannot keep pace with a man walking, let alone a rabbit running.

A dog should not be more than 20 lb. in weight, and a bitch about 18 lb., and neither of them should stand more than 12 inches at the shoulder. Look for a broad, deep chest, a body of medium length, active and flexible, powerful hindquarters, round, cat-like feet on straight, strong legs, a hard coat, and a stern carried well up, "full of guts and ginger." The jaw, above all, should be powerful, square, with level teeth, the eyes dark, and the skull slightly low. Avoid the dog with much black in it.

Once you have something that approximates to these points, although he may not be a show-bench winner, you may be sure you have one of the most sporting terriers and charming companions in the world of small dogs.

CHAPTER XXIII

SOME LITTLE DOGS WHO DESERVE BETTER THINGS

The Over-pampered Cairn and the Tea-table Skye—Give them both a Chance—The Admirable Dandie and the Lion-hearted Irishman—A Word on the Airedale—The Poodle, the Pekinese, and the Pomeranian.

THERE ARE TERRIERS OF SORTS which through long usage as house-dogs and pets have lost most of their essential qualities as outdoor working companions for the man with a gun. But in spite of this decline in their native gifts—no fault of their own—they still preserve the gallant spirit of less urbanized ancestors, and most of them, with a little training and opportunity, can easily be turned into first-rate rabbiters, ratters, and fox-bolters.

I propose to give, therefore, a very few brief, sketchy notes on some of the more promising breeds—the Cairn, the Skye, the Dandie, the Irish terrier, the Airedale, and the poodle, among others.

Although perhaps the oldest of all the terrier breeds, the Cairn has only really become popular since the War. If he is not pampered, this little dog, who weighs only about 12 lb., is a most game little creature. The breed originated in Scotland, where it was used for the destruction of foxes, otters, and other vermin.

In appearance the Cairn is rather 'rugged,' with a foxy head, large stop, and prick ears. The undercarriage is low, and the legs short but sturdy. The coat is of double thickness, a top-coat of long, harsh hair growing up from a close, short under-coat. The most popular colours are brindle-grey and black.

The greatest trouble with the modern Cairn is that many of his owners pamper him. His small size makes him an excellent house-dog for both town and country, and although naturally good-tempered, both towards humans and towards his own kind, pampering will make him snappy.

The Skye terrier originated, as a little severe concentration will suggest, in the islands of the Hebrides. They are short-legged and shaggy-coated, and were used to bolt otters and foxes before sophisticated London women degraded them to the level of tea-table sycophants. The shaggy coat served to protect the wearer from the rocks and gorse on the hillsides of the islands.

It is hard to imagine a present-day specimen being used for bolting any fox or otter. The shaggy coat has now developed into long, flowing tresses, draping the ground and falling over the eyes, and the breed has become a degenerate ornament rather than a worker.

The terrier should measure about 40 inches from nose to tail, and weigh up to 27 lb. The ears may be either erect or pendant; in the latter case they should be larger. The neck should be long, and the tail carried down.

The coat, which is usually dark or light blue-grey, is of double thickness, a long top-coat touching the ground, and a short woolly jacket underneath.

I do not advise procuring a Skye terrier as a pet,

since its coat requires endless care and attention, and in wet weather is liable to become rank and matted. But, apart from this, the Skye is a charming little dog, fearless, obedient, and good-tempered.

Put him in the country, give him plenty of work and sport to sharpen his teeth on, and in no time the miserable park-paddler of London will become a self-respecting gentleman of the best manners.

The Dandie Dinmont takes his name from the character in Scott's *Guy Mannering*, who is described as possessing a large number of small sporting terriers. The actual origin of the breed is obscure, and its appearance quite different from other members of the terrier family.

He is a long-bodied, short-legged dog with a head that seems too large for him, crowned by a silly top-knot of hair. He has large, pleading eyes which one cannot resist, and the spirit which never admits defeat.

The forelegs are short and exceptionally muscular, the back legs slightly longer. The tail is about 9 inches long—curved like a scimitar, but never curled. The head is large, with a gradually tapering muzzle, and large ears set well back.

The best colour is pepper, with lighter patches on the skull and under-carriage, but occasionally a mustard-coloured type is found. The coat is composed of hard and soft hair about 2 inches in length and crisp to the touch.

The puppies are smooth-coated when born, mostly coloured black-and-tan.

The Dandie makes a splendid house-dog, possessing a loud bark guaranteed to scare any aunt, uncle, dun, bailiff, rate-collector, or free-drink connoisseur. Mercifully he does not yap, and is quite at home in town or country. He is, however, rather nervous and suspicious of strangers, and prefers not to be made a fuss of by them.

The Dandie is also rather pugnacious, and will not hesitate to go for another dog, however large, often with disastrous results to him.

Altogether he has a grand spirit, and deserves a better fate than a London flat.

The Irish terrier has, in my opinion, never attained the popularity he deserves, as he is, I believe, the best household companion of all the breeds.

In appearance the Irish terrier is a strongly built, active, and symmetrical dog, free from any appearance of cloddiness, and standing about 2 feet at the shoulder. The head is long with a square muzzle, and small dark eyes full of intelligence. The neck is fairly long, fitting into fine, sloping shoulders; the chest deep, the back straight and level. The coat is hard and wiry, coloured wheaten red.

The outstanding qualities of this breed are an unswerving loyalty to its owner, lion-hearted courage, amounting at times to foolhardiness, and an amusing sense of humour. They make excellent companions for children. They have but one fault—pugnaciousness towards other dogs. This must be cured when young.

I cured mine, which showed signs of becoming a bully at six months, by introducing him to an old retriever. The meeting took place on the bank of a stream, and the young terrier at once flew at the older dog. The retriever proceeded to administer a sound thrashing, ending up by bowling the puppy into the stream. From that time I had no trouble with him.

I like the Airedale. He is one of our youngest breeds, but has won world-wide popularity in the last few years. There is little doubt that the breed originated about fifty years ago from a very ancient breed known as "the old English working terrier," a rather uncouth dog of indefinite size and indefinite appearance.

There is a possibility that this breed was crossed with an otter-hound to give heavier bone. Be that as it may, the result is something to like, trust, and admire.

The Airedale is a strong, active, spruce-looking dog standing about 27 inches at the shoulder, and weighing about 40 lb. The head is long, and should possess very little stop, while the fore-face should be equal in length to the skull.

Eyes should be small and dark, and the forelegs perfectly straight, but sturdy and well muscled at the shoulders. The coat should be close-cropped, hard, and wiry, coloured fawn with a darker shade on back and body.

Airedales are intelligent, courageous, and affectionate, but they need a firm hand or they will become disobedient.

Very good-tempered with children in their own household, they are liable to snap at strange children if pulled about. The Airedale is also rather pugnacious with other dogs, and a sworn enemy of all cats.

Great care should be taken never to let him chase sheep. If not the dog may become a confirmed sheep-worrier—whose end is a charge of shot.

You can laugh at the poodle if you like, but his pedigree is a good deal longer than that of most of us. There were poodles four hundred years ago. They were not merely things that looked like poodles, but real poodles. Dürer drew one in about 1500. Pinturicchio painted a toy poodle in 1490. In 1700 " the Ball of Little Dogs," all of whom were poodles, danced before Queen Anne. These were very aristocratic poodles indeed. They included a " Marquis de Gaillerdain " and a " Madame de Poncette." Just about that time there were several troops of poodles who were up to all sorts of tricks. One troop would conduct a battle, fire small guns. Then there was a poodle who played cards, told the time by the clocks, and was a good hand at dominoes. General Hutchinson in his *Dog-breaking* tells of him. His name was Domini. A highly polished set of poodles took part in a perfect dinner party with servants to wait on them.

But all the time the poodle was busy finding and retrieving duck in the marshes of France and Germany when not otherwise engaged. It is practically certain that they came first of all from Germany to France, and then from France to England, where they had a share in the making of the curly-coated retriever and the Irish water-spaniel.

In Gervase Markham's *Art of Fowling by Water*

and Land, published in 1621, there is a whole chapter
on the " Water Dogge," of whom Markham says that
he had both more character, " excellencie, and a
greater height of vertu " than any other dog. Whether
that was a poodle or not it is difficult to say, for the
description of him, with his very short nose and his
" Lyon-like " appearance, his thick, short neck and his
" brest " like the breast of a " shippe," do not quite
agree with the poodle as we know him to-day; nor do
his " forefeete spatious, full and round, and closed together to the cley, like a water Ducke, they being his
oares to rowe in the water," quite fit the delicate oval
feet of General Bimbo, the poodle who enlivens my
wife's life.

Indeed, the first actual reference that I can find to
the poodle in England is that of Colonel H. Smith,
who writes of them under that name in 1843, and says
that they had been even then " indeed long known to
the middle classes of England and the fishermen on
the North-eastern coast and professional wildfowlers."

The fact is that the poodle is one of the best and
most intelligent gun dogs one can possibly have, particularly in water. The habit of clipping the coat
originated for the purely common-sense reason that in
summer-time and in the hot days of August and September the wretched poodle went swimming after
wounded birds, and found himself hopelessly ham-
pered by the clinging, sodden mass of his coat. Many
sixteenth-century pictures and manuscripts show them
shaven much as they are to-day.

After the poodle the Pekinese and the Pomeranian.

I have a great regard for both. If you have ever seen a Pekinese challenge an Alsatian you will acknowledge him as a gentleman. And if you have seen him in vociferous but gallantly impossible pursuit of a rabbit, rat, or low-flying swallow you will admit that he is a sportsman.

But the Pekinese, after all, is no dog. He is a love-child. The Chinese explained it all some thousands of years ago before the Palace of Pekin had canonized the Pekinese as the dog attendant upon kings and the ladies of kings.

It happened in a Celestial forest. There a lion fell in love with a squirrel. It was a charming but clearly hopeless passion. The gods, however, took pity upon the devoted couple and encompassed their difficulties. The result was the Pekinese. And that is why he has the heart of a lion, the bushy tail and the frisky spirit of the squirrel.

The Pomeranian can claim no such descent. He may or may not be a miniature descendant of a far-off husky strain. The chances are just possible. But when I go to Crabbet Park, in Sussex, and see Lady Wentworth's Pomeranians not only point a rabbit in a rhododendron, but put him out and, at the crack of the .410, retrieve him stertorously but truly, I am filled with admiration for the last on our list of the little dogs who deserve better things.

CHAPTER XXIV

THE ZENITH OF THE DOG

A Final Survey of the Dog's Progress in Sport—The Spectacular
Rise of Greyhound Racing—Twenty Million Pounds' Worth of
Capital—Thirty Million People pay to see it—Back to the Sport
of the Ancient Greeks.

W E HAVE, I HOPE, HIT OFF some sort of general
survey of the part which the dog has played in sport
from the earliest times to the present day. And we
are returning upon the wheel of history. For if you
examine the writings of Arrian and Xenophon you
will find that they write of the greyhound as swiftest
of all dogs, the principal partner in the pursuits of
the individual huntsman and in the mass delights of
the ordinary people. To-day the wheel has turned.
The greyhound is once more the darling of the
ordinary man, greyhound racing the sport of two-
thirds of the population.

Since those days the usages of the dog in sport have
travelled a long way, branched into many diversified
subsidiaries. New breeds have sprung up, been formed
by fashion and killed by neglect. They have served
their time as women's hats serve their butterfly lives.
There are breeds to-day, such as the Italian greyhound, the pocket beagle, the Manchester terrier, the
old English terrier, the Spanish pointer, and the curly-
coated retriever, which are so scarce that you may
search a week or a month before you find a good one.
Some were merely creatures of fashion, clutterers

about women's skirts. The Italian greyhound was never more than a decorative element. The pocket beagle was a pretty fancy. The Manchester terrier was a connoisseur's delight. The Spanish pointer was bred for practical use, with a double nose, which could sift the shifting winds, find a partridge in the longest of long eighteenth-century stubbles. And the curly-coated retriever was popular in an age when men were perhaps hardier, when the bitter delights of winter wildfowling needed a strong and tenacious dog.

All these breeds have either outlived their time or, in the case of the curly coat, endure by reason of sheer quality.

But what dog has lived unchanged throughout the centuries? The foxhound is barely two hundred years old, the Airedale scarcely eighty years of age. The spaniel has broken into so many sub-species that research into his various origins becomes a tiresome omnibus progression among the scarcely dusty records of breed societies. So one might go on to other breeds. They come, they are popular, and they have their brief day.

In the savage background of medieval history, against the snowfields and pine forests of a mythological Northern Europe, stand out the grim, challenging figures of the great Russian Medelan, of the husky, the white Samoyede, the wolfhound and the deerhound, shaggy-haired, noble with the inheritance of ages of rough chivalry. Even the prick-eared, wolfish Alsatian has some claim upon the background of this tapestry of the dog, though no more than that

303

of a herd dog with a whispered inheritance of the wolf.

But these are barbaric memories, rough-cut frescoes on the horizon of history. The wolfhound and the deerhound were born in the mists. The Eskimo husky steps out of the whitened snows, the unwritten history of steppe and tundra behind him. The Medelan is a grim and courtly echo, borne on the breath of dead emperors, of those great dogs of war which fought for Hannibal. But in them all there is little word of written truth, no authentic breath of known ancestry. Pedigrees melt in the glamour of myth. We are left with the echo and the whisper of forgotten songs and the legends of dead bards. But when you walk into the resurrected graves of Chaldean kings; when you tread, by the light of a flickering candle, the stifling, hot, and dusty passages of the tombs of Egyptian Pharaohs; when you burrow at Memphis beneath the hot sands of the desert or walk with flickering ghosts in the "Stables of Antar"; when you tread, awed, among the great pillars of Karnak, and in all these places walk in a world which was the world long before Christ—one thousand to five thousand years before Christ—and find there the pictured story of the greyhound, then the history of the dog suddenly takes on an enormous significance.

It is easy to ask oneself—as I did lately at Luxor—why man for four thousand years has loved, bred, kept, and almost deified this slender, graceful creature of light, gentleness, and action.

I think you have the answer in the last words of

that question. For the greyhound is gentle, is light and graceful in symmetry, supple and strong in action. He answers the æsthetic needs of beauty. He answers, too, the masculine demand for strength and speed. And in gentleness he touches that chord of feminine necessity which long ago made that now almost archaic word 'gentlepeople' a synonym for breeding, strength of purpose, gentleness of manner, and success in achievement.

When we review the races of dog, as we might review the races of men, the greyhound stands out preeminent. Four thousand years ago he had the characteristics which made him a gentleman among dogs, an aristocrat, a person of breeding and beauty. He has kept them to-day.

You find him at the present time in various forms. There is greyhound in the Irish wolfhound, in the Scotch deerhound, in the Russian Borzoi, in the Saluki, in the whippet, and in those very odd dogs with large ears which you find in the Balearic Islands.

It is amusing now to recall the tempest of criticism and abuse which burst from the orthodox coursing world when the plans for greyhound racing in this country were first put forward. I remember the atmosphere. Born and bred in a Fenland county where every squire and farmer kept long dogs, where we never shot hares, in order to save them for coursing, it was uncomfortably easy to sense the reaction against this new form of 'Yankee circus stuff.'

Men to whom Hockwold, the Isle of Ely, Aldeby, Rochford, and our other East Anglian meetings meant months of anxious preparation for their Waterloo—in

U   305

more senses than one—at Altcar naturally could not be expected to welcome an innovation which to them not only seemed to threaten the whole principle of coursing by introducing an artificial element—the stuffed hare—but also, and worse, appeared to threaten the very future of the greyhound itself. For, said they with understandable but panic logic, how was the purity of breeding to be maintained when every Tom, Dick, and Harry in the country was going to sell, breed, and race third-class animals?

It was a natural question to ask. What is the answer? More than a decade of greyhound racing has given it. It has shown on the whole that the new pastime has improved the breed instead of deteriorating it. That, after all, was only logically to be expected. Inferior dogs cannot win prizes, and the introduction of great capital sums and vast public interest has naturally resulted in greater competition to breed and produce the best.

What would bloodstock breeding be to-day without the glittering prizes of the Derby, the Ascot Gold Cup, the Guineas, and the Cesarewitch? It would certainly never have reached its present peak of importance, popularity, and affluence had it continued to rely on small country meetings and provincial attendances.

The same argument can be applied in principle to greyhound racing. As one example of the value of its prize money, it is worth noting that once a year they have a race at the White City known as the "White City." It takes less than thirty seconds to decide, and the prize money is £3500!

A few years ago the greyhound was the property and interest of a few. To-day he is the idol of the million, the property of tens of thousands. Moreover, the dog has answered the main argument himself.

The same animal which races at the White City or at Harringay after a stuffed hare courses a live one at Hockwold or Ely with equal *élan*. The dog is adaptable enough. It was human prejudice which was less malleable. But that has vanished.

To-day if we examine the importance of being a greyhound what do we find? Let me put it in a few potted facts.

There are *twenty million pounds* of British money invested in greyhound racing in this country. The annual turnover of the totalisator at greyhound meetings is estimated at fifty million pounds, approximately five times as much as that of the Racecourse Betting Control Board. The industry or pastime, whichever you like to call it, employs 35,000 people, 20,000 of them in direct employment and 15,000 in indirect work. The annual wages bill is well over two million pounds.

There are sixty-two licensed tracks in this country, and 65,000 registered greyhounds on the books of the National Greyhound Racing Club. They belong to 29,500 individual owners.

To cap these astronomic figures with one even more astral, it is a fact—and I take it from the taxation authorities, who have an uncanny perception in these matters—that no less than *thirty million people* paid to see greyhound racing in 1937. In other words, two-thirds of the population of Britain are going to the dogs—and the dog is the greyhound, the hound of the Greeks, the hound of the Old Testament, one of the four things that were "comely in going."

It all began in 1926, when a man whom I know invested £100 in a greyhound-racing company. He has drawn £6000 a year ever since. Another man put in £2000. He has received £10,000 a year since 1932. That man is an American who brought 'the dogs' to this country. Another man, whom I know well, did not even invest money. He merely guaranteed a few thousands at the bank. To-day he is drawing more than £7000 a year from the sport in which he had faith when others suffered from financial astigmatism.

In 1926 a company was formed with £14,000 capital. All the capital was repaid within a few months, and £1400 was issued in one-shilling shares. Those shilling shares have paid 22s. 6d. each year afterwards. The company itself declared a profit for the year 1937 of £241,236 17s. 7d. This to the shilling shareholders meant a dividend of 40 per cent. That company is the Greyhound Racing Association, Limited, with its partner, the Greyhound Racing Trust, Limited. To-day the capital is £1,500,000.

And this, in a financial peanut, is the story of greyhound racing, one of the most prosperous industries in Britain at the present day.

It started with a whisper some seventy years ago at the Welsh Harp at Hendon. A man stuffed a hare, mounted it on a trolley on a 400-yard rail, and wound it backward and forward with a windlass, while enthusiastic long dogs chased it. That was all very well, but it failed. A straight track is useless. The performance of the dogs was too consistent, and you cannot bet on consistency. So it died. Then in 1890 another man patented a device for a circular dog-racing track. No one took it up. The patent was shelved in the Patent Office.

A few years later O. P. Smith, a farmer of Oklahoma, was entertaining a few Yankee friends to a friendly afternoon's rabbit coursing in the paddock at the back of his house, when he was horrified by the arrival of the State police. O.P. was haled before the sheriff and fined for causing unnecessary cruelty to rabbits—in other words, coursing them in an enclosed space, which is also an offence in Britain.

But O.P.'s pleasant Sunday afternoons were far too much of a social function lightly to be abandoned. So O.P. sought for a substitute. If live rabbits were barred he would course stuffed ones. He hunted the records. The records led him to the Patent Office. The Patent Office disclosed the old patent of 1890. O.P. either acquired it—or improved on it.

A year later Oklahoma City had a brand-new dog-racing track, and O.P. had a brand-new bank balance. So the good work went on. It spread all over the United States.

Then in 1924 Mr Charlie Munn, a self-sacrificing American, took a lot of photographs of the sort of thing that went on in the United States and brought

them to this country. That week-end he met Brigadier-
General Critchley, a live young Canadian, at a country
house party. He showed him the photographs. Before
long Critchley had begged, borrowed, bludgeoned, and
almost stolen £14,000 out of the pockets of his best
friends. It was fortunate that most of them were best
friends—because otherwise he would not have got the
money. Few of them believed in the scheme, but most
of them believed in Critchley. He, the General, so
believed in himself, the scheme, and the power of 'a
bob on a dog' that he threw up a £6000-a-year post
and started to build a greyhound-racing track at Belle
Vue, Manchester. Just as Cochran tries out his revues
at Manchester, so did Critchley try out his dogs in that
shrewd, farseeing, egotistical, uncouth, money-for-
value city.

Half-way through the funds ran out. They had not
even enough to pay another month's wages, let alone
for the hundreds of tons of concrete which were
needed. So he and Munn borrowed another £10,000
—with much blood and sweat. They told their friends
and they told themselves that their average attendance
would be 20,000 people a night. The first night there
were 2000. The next night there were 400 less.
Things looked black. Some of their backers looked
blacker.

For a week or two it was touch and go. Then the
attendances improved. They grew and grew. Once or
twice more than 20,000 people paid to see this spectacle of half a dozen attenuated animals chasing an
inanimate creation of fur and stuffing.

By the end of their thirty-three meetings the attendances had averaged 11,000 people a night. The money was paid back, new shilling shares were created. Almost unheard-of dividends were being contemplated, and the faces of Brigadier-General Critchley, Mr Charles Munn, and others began to wear Rolls-Royce expressions.

Manchester having affixed its Lancastrian *cachet* to the new sport, the General and the Yank decided to seek the shillings of the Cockneys. London was not too easy at first. The White City offered hope, space, and a good name, but the White City directors were a little coy. They remembered that what Manchester does to-day London refers to a committee to-morrow.

Meanwhile the General and Mr Munn went to Harringay. Harringay offered them a dump—45,000 tons of London earth spewed up by the subterranean burrowings of the Underground Railway. There were twenty-five acres of this engineering excreta. General Critchley and Mr Munn had to shift it—by proxy of minions. They did so. That is why, by the time the Harringay track was finished, it had cost not £35,000 —the original estimate—but £150,000, a different and an illuminating figure. To-day it is valued at £450,000.

And in 1937 two million people paid to go in at Harringay alone! No other sport in the world's history, Rome and its arenas included, has ever attracted so vast an attendance to one sports ground.

Then the White City authorities awoke from their coma. The dogs were unleashed on the grounds where

Buffalo Bill had shot glass balls. It opened officially to greyhound racing in June 1927, and averaged an attendance of 50,000 people a night for forty consecutive racing nights—another world record in attendance. To-day it is valued at £750,000.

As for others of these staggering figures, the tale of them is like the bank-book of a Midas. More than £1,000,000 has been paid in prizes, and the same sum in entertainment tax.

The figures I have given are stupendous in their magnitude, but when we come down to the actual question of how much it costs to race a greyhound it is easy to see how this pastime has caught on. The G.R.A. at the outset of their enterprise owned their own greyhounds. They bought a considerable number outright to make sure that there should be a full card every racing night. But as the public interest increased so the desire to own dogs grew. Many people who knew little of the greyhound suddenly became bitten with the desire to own and race one.

The G.R.A. were quick to realize—indeed, they had already contemplated—this desire for individual ownership. So they not only made it easy for patrons to buy greyhounds from the Association kennels, but they also undertook to kennel, keep, and train each dog at an inclusive fee of a pound a week, entry fees included. This immediately solved the problem which would have confronted many people in cities, that of how, and where, to keep and train the dog at home.

The G.R.A. naturally made a point of the fact that, as the dogs were under their supervision, it obviated any attempts at doping or other mischievous work. But the really great benefit which emerged from this principle was that it made it possible for the dogs to be graded. Thus the new patrons and promoters of greyhound racing were able to refute yet one more of the early objections made to the sport—to wit, that it would encourage the breeding and racing of third-class animals.

Soon there was a demand for a controlling body to rule and regulate the actual running of the dogs. The G.R.A., with the best intentions in the world, approached the National Coursing Club and asked them if they would be good enough to co-operate. But the National Coursing Club replied, quite properly, that it existed to safeguard the sport of coursing, and that coursing and greyhound racing had little in common except that both sports employed the same breed of dog.

Then there was a meeting of all the companies interested in greyhound racing. It was held at Wembley. The result was the formation of the National Greyhound Racing Club, which to-day is virtually the Jockey Club of greyhound racing. The stewards include such well-known and reputable men as Brigadier the Hon. A. V. F. V. Russell, who is Senior Steward, Lord Lawrence, Lord Denman, Major-General Sir John Duncan, and Professor Sir Frederick Hobday, the great veterinary surgeon.

The club was established in January 1928, and its objects, which I take from the *Greyhound Racing Year Book*, the official handbook of the National Greyhound Racing Society, are as follows:

" (1) To register all greyhounds racing on tracks approved by the Club, and to take all steps possible for checking the correct identity of greyhounds running on such tracks.

" (2) To investigate all reports of improper practices and breaches of the Rules by owners, trainers, officials, and other persons, and to take disciplinary action against those found guilty, either by warning them off all licensed and approved tracks, or by fining, or by other means.

" (3) To license all tracks and all officials engaged on tracks, and also track trainers and private trainers.

" (4) To publish, as an official journal or record, the *National Greyhound Racing Calendar*, which contains the official announcements of the stewards and a list of every greyhound and every official registered or licensed.

" In regard to the first of these functions—the registration of greyhounds—the N.G.R.C. has established a very elaborate and thorough record of all greyhounds that are sent to the tracks. In the first place, every greyhound has to possess a certificate of the National Coursing Club or the Irish Coursing Club, and before it can race on any track approved by the Club the owner must register the greyhound with the N.G.R.C., while in addition there is for each greyhound an identity book issued by the Club."

The establishment of the Club was followed by that of the National Greyhound Racing Society of Great Britain, the president of which is Lord Askwith. The Vice-Presidents are Sir William Gentle, that grand old

Norfolk sportsman, and Major-General Lord Loch, who, by the way, are two of the best pheasant shots in their respective counties of Norfolk and Suffolk.

The Society is an association of companies which own racecourses that are licensed by the National Greyhound Racing Club and run under its rules. Just as the Club administers matters of racing so the Society has to deal with matters of administration.

I mentioned earlier on that a great many greyhounds are trained under the ægis of the G.R.A., but it is worth noting that during the year 1936, according to the latest figures available, 26 per cent. of the races run were won by greyhounds trained by private trainers, including the Greyhound Derby at the White City, which was won by Mrs M. Yate's Fine Jubilee. This was the first time that the Derby had been won by a privately trained greyhound. Another privately trained dog, Mr J. Walsh's Lone Keel, won the Derby in 1937. Altogether 910 open races were held, with prize money of £51,881 10s.

A lot of nonsense has been talked about the danger which greyhound racing does to the morale of the public. And it is nonsense. Betting on the dogs is what betting has always been in England—" a bob a nob." The man of the artisan or working class who goes to a greyhound meeting seldom bets in anything greater than shillings, and he bets in decent surroundings, in the open air, on a properly regulated race, with no dangers of crookedness, doping, pulling, pocket-picking, rowdyism, drunkenness, three-card-trickery, or any of the other decorative addenda which attached

315

themselves like fleas to flat racing at the London meetings up to only a few years ago. It is impossible to avoid making this comparison.

The greyhound has definitely taken the place of the racehorse in London and many other great cities. And the average well-conducted greyhound meeting is an infinitely more satisfactory and orderly affair than was the suburban race meeting which we knew before the War. One has only to read Pierce Egan's vivid descriptions of the old-time race meetings or to recollect "the things wot went on" at West Drayton to realize that the working man to-day is infinitely better catered for than ever he was in the past so far as his racing and betting are concerned.

But greyhound racing is not merely the sport of the masses. It has attracted the attention of many distinguished people who a few years ago were inclined to sniff a little suspiciously. It is now, in fact, in the full tradition of English sport.

So when I see racing greyhounds in action, the crowds tense, their eyes lit by the sudden vision of such swift grace and beauty of action, I am moved to reflect that the sport which the Greeks knew and loved has returned again upon the wheel of history. The greyhound is still one of the four things "comely in going." He is still in grace a peer with the eagle on wing, the way of a ship upon the sea, or the walking of a maid.

INDEX

Lonsdale, Hugh Lowther, fifth
Earl of, 47, 204
Lucas, Sir Jocelyn, Bart., Sealy-
ham pack of, 286–288, 290–
291, 292
Lurcher, 44, 94

MANCHESTER terrier, 170, 302;
origin of, 170; "Stonehenge"
on points of, 170–172, 174–
177
Margam Hounds, 49, 50
Mastiff, 193, 196
Milton Hounds, 46, 47
Modbury Hounds, 58

NEWFOUNDLAND dog, 189, 190,
195, 203
Norwegian elkhound, 15–16, 23

OTTER-HOUND, 15, 298
Otter-hunting, 161–167, 291

PARTRIDGE-SHOOTING, 35, 122,
123, 142 et seq.
Pekinese, 85, 300; courage of,
301; Chinese on origin of,
301
" Pembrokeshire terrier "—see
Sealyham
Pointer, Spanish breed of, 144,
145, 244, 248, 252, 302,
303; decline of, 244–245;
classic origin of, 245; Arkwright's monograph on, 246;
establishment of, in England,
246; poaching with, 246–
247; three examples of, in
1800, 247–248; Italian breed
of, 248; Hutchinson on
endurance of, 248–249;
Richardson on stamina and
value of, 249; " Idstone "
on, 249–250, 251–256

Pomeranian, 85; origin of, 301
Poodle, ancient pedigree of,
299; accomplishments of,
299; a seventeenth-century
account of, 299–300; in
England, 300; as a gun dog,
300

QUARME HOUNDS, 58

RABBIT-HUNTING, 232, 294;
dachshunds for, 73, 75–76;
Sussex beagles for, 73–75; the
terrier and, 173–174; Sussex
spaniel pack for, 225–227;
Sealyham pack for, 286–288;
Pomeranian and, 301
Rat-killing, 170, 184
Red setter, drawbacks and
charms of, 121–122; deriva-
tion and early records of,
122–126; main strains of,
traced, 126 et seq.; Loftus
diary on, 130–135, 136–138;
black variety of, 138; a
puppy's homing achievement,
138–140; standard of points
for, 140–141; partridge-
shooting with, 146–147,
151–152, 154
Retriever, 302; " Stonehenge "
on origin and points of, 189–
196; " Idstone " on smooth-
coated black variety of, 196–
200; a training tip, 200–201;
" Stonehenge " on origin and
decline of curly-coated black
variety, 202–203; the breed
to-day, 203–204; points of
the Labrador variety, 204–
206; development of flat-
coated variety, 206; golden
variety, 206–207, 209–210

Lightning Source UK Ltd.
Milton Keynes UK
04 May 2010

153696UK00001B/175/P